PRE-APPRENTICE TRAINING

PRE-APPRENTICE TRAINING

A
TEST PREPARATION
MANUAL FOR
THE SKILLED TRADES

Jack Martin
&
Associates
Grand Blanc, Michigan

Previous Editions

© 1993; First published in 1968 with revisions in 1970, 1972, 1980, 1987, 1997, 2013 and 2016 as *Pre-Apprentice Training*

Published by Jack Martin & Associates
9422 South Saginaw
Grand Blanc, MI 48439

Publisher's Cataloging-in-Publication Data
Martin, Jack.

Pre-apprentice training : a test preparation manual for the skilled trades / by Jack Martin & Mary Serich. — Grand Blanc, MI : Jack Martin, ©2006.

p. ; cm.
ISBN: 0-9649530-1-3

1. Apprenticeship programs. 2. Apprentices. 3. Mathematics-Problems, exercises, etc. I. Serich, Mary. II. Title.

HD4881 .M37 2006
331.25/922—dc22   2005900907

Editing and electronic composition by Cindy Wheaton
Cover design by Dawn Dockins, Graphic Press, Inc.

Printed in the United States of America
09 08 07 06 05 · 5 4 3 2

Dedication

A course called Pre-Apprentice Training was first offered by The Mott Adult Education Program of Flint, Michigan in 1968. It was intended to help prepare female and minority job applicants with the skills necessary to pass the General Motors Apprenticeship Test Battery. The class provided training in six areas: (1) Basic Math, (2) Algebra, (3) Geometry, (4) Spatial Skills, (5) Mechanical Comprehension, and (6) Reading Comprehension. The first class used six different text books. The instructor, John Beach and Program Coordinator, Jack Martin wrote a workbook – text that combined all six subjects into what later became known as the **Pre-Apprentice Training Manual**. To their credit, the first class of twenty-two resulted in seventeen apprentices and later, fourteen journeymen.* As a result of this effort, minority and female participation in the Flint Area GM Plants rose from less than 3% in 1968 to more than 16% by 1981.

Currently the text is utilized in training programs across the USA and Canada at the community college, high school and adult education levels to help all applicants pass most skilled trades apprenticeship entry examinations. The text follows a simple step-by-step format and may be used in a classroom setting or as a self-instructional guide.

Since first introduced in 1968, more than 200,000 Apprentice Applicants have used this textbook to prepare for apprenticeship tests. Conscientious instructors including John Mahoney, Ted Baird, Geraldine Haush, Norm Jones, Jessie McKelry and Joanne McGrain have recommended changes and added supplemental materials. There have been two major revisions by Mary Serich, one in 1993 and the other in 2005. This edition was expanded to include the construction trades with new chapters on How To Read A Ruler, Basic Electricity and Technical Reading.

Others share in the textbooks development: The Mott Adult Education Program for providing leadership and direction; The Mott Foundation's Frank Manley, Sr., without whose encouragement this book never would have been written; and finally, General Motors for recognizing the need. Even more important are the students who attended our classes and allowed experimentation with different methods and teaching techniques. It is to those men and women who are aspiring to be today's apprentices and tomorrow's journeypersons that this book is dedicated.

Jack Martin & Mary Serich

*The term "Journeymen" as used occasionally throughout this book is intended to be gender neutral and used to describe any person who completes a formal apprenticeship program and is granted a journeymen's card.

Introduction

The content has been carefully selected to match most skilled trades apprenticeship entry requirements. The text has been designed to assist the apprentice applicant with the basic skills necessary to pass most apprenticeship entry examinations. However, not all apprenticeships utilize the same examination criteria. For example, it's probably not necessary for carpenters to solve Algebraic Equations (Chapter 8), but it is important for them to have a working knowledge of Whole Numbers (Chapter 2), Fractions & Decimals (Chapter 3), Graphic Math (Chapter 10), Geometry (Chapter 9), Measurement and Metric Conversion (Chapter 4). All trades, including carpenters require Mechanical and Spatial Skills (Chapters 13 & 11). Basic Electricity (Chapter 12), while primarily for electricians, is important knowledge for trades that work around electricity, but probably won't be included in most other trades apprenticeship examinations.

Generally speaking the more technical the trade, i.e.: Tool and Die Maker, Machinist, Electrician, etc. the higher the level math that is required. The higher math however, requires a strong base of fractions, decimals and whole numbers. The tendency is for students to want to skip the basic math, but test research shows most incorrect responses on apprenticeship tests are due to simple math errors. The basic math chapters are also important because the student gains confidence in order to deal with the more advanced problems.

The chapter tests have been timed so that students will feel some pressure to finish within the time limits. Probably the best advice we can give to potential test takers is to practice taking tests under timed conditions in order to get used to the pressure.

Applicants for all apprenticeships should spend time on test-taking techniques (Chapter 15) and the apprenticeship-selection interview (Chapter 16). Classroom instructors are also encouraged to arrange for practice interviews in order to prepare students for the actual interview.

Students who are studying independently, should take all of the timed chapter tests before and after they have completed their study. We recommend that classroom instructors use both a pre and post-test to identify areas of concentration and to measure student and class progress. Instructors have the authors' permission to make copies of the chapter tests for classroom use.

While the authors feel that all of the text's content is relevant, and that each chapter builds a knowledge base for future apprenticeship related classroom study, we also recognize that it goes beyond what is essential to do well on the apprenticeship test.

We encourage classroom instructors to do what good teachers have always done, that is, experiment with the content and be innovative in helping your students learn. Examples include using cardboard cut-outs to help develop spatial skills and utilizing alternate mechanical and spatial practice tests. Sharing of these creative ideas can be accomplished on our web site – www.pre-apprenticetraining.com

Good luck and we wish you well,

Jack Martin
Mary Serich

CONTENTS

CHAPTER

1 The Apprenticeship System

Apprenticeship History

Apprenticeship is one of the oldest forms of formalized training. It dates back to the time of Hammurabi. Ancient civilizations relied on some form of apprenticeship to teach the arts and crafts necessary to maintain civilization. The ancient code of Hammurabi stated that "Artisans must teach their crafts to youth".

Historical records indicate that in Great Britain, Parliament passed a law in 1383 officially recognizing apprenticeship training. America's first apprentices were a direct outgrowth of the English system, which provided for formal agreements called indentures. Indentures were signed legal agreements that bound both the master and apprentice to a period of training that lasted from eight to twelve years. Apprentices usually served without pay until they reached journeymen status. Although early indenture papers were legally binding, the USA federal government provided no regulation until Congress passed the National Apprenticeship Law in 1937.

Today, in the USA, The National Apprenticeship System is administered by the U.S. Department of Labor's Office of Apprenticeship Training, Employer and Labor Services (OATELS) who are responsible for the promotion and development of all registered apprenticeship programs. They have offices in all states and most major cities. More information is available from the U.S. Department of Labor Employment and Training Administration at www.doleta.gov.

In Canada, each Province or Territory is responsible for setting the rules and regulations for apprenticeship training. For more information go to www.apprenticetrades.ca.

Modern Apprentices

Todays apprentice is much different than their early counterparts. They are paid an above average wage while they learn their trade. They may be found in one of 800 different apprenticeable occupations, learning their trade on the job and in the classroom. The modern apprentice is still indentured, with both the apprentice and employer signing a formal agreement that establishes the terms of indenture. Upon graduation they are granted a journeymen's* card that is universally recognized by most employers. A holder of a journeymen's card can usually get a job wherever he or she applies. Canadian interprovincial trades mobility requires graduating from a recognized training program and passing The Interprovincial Standards Red Seal Examination for the trade.**

*The term journeymen is intended to be gender neutral and used to describe any person that completes a recognized apprenticeship program and is granted a journeymen's card.
**www.red-seal.ca

Career Development

There is a continuing demand for more and better trained skilled tradespersons. The demand has prompted many states, provinces and territories to initiate career path planning programs that encourage young people to think of apprenticeship as "The other four-year degree". High school counselors can provide students with curriculum choices that will help them meet entry level requirements. Generally, students interested in preparing for a career in construction, industrial or other apprenticeship areas are encouraged to select courses from the following list:

Mathematics
- Shop math
- Algebra
- Geometry
- Trigonometry

Drafting
- Blueprint reading
- Architectural drawing
- Orthographic projection

Communication Skills
- Reading
- Writing
- English/French

Science
- Biology
- Chemistry
- Physical Science
- Applied Physics

Technology
- Computers
- CAD/CAM
- Electronics

Social Science
- Social Studies
- History
- Labor History

Vocational
- Machine shop
- Wood shop
- Welding
- Safety
- Auto mechanics
- Building trades
- Pre-Apprentice Training*

Co-op Education
- On-the-job training
- School-to-Registered Apprenticeship (STRA) Programs — USA only**

Industrial Apprenticeship Programs

The following list of skilled trades are most commonly found at large industrial locations and smaller job shops. Most are four years in length and require on-the-job as well as classroom related instruction:

Auto/Truck Repair	Machine Repair	Stationary Engineer
Die Designer	Millwright	Sheet Metal Worker
Die Maker	Model Maker	Tin Smith
Draftsman	Mold Maker	Tool Designer
Electrician	Pattern Maker	Tool Maker
Machinist	Pipefitter	Welder

The requirements for most industrial apprenticeships include a high school diploma or GED (high school equivalency) and a minimum age of 18 years. Most trades also require some form of aptitude testing and interview as part of the selection process. A typical industrial trades selection system will give a battery of tests and award points in the following areas:

- Reading comprehension: interpreting technical charts, graphs and reading materials
- Arithmetic reasoning: fractions, decimals, algebra and geometry
- Graphic Math: using graphs and charts to solve problems
- Mechanical comprehension: gears, levers, pulleys, friction, gravity, etc.
- Spatial relations: visualizing objects in three dimensions

The industrial apprentice interview will usually include the following topics:
- Job preference and understanding of trade requirements
- Relevance of previous education and classes taken
- Relevance of prior related experience
(See Chapter 15 for more detail on the interview process)

*Pre-Apprentice training utilizing this textbook is available through many high school, community college and adult education programs.

**The School-To-Registered Apprenticeship (STRA) Program is a formal, nationally recognized, USA training program that combines on-the-job training with related classroom instruction for high school students 16 years of age or older. Upon completion, credentials are issued by the U.S. Department of Labor, Office of Apprenticeship Training and Labor Services (OATELS). For more information go to www.stra.org or www.doleta.gov.

Points are awarded based on the test battery and interview. Applicants are ranked according to their point totals and selection is made based on an established list for each trade.

Construction Apprenticeship Programs

There are more than 8 million people that work in the construction industry making it one of the US and Canada's largest employers. The following is a partial list of apprenticeable trades found in the construction industry:

Asbestos Worker	Electrician	Painter/Drywall Finisher
Boilermaker	Elevator Constructor	Plumber/Pipefitter
Bricklayer	Glaziers/Glass Worker	Refrigeration & Air Conditioning
Carpenter/Latherer/Floor Layer	Iron Worker/Structural Steel	Roofer/Waterproofer
Cement Mason	Millwright	Sheet Metal Worker
Construction Craft Laborer	Operating Engineer	Sprinkler Fitter
Drywall Finisher	Plasterer	Tile, Marble & Terrazzo Mason

Most construction apprenticeship entry requirements are similar to the industrial trades, although they vary somewhat from trade to trade. Basic requirements include a high school diploma or GED, a minimum of 16 to 18 years of age, and good health. Some require a valid driver's license and some do drug testing. Most use some form of aptitude testing and interview as part of their selection process. Most construction apprentices tend to work outdoors and move from job to job as work is completed. The ability to work with your hands and your brain is essential. Much of the hiring and training in the construction industry is conducted by a Joint Apprenticeship Training Committee (JATC) composed of both labor and management.

Related Classroom Instruction

Today's apprentice receives a combination of on-the-job and classroom training. The related classroom instruction is provided at a program sponsor's training facility or at a local technical or community college. The period of training can be from three to six years, depending on the trade. Much of the related classroom training also counts as college credit and may be applied towards a two or four-year degree. A registered apprenticeship today is the first step on a career ladder that could lead to an administrative position, or even owning your own company.

How to Select an Apprenticeship

The more than 800 apprenticeable trades make it extremely difficult to have an in-depth knowledge about all of the different trades. The following are steps to help you learn more about the opportunities available:

1. **Read** - Make a list of available trades in your area and visit the library to read as much as you can about the trade. An excellent resource is The Occupational Outlook Handbook www.bls.gov/oco.
2. **Observe** - Visit factories and construction sites to observe tradespersons and what they do for a living.
3. **Interview** - Don't be afraid to ask skilled tradespersons about their jobs. Most take pride in their work and enjoy talking about what they do.
4. **Assimilate** - Try to match the work traits to what you know about yourself. Does the trade require outdoor work? Do you like to work outdoors? Does the trade require advanced math? Can you handle algebra and geometry?
5. **Odds** - How many persons are hired annually, and what are your chances of being selected? If given the opportunity, will you be able to do the work?
6. **Application** - It doesn't cost anything to fill out an application. In the process, you might learn something about yourself and the trade.
7. **Internet** - To learn more about specific trades and their entry requirements, go the the U.S. Department of Labor's website at www.doleta.gov or do an Internet search for a specific trade. In Canada, go to www.apprenticetrades.ca.

How To Apply

Apprenticeship opportunities are usually posted on company and union bulletin boards. Information regarding anticipated openings is usually sent to the U.S. Department of Labor, Office of Apprenticeship and Training, as well as State, Provincial and Territorial employment agencies, local schools, various women's centers and community outreach centers. Often openings are advertised in local trade newspapers and magazines. Many joint labor-management trade associations also list job openings on the Internet.

Today, most hiring of apprentices is done by the employer without regard to race, color, religion, national origin, or sex.

How to Improve Your Chances of Being Hired

There are many ways to improve your chances of being selected as an apprentice. All involve increasing your selection point totals. Not all, however, are accepted by every trade. Consider the following and check to see if they apply in your area:

1. Selection starts by taking the right courses in high school, having good attendance and developing a strong work ethic. Actual job related work experience is also a plus.

2. Extra Courses - Most selection systems provide credit for extra job related courses. Applicants may improve their chances by selecting the right classes in preparation for the test.

3. Test and Retest - Many selection systems allow for retest after a given period of time or the completion of specific classes. The applicant should get as much practice as possible by taking practice tests and reviewing subject matter before testing. Chapter 15 of this text will help you prepare to take tests.

4. G.E.D. - Many selection systems allow applicants to submit a high school equivalency score in place of high school grades. This is an advantage to the person who didn't do well in high school. G.E.D. tests are usually given by local school boards. There are also many study guides available to help prepare for the G.E.D. test.

5. Interview - Preparation for the interview is important. There are several books available at your local library to help you prepare for the interview, as well as Chapter 15 of this text.

6. Following Directions - It is important that you follow all directions exactly as they are given or risk being eliminated from consideration.

7. Pre-Apprentice Training - Special courses are often available through local education programs, community agencies and various outreach programs. Most pre-apprentice programs review and strengthen skills necessary for successful apprenticeship application.

Canadian Apprenticeships

The government of Canada is keenly aware that it's future competitiveness depends on a highly skilled and mobile work force. Consequently, they have programs in place that support and encourage both pre-apprentice and apprenticeship training. For more specific information, contact any of the following organizations:

• Human Resources and Skills Development Canada — www.hrsdc.gc.ca
• The Canadian Apprenticeship Forum — www.caf-fca.org
• Promoting Skilled Trades and Apprenticeship Project — www.careerintrades.ca
• The Interprovincial Standards Red Seal Program — www.red-seal.ca

CHAPTER
2

Whole Numbers

ARITHMETIC

A review of basic arithmetic is an important factor in gaining skills in other areas of math. Although you may be perfectly aware of the rules for addition, subtraction, multiplication, and division, accuracy and speed can be gained in this section.

Be aware that most simple mistakes occur in the simple arithmetic problems. This probably happens because the student does not give the simple math problems the same amount of mental concentration that is applied to the more difficult problems. The basic arithmetic problems usually count for just as many points as the more difficult ones, so you cannot afford to make errors on them. Do not take the easy problems for granted.

Incorrectly copying the problem from the book or test to the scratch paper is a common error. You cannot get the answer right if you copy the problem wrong. Apply the following tips whenever you copy from one page to another to eliminate this problem.

Tip 1. Keep the scratch paper as close as possible to the book or test you are copying from.

Tip 2. Use your non-writing hand to point to each number in the problem as you copy it.

Tip 3. Number the problems on the scratch paper to correspond to the book or test problem numbers.

ADDITION

All arithmetic operations have specific terms for the different numbers in a problem. The terms used in addition are addend and sum. Addend refers to each number being added, and sum refers to the answer of an addition problem.

$$
\begin{array}{cll}
\textbf{EXAMPLE:} & 56 & \text{Addend} \\
& +72 & \text{Addend} \\
\hline
& 128 & \text{Sum}
\end{array}
$$

EXERCISE 1

Add:

1.	8 +4	3.	8 +3	5.	9 +8	7.	9 +4	9.	6 +6
2.	5 +6	4.	9 +7	6.	2 +9	8.	7 +9	10.	7 +4

Addition is not limited to problems having two terms. The number of terms possible in an addition problem is infinite. In adding a column of numbers, it is best to begin at the top (or bottom) and add straight to the end.

```
  8       1. Start by adding 8 & 7
  7       2. That sum (15) should be added to 6
  6       3. This new sum should be added to the next number and this
  9          procedure continued to the conclusion of the problem.
  3
  5
 +2
 40
```

In order to check the answer, add again in the reverse order. (If the answer was found by adding down, check by adding up.) If the check result is the same as the answer, the answer is probably right. If it is different, try both again.

EXERCISE 2

1.
```
  9
  2
  3
 +5
```

2.
```
  5
  7
  3
 +9
```

3.
```
  8
  2
  1
 +6
```

4.
```
  7
  4
  8
  3
 +6
```

5.
```
  9
  4
  5
  6
  1
 +3
```

6. $5 + 8 + 2 + 7 + 6 + 3 =$

7. $8 + 7 + 2 + 4 + 6 + 9 =$

8. $7 + 2 + 6 + 7 + 7 + 8 =$

9. $4 + 5 + 3 + 3 + 8 + 2 =$

10. $2 + 8 + 5 + 7 + 2 + 1 =$

11. $8 + 9 + 8 + 6 + 9 + 6 =$

12. $3 + 9 + 4 + 8 + 4 + 5 =$

Addition of numbers of more than one digit require "carrying." In order to understand carrying, the following chart will be helpful:

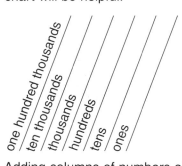

Notice that from right to left, each place is ten times greater than the one before.

Adding columns of numbers always begins with the "ones" column (the extreme right hand column).

EXAMPLE:

4. Take the 1 (a ten) and place it in the problem at the top of the "tens column"

1

76

+58

134

1. Add the digits in the "ones column"

2. The result is 14

5. Add the "tens" and put sum in the answer

3. Place the 4 in the answer

EXERCISE 3

Add and check:

| 1. 36
+7 | 8. 88
+43 | 15. 56
+49 | 21. 18
49
15
9
26
+29 | 27. 91432
54687
79865
+63279 |

| 2. 24
+9 | 9. 52
+47 | 16. 45
+48 | 22. 143
237
486
315
+987 | 28. 42356
98762
35491
+45936 |

| 3. 8
+31 | 10. 63
+38 | 17. 76
+213 | 23. 642
437
578
+267 | 29. 10090
37128
21010
+49850 |

| 4. 98
+4 | 11. 17
+46 | 18. 127
+287 | 24. 1286
1523
+8216 | 30. 97856
87965
67875
+47685 |

| 5. 76
+27 | 12. 73
+94 | 19. 32
16
+5 | 25. 81632
92139
13269
+45936 | |

| 6. 57
+7 | 13. 16
+47 | 20. 41
28
16
9
+37 | 26. 39218
94321
62572
+84235 | |

| 7. 97
+30 | 14. 42
+69 | | | |

Subtraction

The terms in subtraction are as follows:

$$
\begin{array}{r}
47 \\
-36 \\
\hline
11
\end{array}
\quad
\begin{array}{l}
\text{minuend} \\
\text{subtrahend} \\
\text{difference}
\end{array}
$$

As in addition, there are certain subtraction facts that must be committed to memory. Some of the more difficult appear in the next exercise.

EXERCISE 4

Subtract:

1. 12 − 5	8. 14 − 5	15. 11 − 8	22. 12 − 7	29. 12 − 8
2. 11 − 6	9. 13 − 9	16. 13 − 8	23. 15 − 6	30. 11 − 7
3. 18 − 9	10. 17 − 8	17. 13 − 5	24. 16 − 8	31. 12 − 3
4. 14 − 8	11. 14 − 9	18. 14 − 7	25. 17 − 9	32. 11 − 4
5. 15 − 9	12. 15 − 7	19. 12 − 9	26. 16 − 9	33. 11 − 3
6. 11 − 2	13. 11 − 9	20. 11 − 5	27. 16 − 7	34. 15 − 8
7. 13 − 7	14. 12 − 4	21. 13 − 6	28. 12 − 6	35. 17 − 6

When subtracting numbers, if the number being subtracted in the "ones" column is greater than the number which it is being subtracted from, it becomes necessary to borrow.

EXAMPLE 1:

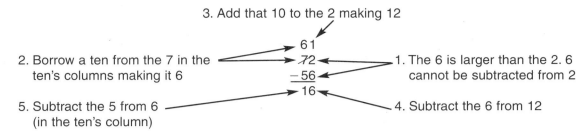

3. Add that 10 to the 2 making 12

2. Borrow a ten from the 7 in the ten's columns making it 6

1. The 6 is larger than the 2. 6 cannot be subtracted from 2

6 1
7̸2
− 5 6
16

5. Subtract the 5 from 6 (in the ten's column)

4. Subtract the 6 from 12

EXAMPLE 2:

```
6 14 11 16 11
7̸  5̸  2̸  7̸  1̸
−6  6  3  8  5
   8  8  8  6
```

Care must be exercised when borrowing in a problem of this kind. Starting on the right, notice that each borrowing operation is based on the previous borrow.

To check subtraction problems, the difference and the subtrahend are added. Their sum should equal the minuend if the operations are correct.

EXAMPLE 3:

```
      6  ⁹9  ⁹9  1
  5   7̸   0̸   0̸  0
 −4   3   1   5  2
  1   3   8   4  8
```

EXAMPLE 4:

```
  2₁
  3̸27     minuend
 − 56     subtrahend
  271     difference
```

1. Add subtrahend and difference.

2. This sum should be equal to the minuend if correct.

Add
```
   56
 +271
  327
```

EXERCISE 5

1.	62 −20	6.	83 −18	11.	388 −99	16.	4000 −1837
2.	97 −39	7.	119 −70	12.	201 −63	17.	672 −138
3.	156 −39	8.	61 −25	13.	837 −470	18.	600000 −129493
4.	83 −37	9.	47 −29	14.	7846 −1379	19.	4582 −694

5. 23 − 19 =   10. 273 − 194 =   15. 1439 − 983 =   20. 5006 − 1638 =

Multiplication

Terms for multiplication:

$$
\begin{array}{rl}
27 & \text{multiplicand} \\
\times 4 & \text{multiplier} \\
\hline
108 & \text{product}
\end{array}
$$

The following multiplication tables must be committed to memory:

1's	2's	3's	4's
$1 \times 1 = 1$	$2 \times 2 = 4$	$3 \times 3 = 9$	$4 \times 4 = 16$
$1 \times 2 = 2$	$2 \times 3 = 6$	$3 \times 4 = 12$	$4 \times 5 = 20$
$1 \times 3 = 3$	$2 \times 4 = 8$	$3 \times 5 = 15$	$4 \times 6 = 24$
$1 \times 4 = 4$	$2 \times 5 = 10$	$3 \times 6 = 18$	$4 \times 7 = 28$
$1 \times 5 = 5$	$2 \times 6 = 12$	$3 \times 7 = 21$	$4 \times 8 = 32$
$1 \times 6 = 6$	$2 \times 7 = 14$	$3 \times 8 = 24$	$4 \times 9 = 36$
$1 \times 7 = 7$	$2 \times 8 = 16$	$3 \times 9 = 27$	$4 \times 10 = 40$
$1 \times 8 = 8$	$2 \times 9 = 18$	$3 \times 10 = 30$	$4 \times 11 = 44$
$1 \times 9 = 9$	$2 \times 10 = 20$	$3 \times 11 = 33$	$4 \times 12 = 48$
$1 \times 10 = 10$	$2 \times 11 = 22$	$3 \times 12 = 36$	
$1 \times 11 = 11$	$2 \times 12 = 24$		
$1 \times 12 = 12$			

5's	6's	7's	8's
$5 \times 5 = 25$	$6 \times 6 = 36$	$7 \times 7 = 49$	$8 \times 8 = 64$
$5 \times 6 = 30$	$6 \times 7 = 42$	$7 \times 8 = 56$	$8 \times 9 = 72$
$5 \times 7 = 35$	$6 \times 8 = 48$	$7 \times 9 = 63$	$8 \times 10 = 80$
$5 \times 8 = 40$	$6 \times 9 = 54$	$7 \times 10 = 70$	$8 \times 11 = 88$
$5 \times 9 = 45$	$6 \times 10 = 60$	$7 \times 11 = 77$	$8 \times 12 = 96$
$5 \times 10 = 50$	$6 \times 11 = 66$	$7 \times 12 = 84$	
$5 \times 11 = 55$	$6 \times 12 = 72$		
$5 \times 12 = 60$			

9's	10's	11's	12's
$9 \times 9 = 81$	$10 \times 10 = 100$	$11 \times 11 = 121$	$12 \times 12 = 144$
$9 \times 10 = 90$	$10 \times 11 = 110$	$11 \times 12 = 132$	
$9 \times 11 = 99$	$10 \times 12 = 120$		
$9 \times 12 = 108$			

Multiplication is a form of addition. It simply shortens the process of adding a given number many times.

EXAMPLE:

```
              12      12
              12     ×4     Multiplied
      Added   12      48
             +12
              48
```

Four 12s added together in the first case, but in the second, through multiplication, the same result is found by finding 4 twelves.

To multiply numbers other than those found on the tables, certain steps must be followed. In multiplying 47 by 4, the first thing is to write the problem in proper form.

```
              47
             ×4
```

Once the problem is set, multiply each number in the multiplicand, from right to left, by the multiplier.

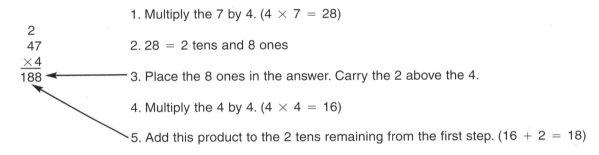

```
   2
  47
 ×4
 188
```

1. Multiply the 7 by 4. (4 × 7 = 28)

2. 28 = 2 tens and 8 ones

3. Place the 8 ones in the answer. Carry the 2 above the 4.

4. Multiply the 4 by 4. (4 × 4 = 16)

5. Add this product to the 2 tens remaining from the first step. (16 + 2 = 18)

EXAMPLE:

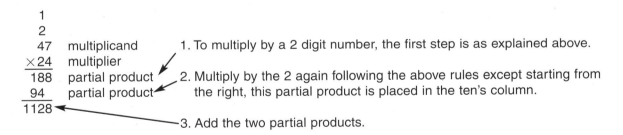

```
    1
    2
   47    multiplicand
  ×24    multiplier
  188    partial product
   94    partial product
 1128
```

1. To multiply by a 2 digit number, the first step is as explained above.

2. Multiply by the 2 again following the above rules except starting from the right, this partial product is placed in the ten's column.

3. Add the two partial products.

Multiply:

1.　　11 　　×4	9.　　227 　　× 8	17.　　86 　　×86	25.　437269 　×　　38
2.　　91 　　×9	10.　6573 　　×　6	18.　　71 　　×18	26.　　437 　　×186
3.　　82 　　×6	11.　42109 　　×　　4	19.　　55 　　×25	27.　　563 　　×416
4.　　40 　　×4	12.　　800 　　×　9	20.　　800 　　×99	28.　86234 　×　359
5.　　39 　　×8	13.　　37 　　×29	21.　　137 　　×46	29.　3937137 　×　　2283
6.　　73 　　×8	14.　　28 　　×13	22.　　329 　　×14	30.　7328546 　×　13468
7.　　350 　　×3	15.　　69 　　×33	23.　　387 　　×78	31.　98764 　×　329
8.　　84 　　×5	16.　　78 　　×46	24.　9994 　×　22	32.　73698 　×　576

Division

Terms used in division:

$$\begin{array}{r} 4 \quad \text{quotient} \\ \text{divisor} \quad 6\,/\,\overline{25} \quad \text{dividend} \\ \underline{24} \\ 1 \quad \text{remainder} \end{array}$$

Division is a short form of subtraction. The answer to the above example can be determined as follows. How many times does 6 go into 25?

$$\begin{array}{r} 25 \\ \underline{-6} \quad \text{once} \\ 19 \\ \underline{-6} \quad \text{twice} \\ 13 \\ \underline{-6} \quad \text{three times} \\ 7 \\ \underline{-6} \quad \text{four times} \\ 1 \quad \text{remainder} \end{array}$$

Understanding the division process greatly shortens the above subtraction method. The same problem can be divided as follows:

1. Will 6 (divisor) go into 2 (first number of dividend)? It doesn't!

2. Will the 6 go into 25 (second number of the dividend)? Yes, it does. 6 divides into 25 four times with one remainder.

$$\begin{array}{r} 4 \\ 6\,/\,\overline{25} \\ \underline{24} \\ 1 \end{array}$$

3. Place the 4 above the 5.

4. Multiply the 4 in the quotient by the divisor, 6, and place below dividend.

5. Subtract - This difference is the remainder and can be placed in the quotient.

The remainder in this problem is 1. It can also be written as a fraction by placing the remainder over the divisor.

$$\frac{\text{remainder}}{\text{divisor}} = \frac{1}{6}$$

The answer could be correctly expressed 4R1 or 4⅙. The fractional form is more useful in further calculations in most cases.

EXAMPLE:

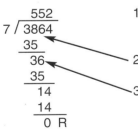

1. Proceed as in above example. 7 does not go into 3, but it will go into 38. Multiply this result by the divisor, and subtract.

2. Bring the next number in the dividend down to the remainder.

3. Divide 7 into this 36 and repeat after multiplication and subtraction until all numbers in dividend are used.

```
        164 R20
22 / 3628
     22
     142
     132
     108
      88
      20 R
```

1. A trial would be to divide 20 into 36. This trial quotient is 1. If after multiplication this product can be subtracted from the dividend with a remainder less than the divisor, the number in the quotient can be assumed correct.

2. Proceed as above example.

EXERCISE 7

Divide:

1. $2 \overline{)26}$

2. $2 \overline{)17}$

3. $6 \overline{)77}$

4. $40 \div 3 =$

5. $72 \div 7 =$

6. $8 \overline{)224}$

7. $7 \overline{)364}$

8. $5 \overline{)736}$

9. $2136 \div 4 =$

10. $738 \div 9 =$

11. $9 \overline{)2638}$

12. $4 \overline{)8247}$

13. $2 \overline{)13469}$

14. $5274 \div 6 =$

15. $627345 \div 5 =$

PRE-APPRENTICE TEST

Time - 8 minutes

Part 1 - Whole Numbers

1.
$$48$$
$$+31$$

2.
$$79$$
$$+8$$

3.
$$65$$
$$+43$$

4.
$$845$$
$$+376$$

5.
$$34$$
$$346$$
$$8$$
$$+4371$$

6.
$$74$$
$$-33$$

7.
$$52$$
$$-14$$

8.
$$481$$
$$-92$$

9.
$$424$$
$$-375$$

10.
$$5682$$
$$-683$$

11.
$$43$$
$$\times 3$$

12.
$$56$$
$$\times 48$$

13.
$$507$$
$$\times 62$$

14.
$$491$$
$$\times 240$$

15.
$$6060$$
$$\times 7009$$

16. $7 \overline{\smash{\big)}\ 2163}$

17. $8 \overline{\smash{\big)}\ 174}$

18. $45 \overline{\smash{\big)}\ 810}$

19. $37 \overline{\smash{\big)}\ 3850}$

20. $391 \overline{\smash{\big)}\ 71202}$

ANSWERS

1. _____
2. _____
3. _____
4. _____
5. _____
6. _____
7. _____
8. _____
9. _____
10. _____
11. _____
12. _____
13. _____
14. _____
15. _____
16. _____
17. _____
18. _____
19. _____
20. _____

Fractions and Decimals

Fractions - Common and Decimal

A complete understanding of fractions is necessary for a skilled tradesperson. They must be able to use them in order to read and understand blueprints. They also use them in calculations of various problems that occur on the job. Without a working knowledge of fractions, they cannot function as a journeyperson.

Because of this reliance on fractions, a review of definitions will be helpful.

What is a Fraction?

A fraction is a method of showing a part of a whole item.

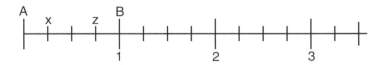

The scale shown above is in inches. From point A to point B represents the whole inch. The inch on this scale is divided into 4 equal parts. The distance shown between A and X is $\frac{1}{4}$ of the total inch.

The distance A to Z can also be represented as a fraction of an inch. It is $\frac{3}{4}$ of the total inch.

The scale could have been divided into any number of equal parts and fractions could be written representing any number of these parts. The common divisions used on scales are fourths, ($\frac{1}{4}$), eighths, ($\frac{1}{8}$), sixteenths, ($\frac{1}{16}$), thirty-secondths, ($\frac{1}{32}$), and sixty-fourths, ($\frac{1}{64}$).

All the fractions written above have certain things in common. They contain two terms, one above the line and one below. The term above the line is called the numerator. The term below the line is called the denominator.

$$\text{Numerator} - \frac{1}{4} - \text{Denominator (the number of parts in a whole)}$$

Kinds of Common Fractions

Fractions appear in a number of forms. A proper fraction is a fraction whose numerator is smaller than the denominator. This type of fraction represents a value less than the whole unit. (Less than one.)

$\frac{1}{4}$, $\frac{3}{4}$, $\frac{13}{16}$, $\frac{27}{64}$

An improper fraction is one whose top term is equal to or greater than the bottom term. The value indicated by this type of fraction is equal to or larger than one.

EXAMPLES:

$\frac{5}{4}$, $\frac{16}{16}$, $\frac{35}{32}$, $\frac{27}{25}$, $\frac{322}{64}$

A mixed number is one which contains both a whole number and a fraction. The value of the fraction is greater than one.

EXAMPLES:

$5\frac{1}{4}$ $13\frac{3}{8}$ $1\frac{1}{64}$

Lowest Terms - Proper Fractions

Fractions given to the tradesperson on prints and sketches are always given in their lowest terms. When the tradesperson, through calculation, has an answer to a problem expressed as a fraction, it is best to always reduce this answer to the lowest terms before using.

A fraction is in its lowest terms when neither the numerator nor the denominator can be divided by a common factor other than one.

EXAMPLES:

$\frac{5}{8}$ is in its lowest terms. Neither the 5 nor 8 can be divided by any common factor without a remainder.

EXAMPLES:

$\frac{10}{16}$ is not in its lowest terms. Both the 10 and the 16 can be divided by the common factor 2.

$$\frac{10}{16} = \frac{10}{16} \div \frac{2}{2} = \frac{5}{8}$$

$\frac{5}{8}$ is in its lowest terms and ready to use.

It is not always possible to see a common factor that will reduce a fraction to its lowest terms in one step as in the previous example. It is sometimes necessary to reduce the fraction a number of times to achieve lowest terms. To reduce $\frac{120}{192}$ to lowest terms, the following procedure might take place.

$$\frac{120}{192}$$

$$\frac{120 \div 4 = 30}{192 \div 4 = 48} \longleftarrow \text{Divide both the numerator and denominator by common factor 4.}$$

$$\frac{30 \div 6 = 5}{48 \div 6 = 8} \longleftarrow \text{Divide new factor by common factor 6.}$$

$\frac{5}{8}$ is a common fraction in its lowest terms.

The fraction $^{120}/_{192}$ can be reduced to lowest terms by using the same common factors but in another order, or by using other factors which would be common to both numerator and denominator. Regardless of the order or factors, it will always reduce to $^5/_8$.

EXERCISE 1

Reduce the following fractions to their lowest terms. If they cannot be reduced as given, write L.T.

_____ 1. $\dfrac{4}{8}$	_____ 9. $\dfrac{64}{128}$	_____ 17. $\dfrac{48}{93}$	_____ 25. $\dfrac{42}{700}$
_____ 2. $\dfrac{2}{8}$	_____ 10. $\dfrac{84}{144}$	_____ 18. $\dfrac{14}{19}$	_____ 26. $\dfrac{15}{147}$
_____ 3. $\dfrac{5}{8}$	_____ 11. $\dfrac{125}{1000}$	_____ 19. $\dfrac{287}{700}$	_____ 27. $\dfrac{2844}{5632}$
_____ 4. $\dfrac{14}{16}$	_____ 12. $\dfrac{636}{1536}$	_____ 20. $\dfrac{96}{216}$	_____ 28. $\dfrac{284}{2740}$
_____ 5. $\dfrac{28}{64}$	_____ 13. $\dfrac{11}{222}$	_____ 21. $\dfrac{8125}{10,000}$	_____ 29. $\dfrac{2000}{40,000}$
_____ 6. $\dfrac{12}{32}$	_____ 14. $\dfrac{625}{1000}$	_____ 22. $\dfrac{15,625}{1,000,000}$	_____ 30. $\dfrac{6875}{10,000}$
_____ 7. $\dfrac{35}{80}$	_____ 15. $\dfrac{9375}{10,000}$	_____ 23. $\dfrac{13}{23}$	
_____ 8. $\dfrac{37}{80}$	_____ 16. $\dfrac{23}{25}$	_____ 24. $\dfrac{1}{2}$	

Lowest Terms - Improper Fractions

To reduce improper fractions to lowest terms requires the same principles used in the previous exercise plus the knowledge of how to change improper fractions to mixed numbers.

In order to accomplish this in the most direct manner, it will help to know that any fraction can be read as the numerator divided by the denominator.

EXAMPLE: $^4/_5$ also means 4 divided by 5.

Putting this information to work in reducing improper fractions gives:

$$\frac{8}{8} = 8 \div 8 = 1$$

Or in the case of the numerator being larger than the denominator:

$$\frac{11}{8} = 11 \div 8 = 1\frac{3}{8}$$

Change improper fractions to whole or mixed numbers. Reduce first when possible.

_____ 1. $\dfrac{5}{4}$	_____ 6. $\dfrac{8}{5}$	_____ 11. $\dfrac{2125}{1000}$	_____ 16. $\dfrac{29}{7}$	_____ 21. $\dfrac{5500}{55}$
_____ 2. $\dfrac{6}{4}$	_____ 7. $\dfrac{133}{11}$	_____ 12. $\dfrac{1000}{1000}$	_____ 17. $\dfrac{237}{51}$	_____ 22. $\dfrac{732}{143}$
_____ 3. $\dfrac{15}{9}$	_____ 8. $\dfrac{43}{16}$	_____ 13. $\dfrac{427}{66}$	_____ 18. $\dfrac{2800}{130}$	_____ 23. $\dfrac{13,125}{10,000}$
_____ 4. $\dfrac{15}{8}$	_____ 9. $\dfrac{97}{32}$	_____ 14. $\dfrac{87}{13}$	_____ 19. $\dfrac{536}{28}$	_____ 24. $\dfrac{496}{96}$
_____ 5. $\dfrac{7}{4}$	_____ 10. $\dfrac{87}{64}$	_____ 15. $\dfrac{54}{5}$	_____ 20. $\dfrac{84}{14}$	_____ 25. $\dfrac{325}{5}$

Certain math calculations require that the fraction not be in its lowest terms. In fact, they dictate that the denominator must be a specific number. In order to raise the denominator to this number, the numerator must also be raised by the same value in order for the value of the fraction remain the same.

In reducing a fraction, both the numerator and denominator were divided by the same number (common factor). This procedure did not change the value of the fraction.

To raise the denominator to a given number without changing the value of the fraction, both the numerator and denominator must be multiplied by a common factor. This is the reverse of the reducing operation.

EXAMPLE:

Change ⅝ to a fraction with 32 as the denominator.

To change the denominator (8) to 32 it must be multiplied by 4.

The numerator must be multiplied by 4 also.

$$\dfrac{5}{8} = \dfrac{5 \times 4}{8 \times 4} = \dfrac{20}{32}$$

EXERCISE 3

Change the following fractions to fractions of equal value having denominators as indicated.

1. $\dfrac{1}{2} = \dfrac{}{8}$ 3. $\dfrac{1}{4} = \dfrac{}{32}$ 5. $\dfrac{3}{4} = \dfrac{}{36}$ 7. $\dfrac{13}{64} = \dfrac{}{128}$ 9. $\dfrac{5}{8} = \dfrac{}{144}$

2. $\dfrac{1}{4} = \dfrac{}{16}$ 4. $\dfrac{3}{4} = \dfrac{}{24}$ 6. $\dfrac{2}{5} = \dfrac{}{60}$ 8. $\dfrac{13}{64} = \dfrac{}{448}$ 10. $\dfrac{13}{32} = \dfrac{}{96}$

11. $\dfrac{11}{18} = \dfrac{\rule{1.5cm}{0.4pt}}{144}$ 16. $\dfrac{1}{2} = \dfrac{\rule{1.5cm}{0.4pt}}{10}$ 21. $\dfrac{7}{32} = \dfrac{\rule{1.5cm}{0.4pt}}{160}$ 26. $\dfrac{4}{5} = \dfrac{\rule{1.5cm}{0.4pt}}{100}$ 31. $\dfrac{4}{8} = \dfrac{\rule{1.5cm}{0.4pt}}{32}$

12. $\dfrac{1}{8} = \dfrac{\rule{1.5cm}{0.4pt}}{1000}$ 17. $\dfrac{1}{2} = \dfrac{\rule{1.5cm}{0.4pt}}{100}$ 22. $\dfrac{11}{32} = \dfrac{\rule{1.5cm}{0.4pt}}{352}$ 27. $\dfrac{13}{16} = \dfrac{\rule{1.5cm}{0.4pt}}{10,000}$ 32. $\dfrac{12}{48} = \dfrac{\rule{1.5cm}{0.4pt}}{96}$

13. $\dfrac{23}{25} = \dfrac{\rule{1.5cm}{0.4pt}}{175}$ 18. $\dfrac{1}{2} = \dfrac{\rule{1.5cm}{0.4pt}}{1000}$ 23. $\dfrac{3}{5} = \dfrac{\rule{1.5cm}{0.4pt}}{1000}$ 28. $\dfrac{15}{16} = \dfrac{\rule{1.5cm}{0.4pt}}{144}$

14. $\dfrac{1}{32} = \dfrac{\rule{1.5cm}{0.4pt}}{100,000}$ 19. $\dfrac{5}{6} = \dfrac{\rule{1.5cm}{0.4pt}}{42}$ 24. $\dfrac{4}{9} = \dfrac{\rule{1.5cm}{0.4pt}}{189}$ 29. $\dfrac{5}{15} = \dfrac{\rule{1.5cm}{0.4pt}}{90}$

15. $\dfrac{31}{64} = \dfrac{\rule{1.5cm}{0.4pt}}{896}$ 20. $\dfrac{5}{32} = \dfrac{\rule{1.5cm}{0.4pt}}{64}$ 25. $\dfrac{1}{16} = \dfrac{\rule{1.5cm}{0.4pt}}{10,000}$ 30. $\dfrac{9}{16} = \dfrac{\rule{1.5cm}{0.4pt}}{320}$

Addition and Subtraction of Common Fractions

In the addition and subtraction of fractions, the most important consideration is that all fractions involved have the same denominator. Adding and subtracting cannot take place until this has been accomplished. In order to get the fractions to their lowest common denominator, it is first necessary to determine what it will be.

Method 1 - By Sight

In the fractions, ½, ¾, ⅝, ¹¹⁄₁₆, the denominators can be divided equally into 16. Therefore, 16 is the lowest common denominator.

$$\frac{1}{2} = \frac{1 \times 8}{2 \times 8} = \frac{8}{16}$$

$$\frac{3}{4} = \frac{3 \times 4}{4 \times 4} = \frac{12}{16}$$

$$\frac{5}{8} = \frac{5 \times 2}{8 \times 2} = \frac{10}{16}$$

$$\frac{11}{16} = \frac{11}{16} = \frac{11}{16}$$

Also, the fractions ¾ and ⁷⁄₁₀ present no great problem since it can be readily seen that both 4 and 10 can be divided evenly into 20.

$$\frac{3}{4} = \frac{3 \times 5}{4 \times 5} = \frac{15}{20} \qquad \frac{7}{10} = \frac{7 \times 2}{10 \times 2} = \frac{14}{20}$$

Method 2 - Reducing to Prime

In this case, fractions whose lowest common denominator cannot be identified by sight, such as ⅝, ⁷⁄₁₀, and ⅚, the denominator must first be reduced to prime factors.

Denominator	Prime Factors
8 =	(2) (2) (2)
10 =	(2) (5)
6 =	(2) (3)

By taking the factors the greatest number of times they appear in any single denominator and multiplying these together, the lowest common denominator can be obtained.

$$(2)\ (2)\ (2)\ (5)\ (3) = 120 = \text{lowest common denominator}$$

The factor 2 appears 3 times in the first denominator   The factor 5 appears once in the second denominator   The factor 3 appears in the third denominator

Therefore:

$$\frac{5}{8} = \frac{5 \times 15}{8 \times 15} = \frac{75}{120}$$

$$\frac{7}{10} = \frac{7 \times 12}{10 \times 12} = \frac{84}{120}$$

$$\frac{5}{6} = \frac{5 \times 20}{6 \times 20} = \frac{100}{120}$$

EXERCISE 4

Change the following fractions to fractions of equal value having the lowest common denominators.

_____1. $\dfrac{7}{8}$ $\dfrac{11}{16}$

_____2. $\dfrac{3}{4}$ $\dfrac{13}{16}$

_____3. $\dfrac{15}{32}$ $\dfrac{7}{8}$ $\dfrac{5}{16}$

_____4. $\dfrac{1}{2}$ $\dfrac{3}{6}$ $\dfrac{2}{5}$

_____5. $\dfrac{4}{5}$ $\dfrac{2}{7}$

_____6. $\dfrac{5}{16}$ $\dfrac{17}{24}$

_____7. $\dfrac{5}{16}$ $\dfrac{3}{18}$

_____8. $\dfrac{1}{2}$ $\dfrac{4}{5}$ $\dfrac{3}{7}$

_____9. $\dfrac{1}{2}$ $\dfrac{4}{35}$ $\dfrac{3}{14}$

_____10. $\dfrac{1}{4}$ $\dfrac{4}{35}$ $\dfrac{3}{14}$

_____11. $\dfrac{31}{32}$ $\dfrac{63}{64}$ $\dfrac{15}{16}$

_____12. $\dfrac{2}{3}$ $\dfrac{2}{7}$ $\dfrac{3}{12}$ $\dfrac{1}{4}$

_____13. $\dfrac{7}{12}$ $\dfrac{4}{5}$ $\dfrac{7}{15}$

_____14. $\dfrac{3}{32}$ $\dfrac{21}{125}$ $\dfrac{7}{10}$

_____15. $\dfrac{5}{16}$ $\dfrac{7}{32}$ $\dfrac{17}{100}$ $\dfrac{33}{1000}$

_____16. $\dfrac{5}{8}$ $\dfrac{23}{100}$ $\dfrac{3}{10}$

_____17. $\dfrac{1}{4}$ $\dfrac{3}{5}$ $\dfrac{6}{7}$

_____18. $\dfrac{1}{3}$ $\dfrac{1}{4}$ $\dfrac{1}{8}$ $\dfrac{2}{5}$

_____19. $\dfrac{4}{9}$ $\dfrac{5}{13}$ $\dfrac{15}{26}$ $\dfrac{1}{3}$

_____20. $\dfrac{13}{18}$ $\dfrac{1}{16}$ $\dfrac{3}{20}$ $\dfrac{5}{13}$

_____21. $\dfrac{3}{19}$ $\dfrac{5}{57}$ $\dfrac{1}{3}$

Having obtained the lowest common denominator for the fractions involved, adding or subtracting can follow by doing the indicated operation to the numerators, placing the result over the denominator, and reducing to the lowest terms.

EXAMPLE: Add ¾ and ⁷⁄₁₀

$$\frac{3}{4} = \frac{3 \times 5}{4 \times 5} = \frac{15}{20}$$

$$\frac{7}{10} = \frac{7 \times 2}{10 \times 2} = \frac{14}{20}$$

1. Expand to fractions having a common denominator

2. Add numerators and place sum over common denominator

$$\frac{29}{20} = 1\tfrac{9}{20}$$ 3. Reduce

EXAMPLE: Subtract ⅔ from ⅘

$$\frac{4}{5} = \frac{12}{15}$$

1. Expand the fractions having a common denominator

2. Subtract and place remainder over common denominator

$$\frac{2}{3} = \frac{10}{15}$$

$$\frac{2}{15}$$

3. Answer in lowest terms and cannot be reduced

EXERCISE 5

Add or subtract the following fractions. Reduce the answers to the lowest terms.

_____ 1. $\dfrac{2}{3} + \dfrac{1}{3}$

_____ 2. $\dfrac{1}{2} + \dfrac{5}{8}$

_____ 3. $\dfrac{7}{16} - \dfrac{5}{16}$

_____ 4. $\dfrac{1}{2} - \dfrac{1}{4}$

_____ 5. $\dfrac{2}{3} - \dfrac{1}{7}$

_____ 6. $\dfrac{3}{32} + \dfrac{11}{64} + \dfrac{7}{8}$

_____ 7. $\dfrac{5}{12} + \dfrac{7}{15}$

_____ 8. $\dfrac{3}{4} + \dfrac{1}{35} + \dfrac{3}{7}$

_____ 9. $\dfrac{9}{16} - \dfrac{3}{18}$

_____ 10. $\dfrac{17}{24} - \dfrac{5}{16}$

_____ 11. $\dfrac{1}{3} + \dfrac{3}{4} + \dfrac{2}{7}$

_____ 12. $\dfrac{1}{12} - \dfrac{1}{144}$

_____ 13. $\dfrac{1}{12} + \dfrac{2}{6}$

_____ 14. $\dfrac{14}{15} - \dfrac{7}{8}$

_____ 15. $\dfrac{48}{49} - \dfrac{2}{3}$

_____ 16. $\dfrac{13}{64} - \dfrac{3}{24}$

_____ 17. $\dfrac{5}{8} - \dfrac{3}{18}$

_____ 18. $\dfrac{4}{5} + \dfrac{3}{25} + \dfrac{7}{45}$

_____ 19. $\dfrac{17}{45} - \dfrac{1}{3}$

_____ 20. $\dfrac{9}{16} + \dfrac{7}{8} + \dfrac{15}{32}$

_____ 21. $\dfrac{3}{19} + \dfrac{5}{57} + \dfrac{1}{3}$

Adding and subtracting of mixed numbers follows the same steps used for common fractions except now a whole number is also involved. The process is exactly the same as with proper fractions except that the whole numbers must be added or subtracted.

EXAMPLE: Add 2⅖ to 3⅚

$$2\frac{2}{5} = 2\frac{2 \times 6}{5 \times 6} = 2\frac{12}{30}$$

$$+3\frac{5}{6} = 3\frac{5 \times 5}{6 \times 5} = 3\frac{25}{30}$$

$$5\frac{37}{30} = 6\frac{7}{30}$$

EXAMPLE: Subtract 2¼ from 5⅚

$$5\frac{5}{6} = 5\frac{10}{12}$$

$$-2\frac{1}{4} = 2\frac{3}{12}$$

$$3\frac{7}{12}$$

EXAMPLE: Subtract 2¾ from 3⅖

$$3\frac{2}{5} = 3\frac{8}{20} = 2\frac{28}{20}$$

$$-2\frac{3}{4} = 2\frac{15}{20} = 2\frac{15}{20}$$

$$\frac{13}{20}$$

3. This is accomplished by taking one whole unit from the 3 making it a 2.

4. Making the whole unit borrowed into a fraction having the same denominator as in the other fraction ($^{20}/_{20} = 1$) and adding this to the fraction $^8/_{20}$.

1. Expand to fractions having common denominators.

2. Since it is impossible to subtract the numerator 15 from the numerator 8, the 8 must borrow from the whole units.

5. Subtract numerators, place the answer over the common denominator.

EXERCISE 6

Do the indicated operation and reduce to the lowest terms.

_____1. $2\frac{7}{8} + 3\frac{1}{2}$

_____2. $4\frac{11}{16} - 1\frac{1}{2}$

_____3. $3\frac{1}{5} + 2\frac{1}{4}$

_____4. $4\frac{5}{6} - 2\frac{1}{5}$

_____5. $7\frac{7}{8} + 4\frac{1}{16}$

_____6. $2\frac{1}{3} + 4\frac{5}{6}$

_____7. $2\frac{1}{2} + 3\frac{2}{5} + \frac{3}{7}$

_____8. $4\frac{1}{2} - 3\frac{3}{4}$

_____9. $\frac{5}{16} + \frac{3}{12} + 1\frac{1}{3}$

_____10. $2\frac{5}{18} - 1\frac{7}{16}$

_____11. $\frac{25}{32} + \frac{63}{64}$

_____12. $1\frac{5}{8} - \frac{7}{8}$

_____13. $\frac{13}{16} + 2\frac{63}{64} + \frac{1}{2}$

_____14. $11\frac{4}{5} + \frac{5}{6} + 5\frac{3}{4}$

_____15. $\frac{31}{32} + \frac{15}{16} + \frac{63}{64} + 1$

_____16. $7 - \frac{5}{16}$

_____17. $5\frac{2}{5} - 3\frac{7}{8}$

_____18. $3\frac{27}{64} - 1\frac{19}{144}$

_____19. $4\frac{3}{4} - \frac{9}{16}$

_____20. $2\frac{1}{8} + 2\frac{1}{5} + 2\frac{1}{6} + 2\frac{1}{2}$

_____21. $\frac{1}{2} - \frac{1}{13}$

_____22. $\frac{3}{5} + \frac{5}{7} + \frac{4}{9}$

_____23. $4\frac{5}{54} - 2\frac{5}{36}$

_____24. $4\frac{5}{32} - \frac{17}{64}$

A further possibility that occurs in adding and subtracting of fractions is when both addition and subtraction appear in the same problem. The order in which the operations are done has no affect on the answer.

EXAMPLE: 2¼ + 3⁵⁄₁₆ − 2¹⁄₃₂ − ⅛

By taking the operations in the order they occur:

$$2\frac{1}{4} = 2\frac{4}{16}$$
$$3\frac{5}{16} = 3\frac{5}{16}$$ ⟵ The sum of the first two terms
$$\overline{\quad 5\frac{9}{16} = 5\frac{18}{32}}$$
$$2\frac{1}{32} = 2\frac{1}{32}$$
$$\overline{\quad 3\frac{17}{32} = 3\frac{17}{32}}$$ ⟵ The remainder when the third term is subtracted
$$\frac{1}{8} = -\frac{4}{32}$$
$$\overline{\quad 3\frac{13}{32}}$$ ⟵ The answer when the last operation is accomplished

Or in a simpler approach might be to first add all those terms which are to be added (any number without a sign, or + in front is considered as added). Next subtract all terms to be subtracted. Finally solve for the answer by subtracting the results.

$$2\frac{1}{4} = 2\frac{4}{16}$$
$$+3\frac{5}{16} = 3\frac{5}{16}$$ ⟵ All added terms come to 5⁹⁄₁₆
$$\overline{\quad 5\frac{9}{16}}$$

$$-2\frac{1}{32} = 2\frac{1}{32}$$
$$-\frac{1}{8} = \frac{4}{32}$$ ⟵ All subtracted terms come to 2⁵⁄₃₂
$$\overline{\quad 2\frac{5}{32}}$$

$$5\frac{9}{16} = 5\frac{18}{32}$$
$$-2\frac{5}{32} = 2\frac{5}{32}$$ ⟵ Subtract these two problems, the answer is 3¹³⁄₃₂
$$\overline{\quad 3\frac{13}{32}}$$

EXERCISE 7

Solve the following:

_____1. $2\frac{1}{3} + 1\frac{2}{5} - \frac{15}{16}$

_____2. $1\frac{3}{5} - \frac{1}{2} + 2\frac{3}{16}$

_____3. $\frac{4}{5} + \frac{5}{6} - \frac{3}{4} - \frac{3}{15}$

_____4. $4\frac{7}{16} - 2\frac{1}{3} + 6\frac{13}{16} + \frac{63}{64}$

_____5. $2\frac{1}{2} - 4\frac{3}{4} + 5\frac{5}{8}$

_____6. $7\frac{1}{4} + 11\frac{3}{8} - 5\frac{15}{16} - 4\frac{1}{2}$

_____ 7. $\dfrac{7}{9} + \dfrac{2}{5} - \dfrac{1}{3} - \dfrac{11}{18}$

_____ 10. $3\dfrac{5}{6} - \dfrac{1}{4} + 1\dfrac{4}{5} - \dfrac{3}{8}$

_____ 8. $\dfrac{3}{8} + \dfrac{4}{5} + 1\dfrac{1}{2} + \dfrac{13}{16}$

_____ 11. $4\dfrac{3}{8} - 7\dfrac{1}{15} + 4\dfrac{4}{5}$

_____ 9. $\dfrac{15}{32} - \dfrac{6}{32} + \dfrac{11}{32} - \dfrac{1}{32}$

_____ 12. $\dfrac{24}{15} + \dfrac{35}{45} - \dfrac{4}{5}$

Multiplying and Dividing Common Fractions

Unlike addition and subtraction, it is not necessary to find a lowest common denominator in order to multiply and divide. These operations can be done to proper and improper fractions as given.

TO MULTIPLY:

First, multiply the numerators. This product becomes the numerator of the answer. Second, multiply the denominators. This product is the denominator of the answer. Third, reduce if necessary.

EXAMPLE: $\frac{7}{8} \times \frac{1}{4}$

$$\dfrac{7}{8} \times \dfrac{1}{4} = \dfrac{7 \times 1}{8 \times 4} = \dfrac{7}{32}$$

EXAMPLE: $\dfrac{2}{5} \times \dfrac{3}{8}$

$$\dfrac{2}{5} \times \dfrac{3}{8} = \dfrac{2 \times 3}{5 \times 8} = \dfrac{6}{40} = \dfrac{3}{20}$$

This problem can be reduced before multiplying by dividing any numerator and any denominator by a common factor. If all possible reductions are made prior to multiplication, the answer will be in lowest terms.

$$\dfrac{\overset{1}{\cancel{2}} \times 3}{5 \times \underset{4}{\cancel{8}}} = \dfrac{3}{20}$$ Both the numerator "2" and the denominator "8" can be divided by the common factor "2".

EXAMPLE:

When a mixed number appears in a multiplication problem, it is first necessary to change it to an improper fraction. This is done as follows:

    a. multiply the whole number by the denominator.
    b. add this result to the numerator.
    c. set this sum over the denominator.

Change 2¼ to an improper fraction   1. $2\dfrac{1}{4} = 8$ 2. $8 + 1 = 9$ 3. answer $= \dfrac{9}{4}$

Multiply

EXAMPLE: 2¼ × 3⅔   2. Reduce by common factor "3".

$$2\frac{1}{4} \times 3\frac{2}{3} = \frac{\overset{3}{\cancel{9}}}{4} \times \frac{11}{\underset{1}{\cancel{3}}} = \frac{33}{4} = 8\frac{1}{4}$$

1. Change mixed numbers to improper fractions.

EXERCISE 8

Multiply and reduce to lowest terms.

_____1. $2 \times \frac{3}{4}$ _____10. $\frac{3}{7} \times 35$

_____2. $\frac{1}{2} \times \frac{2}{5}$ _____11. $15\frac{1}{3} \times 4\frac{1}{2}$

_____3. $\frac{5}{8} \times \frac{2}{15}$ _____12. $\frac{7}{16} \times 10 \times 2\frac{1}{2}$

_____4. $\frac{1}{3} \times \frac{3}{4} \times \frac{2}{5}$ _____13. $13\frac{1}{3} \times 9\frac{1}{2}$

_____5. $\frac{7}{16} \times \frac{32}{49}$ _____14. $\frac{13}{16} \times \frac{1}{8} \times \frac{32}{52}$

_____6. $1\frac{2}{3} \times 1\frac{1}{4}$ _____15. $6\frac{1}{2} \times 7\frac{1}{2} \times 1\frac{2}{3}$

_____7. $\frac{1}{2} \times \frac{1}{2} \times \frac{1}{2}$ _____16. $\frac{121}{144} \times \frac{72}{132}$

_____8. $\frac{3}{4} \times \frac{2}{3} \times \frac{1}{3}$ _____17. $\frac{5}{8} \times \frac{3}{15} \times \frac{2}{3} \times \frac{6}{8} \times \frac{9}{32} \times 5$

_____9. $\frac{34}{39} \times \frac{26}{51}$ _____18. $4 \times \frac{7}{8} \times \frac{3}{10}$

Division of Common Fractions

Once the principles of multiplication are mastered, going to division of common fractions is only a small step. Division requires the inversion of the divisor (the number being divided by) or the denominator. Finally, cross cancel if possible and multiply the fractions.

DEFINITION: Invert ⅝ (Invert means to turn upside down)

⅝ inverted becomes ⁸⁄₅

Once the divisor is inverted, drop the division sign, put a multiplication sign in its place and multiply.

EXAMPLE 1:

Divide: ¾ by ⅝

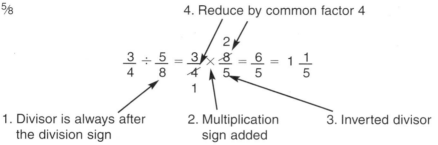

4. Reduce by common factor 4

$$\frac{3}{4} \div \frac{5}{8} = \frac{3}{4} \times \frac{8}{5} = \frac{6}{5} = 1\frac{1}{5}$$

1. Divisor is always after the division sign

2. Multiplication sign added

3. Inverted divisor

EXAMPLE 2: Proceed with division.

Divide: 2½ ÷ 1⅜

$$2\frac{1}{2} \div 1\frac{3}{8} = \frac{5}{2} \div \frac{11}{8} = \frac{5}{2} \times \frac{8}{11} = \frac{20}{11} = 1\frac{9}{11}$$

In mixed numbers change to improper fraction first.

EXAMPLE 3:

When the problem calls for division of more than two fractions invert all of the fractions following a division sign. Do **NOT** invert the first fraction.

When the problem includes a combination of division and multiplication invert all fractions following a division sign, but do **NOT** invert fractions following a multiplication sign. Do **NOT** invert the first fraction.

$$\frac{1}{2} \div \frac{3}{8} \times \frac{9}{12} = \frac{1}{2} \times \frac{8}{3} \times \frac{9}{12} = \frac{1}{2} \times \frac{8}{3} \times \frac{9}{12} = 1$$

EXERCISE 9

Solve and reduce to lowest terms.

_____1. $\frac{2}{3} \div \frac{1}{2}$ _____6. $2\frac{1}{8} \div 1\frac{5}{16}$

_____2. $4 \div \frac{5}{8}$ _____7. $\frac{15}{16} \div 5$

_____3. $\frac{5}{8} \div 4$ _____8. $\frac{7}{9} \div 4\frac{2}{3}$

_____4. $1\frac{1}{2} \div \frac{3}{5}$ _____9. $18 \div \frac{6}{7}$

_____5. $4 \div \frac{4}{9}$ _____10. $2\frac{41}{64} \div 4\frac{1}{3}$

_____11. $7 \frac{2}{3} \div 4 \frac{3}{6}$

_____12. $3 \frac{3}{7} \div 1 \frac{5}{7}$

_____13. $18 \div \frac{3}{8}$

_____14. $18 \frac{2}{3} \div \frac{2}{3}$

_____15. $\frac{21}{100} \div 3 \frac{3}{5}$

_____16. $3 \frac{3}{8} \div \frac{3}{32}$

_____17. $\frac{1}{16} \div \frac{1}{16}$

_____18. $\frac{1}{10} \div \frac{1}{100}$

_____19. $\frac{31}{32} \div \frac{5}{8}$

_____20. $4 \frac{7}{8} \div \frac{13}{16}$

_____21. $\frac{2}{5} \div \frac{5}{6} \div \frac{3}{4}$

_____22. $\frac{7}{8} \div \frac{3}{8} \div \frac{21}{64}$

_____23. $\frac{22}{7} \div \frac{4}{5} \div 64$

_____24. $\frac{1}{64} \div \frac{7}{8} \times \frac{3}{4}$

Complex Fractions

A complex fraction is one which has a fraction or mixed number as its numerator, denominator, or both.

EXAMPLES:
$$\frac{\frac{7}{8}}{\frac{3}{5}} \qquad \frac{2\frac{1}{8}}{2} \qquad \frac{2}{2\frac{1}{8}}$$

A fraction can be read as a numerator divided by denominator.

$$\frac{N}{D} = N \div D$$

or

$$\frac{\frac{7}{8}}{\frac{3}{5}} = \frac{7}{8} \div \frac{3}{5}$$

The above step will place a complex fraction into a form that can be readily divided.

EXAMPLES:

$$\frac{\frac{7}{8}}{\frac{3}{5}} = \frac{7}{8} \div \frac{3}{5} = \frac{7}{8} \times \frac{5}{3} = \frac{35}{24} = 1 \frac{11}{24}$$

$$\frac{2\frac{1}{8}}{2} = 2\frac{1}{8} \div 2 = \frac{17}{8} \times \frac{1}{2} = \frac{17}{16} = 1\frac{1}{16}$$

$$\frac{2\frac{1}{8}}{\frac{1}{2}} = 2\frac{1}{8} \div \frac{1}{2} = \frac{17}{\overset{}{\cancel{8}}_{4}} \times \frac{\overset{1}{\cancel{2}}}{1} = \frac{17}{4} = 4\frac{1}{4}$$

EXERCISE 10

Compute the following:

_____ 1. $\dfrac{\dfrac{2}{3}}{\dfrac{1}{16}}$

_____ 6. $\dfrac{2 + \dfrac{1}{2}}{\dfrac{3}{4} + \dfrac{2}{3}}$

_____ 2. $\dfrac{4\dfrac{7}{8}}{3\dfrac{1}{7}}$

_____ 7. $\dfrac{\dfrac{7}{8} + \dfrac{21}{64}}{2\dfrac{3}{8}}$

_____ 3. $\dfrac{\dfrac{31}{32}}{\dfrac{5}{8}}$

_____ 8. $\dfrac{2\dfrac{1}{32}}{\dfrac{1}{16} \times \dfrac{4}{5}}$

_____ 4. $\dfrac{7\dfrac{1}{2}}{\dfrac{5}{16}}$

_____ 9. $\dfrac{\dfrac{3}{8} \times \dfrac{4}{9}}{\dfrac{7}{9} \div \dfrac{21}{35}}$

_____ 5. $\dfrac{\dfrac{41}{64}}{\dfrac{16}{21}}$

_____ 10. $\dfrac{\dfrac{7}{8} + \dfrac{3}{5} - \dfrac{1}{2}}{\dfrac{7}{8} \times \dfrac{2}{3} \times \dfrac{9}{14}}$

Review

1. A fraction is a method of showing part of a whole item.

2. Terms - $\dfrac{\text{Numerator}}{\text{Denominator}}$

3. A **proper fraction** represents **less** than a whole unit.

4. An **improper fraction** represents a value **equal** to or **greater** than the whole unit.

5. A **mixed number** is one which contains a whole number and a fraction.

6. A fraction is in its lowest terms when both the numerator and denominator cannot be divided by a common factor.

7. To add and subtract, change to fractions of equal value having lowest common denominator. Place answer over common denominator and reduce if possible.

8. To multiply fractions, the product of the numerators becomes the numerator of the answer and the product of the denominators becomes the denominator of the answer. Reduce if possible.

9. To divide fractions, invert the divisor and proceed as multiplication.

Decimal Fractions

Because precision is necessary for parts in today's machines and tools, it is required that some standard method be used to represent very small parts of an inch other than common fractions. Fractions representing much smaller divisions of the inch are used for this purpose. In these cases, the inch is divided, instead of 8, 16, 32, and 64 parts, into 100, 1000, etc. parts. This then provides much greater accuracy in parts.

The system of decimal fractions is one which employs as a denominator 10, 100, 1000, 10,000 and up by multiples of ten as the need for accuracy dictates.

A decimal fraction, however, is not written with a numerator and denominator. Only the numerator is written with a rather simple code for designating the denominator.

This code is best explained by the following chart.

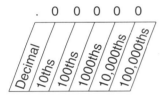

This chart committed to memory will greatly aid the beginning tradesperson in correctly reading dimensions presented out in prints and sketches.

Reading Decimals

To read decimals, the number is read as the numerator and the denominator is read as the place of the last digit to the right of the decimal point.

EXAMPLE:
.8 is read as eight tenths
.47 is read as forty-seven hundredths
.102 is read as one hundred two thousandths
6.535 is read 6 **and** five hundred thirty-five thousandths

Notice in reading this last example the word **and** was inserted to represent the decimal point. It could also have been correctly read as 6 **point** five hundred thirty-five thousandths.

Sometimes these same decimals might be referred to as:

.8 - point eight
.47 - point forty-seven
.102 - point one "0" two
6.535 - six point five three five

In this case, no attempt is made to establish a relationship between the numbers to the right of the decimal point and the indicated denominator. The digits are simply read in their locations.

$\frac{1}{100}$ is written .01

In like manner, any numerator having a denominator of 100 is written so that its last digit is **two** places removed from the decimal point.

EXAMPLE: $\frac{3}{100}$ = .03 $\frac{15}{100}$ = .15

$\frac{1}{1000}$ is written .001

The numerator's last digit is three spaces to the right of the decimal point.

$\frac{1}{1,000,000}$ is written .000001, $\frac{1}{10,000}$ is written .0001

EXERCISE 11

Write the following decimals in words giving the numerator and denominator.

1.   .7 _____

2.   .22 _____

3.   .02 _____

4.   .003 _____

5.   .3 _____

6.   .1375 _____

7.   6.134 _____

8.   .99 _____

9.   .888 _____

10.   5.675 _____

11.   .8 _____

12.   7.8 _____

13.   7.0023 _____

14.   .4 _____

15.   3.012 _____

16.   .00001 _____

17.   .125 _____

18.   .9375 _____

19.   .28125 _____

20.   .500 _____

Rewrite the following as decimals:

_____1. two tenths

_____2. seven thousandths

_____3. one hundred thirty-six ten-thousandths

_____4. fifteen hundredths

_____5. five and forty-seven thousandths

_____6. one thousand and one thousandths

_____7. two hundred twenty-five and two hundred twenty-five thousandths

_____8. two thousand one hundred twenty-four ten-thousandths

_____9. seven point six five four five

_____10. forty-seven point one two five

EXERCISE 13

Rewrite the following as decimals:

_____1. $\dfrac{5}{10}$

_____2. $\dfrac{7}{10}$

_____3. $\dfrac{43}{100}$

_____4. $\dfrac{6}{100}$

_____5. $\dfrac{5}{10000}$

_____6. $\dfrac{125}{1000}$

_____7. $\dfrac{4875}{10000}$

_____8. $\dfrac{125}{10000}$

_____9. $25\dfrac{125}{10000}$

_____10. $1000\dfrac{1}{1000}$

_____11. $2\dfrac{6023}{1,000,000}$

_____12. $1515\dfrac{15}{1000}$

_____13. $5\dfrac{7}{1,000,000}$

_____14. $\dfrac{406}{1000}$

_____15. $\dfrac{5260}{10000}$

_____16. $\dfrac{832}{1000}$

Conversion - Decimals and Common Fractions

Many prints have both decimal and common fractions. Before computations can be made, it is necessary to change to all decimals or all common fractions.

In changing a common fraction to a decimal fraction, divide the numerator by the denominator with long division.

EXAMPLE: Change ⅜ to a decimal

Divide the numerator by the denominator $8\overline{)3.000}$ with quotient $.375$

EXERCISE 14

Rewrite the following as decimals:

_____1. $\dfrac{3}{16}$	_____5. $\dfrac{5}{8}$	_____9. $\dfrac{27}{64}$
_____2. $\dfrac{45}{64}$	_____6. $\dfrac{21}{64}$	_____10. $\dfrac{1}{3}$
_____3. $\dfrac{3}{4}$	_____7. $\dfrac{3}{5}$	
_____4. $\dfrac{1}{16}$	_____8. $\dfrac{27}{32}$	

If, on the other hand, it is better to change decimal fractions to common fractions, set the decimal, as the numerator of a fraction, over the denominator, from the earlier chart, and reduce.

EXAMPLE: Change .625 to a common fraction and reduce.

$$.625 = \frac{625}{1000} = \frac{5}{8}$$

EXERCISE 15

Change the following decimals to common fractions and reduce to lowest terms.

_____1. .5	_____6. 3.05
_____2. .24	_____7. 4.9375
_____3. .096	_____8. .6875
_____4. .0625	_____9. .015625
_____5. .625	_____10. 3.08125

Addition and Subtraction of Decimals

In order to add or subtract common fractions, the denominators must be the same. In the case of decimal fractions, the denominators must be aligned. An easy way to accomplish this is to first line the decimal points one below the other. The numbers will then be in the proper columns.

EXAMPLE: Add 3.75 to 2.9375

$$\begin{array}{r} 3.75 \\ +2.9375 \\ \hline 6.6875 \end{array}$$

EXAMPLE: Subtract .01625 from 1

$$\begin{array}{r} 1.00000 \\ -.01625 \\ \hline .98375 \end{array}$$

Add and subtract as indicated. If necessary, change common fractions to decimals.

_____1. .12 + .037

_____2. .756 + 1.3705

_____3. $2\frac{1}{8}$ + 1.375

_____4. .98 − .099

_____5. $3\frac{4}{5}$ + .002 + $\frac{15}{16}$

_____6. $1\frac{1}{2}$ + 1.475

_____7. 5.216 + $\frac{3}{8}$ − 5.505

_____8. 5.703 + 4.256 + $\frac{13}{32}$

_____9. .030303 + 3.0303

_____10. 2.335 + $\frac{1}{2}$ + $2\frac{5}{8}$

_____11. 5.728 + .00035 − $\frac{1}{2}$

_____12. 5.835 − $5\frac{13}{16}$

_____13. .123 + 1.23 + 12.3 + 123

_____14. $\frac{5}{8}$ + $\frac{13}{16}$ − 1.025

_____15. $\frac{17}{64}$ + 5.00365

_____16. 165423 + 1654.23 + .165423

_____17. 522.45 + 8.1 + 365 + .021

_____18. 6.7 − 5.83215794368

_____19. 6.7 + 235 + .0365 + 1000.001

_____20. 4.368 + 4.503 + .7646

Multiplying Decimals

When two numbers containing decimal fractions must be multiplied, the computation is made with no regard to the decimal points. However, the answer must contain the same number of decimal places as found in both numbers being multiplied.

EXAMPLE: Multiply 6.375 by .75

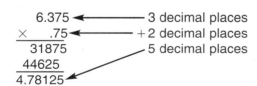

```
        6.375 ◄─────────── 3 decimal places
    ×    .75 ◄─────────── +2 decimal places
      31875          ┌─── 5 decimal places
      44625          │
      4.78125 ◄──────┘
```

Multiply.

_____1. 2.67 × 3.02

_____2. 4.125 × 11.6

_____3. $4\frac{7}{8}$ × 1675.3

_____4. .2 × .2

_____5. 6.78 × .875

_____6. 3.14156 × 314

_____7. .03125 × 6.3

_____8. .0625 × 3.679

_____9. .4375 × $3\frac{1}{2}$

_____10. 3.357 × 6.02

_____11. 6.753 × 10

_____12. 6.753 × 100

_____13. 6.753 × 1000

_____15. .125 × .125

_____14. $3\frac{5}{6}$ × 1.35

_____16. 8.5 × 3.2

Division of Decimals

The division of decimals is basically the same as the division of whole numbers. The only difference is that consideration must be given to the placement of the decimal in the answer.

EXAMPLE: Divide 12.5 by 6.25

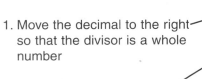

1. Move the decimal to the right so that the divisor is a whole number

2. Move the decimal an equal number of places.

3. Raise the decimal to the quotient.

4. Divide as a whole number.

$$625\overline{)\,1250\,}^{2.}$$

EXERCISE 18

Divide.

_____1. $.5\overline{)\,.875\,}$

_____6. $7\frac{5}{8}$ ÷ 3.14

_____11. 2867 ÷ 10,000

_____2. $.125\overline{)\,.125\,}$

_____7. $.6\overline{)\,.006\,}$

_____12. 7.335 ÷ .006

_____3. $3.75\overline{)\,.375\,}$

_____8. 2867 ÷ 10

_____13. $30.3\overline{)\,.0303\,}$

_____4. $375\overline{)\,37.5\,}$

_____9. 2867 ÷ 100

_____14. $\frac{3}{16}$ ÷ .375

_____5. 6.25 ÷ $1\frac{1}{4}$

_____10. 2867 ÷ 1000

_____15. 1 ÷ $\frac{5}{8}$

Comparing Fractions

Given two or more fractions and asked to determine which fraction is larger (or smaller) the fractions must be converted into fractions with a common denominator before they can be compared.

EXAMPLE: Which is larger ⅜ or ⅗?

$$\frac{3}{8} = \frac{15}{40}$$

$$\frac{3}{5} = \frac{24}{40}$$

Answer: ⅗ (24 parts of 40 is larger than 15 parts of 40.)

Comparing Decimals

Given two or more decimals and asked to arrange decimals numbers in order from smallest to largest the numbers must be converted into decimals with an equal number of decimal places before they can be compared.

EXAMPLE: Arrange those numbers in order from smallest to the largest value.
2.045, 2.4, 2.05, 2.325, 3.2, 1.675

The longest decimal has 3 decimal places, rewrite each decimal to the thousandths place by filling in with zeros.

2.045, 2.400, 2.050, 2.325, 3.200, 1.675

Now arrange the numbers in order from smallest to the largest value.

1.675, 2.045, 2.050, 2.400, 3.200

EXERCISE 19

Circle the largest fraction in each set:

1. $\frac{1}{4}$ $\frac{5}{8}$ 3. $\frac{7}{8}$ $\frac{5}{6}$ $\frac{2}{4}$ 5. $\frac{5}{8}$ $\frac{2}{6}$ $\frac{3}{4}$

2. $\frac{6}{8}$ $\frac{11}{16}$ 4. $\frac{11}{16}$ $\frac{5}{8}$ $\frac{3}{4}$ 6. $\frac{1}{4}$ $\frac{1}{2}$ $\frac{1}{6}$

Rearrange the following values in ascending order:

7. .635, .65, 6.1, .069   10. .76, .7, .076, .071   13. 4.504, 4.5

8. 2.25, .253, .2485, 2.249   11. .006, 5.02, .503, .1483   14. .091, .0909

9. .51, .583, .6, .5126   12. 2.0439, 2.04395   15. .21, .201

BASIC MATH

Time: 12 Minutes

_____1. $8 + 11$

_____2. $71 - 19$

_____3. 8×5

_____4. 9×13

_____5. $54 \div 6$

_____6. $112 \div 4$

_____7. $1.75 - .017$

_____8. $72 + 59$

_____9. 18×4

_____10. $1.768 + .189$

_____11. 1.008×3.5

_____12. $47 - 21$

_____13. $18 \div 4$

_____14. $\frac{1}{3} + \frac{1}{2}$

_____15. $74 + 113$

_____16. $9 \div .3$

_____17. $.017 + .504$

_____18. $.671 - .659$

_____19. $\frac{1}{5} \times \frac{1}{12}$

_____20. $.72 \times 1.8$

_____21. $\frac{29}{42} + \frac{12}{21}$

_____22. $1.67 \times \frac{3}{4}$

_____23. $67 + 23$

_____24. $84 \div 4$

_____25. $1.68 \div 1.2$

_____26. $\frac{1}{6} \div \frac{1}{2}$

_____27. $175 - 143$

_____28. $\frac{29}{72} - \frac{5}{36}$

_____29. 17×12

_____30. 1.9×4.5

_____31. $4 \div .25$

_____32. $.4 \times \frac{1}{4}$

_____33. $139 - 67$

_____34. $4.5 - \frac{6}{8}$

_____35. $18 + 76$

_____36. $\frac{1}{1000} \times 3.616$

_____37. $7.3 - .017$

_____38. $.6 \times .8$

_____39. $\frac{1}{3} \div \frac{1}{6}$

_____40. $76 - 52$

CHAPTER 4

Measurement and Metric Conversion

English and Metric Units

Whether you are reading blueprints, checking parts for quality, siding a house, or plotting out a piece of property you need to know how to read and use some form of a measurement tool. Most of the Skilled Trades require a working knowledge of a variety of measurement tools. A ruler or measuring tape is the carpenters' most commonly used tool. Rulers are used to measure objects and to draw lines of specific length. Many rulers sold in the United States have both the English and the Metric units of measurement. Typically the English measurements are written in fraction form while the metric system uses decimal numbers. Construction trades often use measurements in feet and inches in their line of work. Most of the machine trades use the metric system as their standard unit of measurement. A working knowledge of both systems is important, especially when preparing to take the Apprenticeship Entrance Examination. Both the English and metric units of measurement are written as a number or value followed by a unit of measurement.

EXAMPLES: 12 ft   10 in   45 mi   6 cm   24 mm   82 m   17 km

English Measurement Units

In the English measurement system the basic unit of length is the inch. The abbreviation for the inch is in. Often the period is left off when used in drafting applications. The numerical portion of an English length unit is typically in mixed number, fraction, or whole number format; no decimals.

EXAMPLES: 3 in   6 in   ½ in   5¼ in

A double " mark is also an acceptable symbol for the inch.

EXAMPLES: 3"   6"   ½"   5¼"

Mixed units may also be used for measurements of greater than 12 inches or 1 foot. The abbreviation for foot is ft.

EXAMPLES: 10 ft 8 in   5 ft 4 in   9 ft 10 in

A single ' mark is also an acceptable symbol for the foot.

EXAMPLES: 10' 8"   5' 4"   9' 10"

Metric Measurement Units

In the metric system of measurement the basic unit of length is the centimeter. The abbreviation for the centimeter is cm. The numerical portion of a metric length unit is typically in whole number, or decimal number format as opposed to fractions.

EXAMPLES: 3 cm   6.5 cm   .8 cm   5.3 cm

The millimeter is another commonly used unit of length in the metric system. The abbreviation for millimeter is mm.

EXAMPLES: 1 mm   18 mm   5 mm   29 mm

The English Ruler

A standard ruler is divided into 16ths, that is to say, each inch is subdivided into 16 equal parts, and each part is one sixteenth or $\frac{1}{16}$ of an inch. See the diagram below. A measurement of 3 lines past the 0 mark represents $\frac{3}{16}$ of an inch or $\frac{3}{16}$ in. A measurement of 5 lines past the 0 mark would be $\frac{5}{16}$ in. Notice that the denominator of the fraction is always 16 because each inch is divided into 16 equal parts. However, to be proper, all fractions must be reduced to lowest terms whenever possible. A reading of 6 lines past the 0 mark would be $\frac{6}{16}$ in, but must be reduced to $\frac{3}{8}$ in. Any time a measurement has an even number in the numerator (top number) on a 16ths scale such as $\frac{2}{16}$, $\frac{4}{16}$, $\frac{6}{16}$, $\frac{8}{16}$, $\frac{10}{16}$, $\frac{12}{16}$, $\frac{14}{16}$, and $\frac{16}{16}$ the fraction must be reduced to lowest terms. See the diagram below for reduced fractions. The fraction $\frac{16}{16}$ is equal to 1 inch. Measurements of less than one inch are written in reduced fraction form, such as $\frac{2}{3}$ in, $\frac{5}{16}$ in, $\frac{3}{8}$ in etc. Measurements of an exact number of inches are written in whole number form, such as 3 in, 6 in, 8 in, and so on.

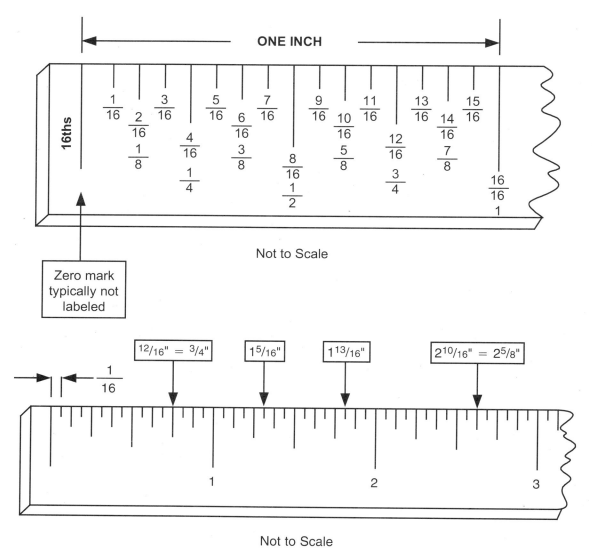

Not to Scale

Zero mark typically not labeled

Not to Scale

In the diagram above, the readings beyond the 1-inch mark are written in mixed number format. A measurement of 5 lines past the 1-inch mark would be written as $1\frac{5}{16}$ in. A measurement of 13 lines past the 1-inch mark would be written as $1\frac{13}{16}$ in. A measurement of 10 lines past the 2-inch mark would be written as $2\frac{10}{16}$ in and must be reduced to $2\frac{5}{8}$ in. A measurement of 8 lines past the 3-inch mark would be written as $3\frac{8}{16}$ in and must be reduced to $3\frac{1}{2}$ in.

When using a ruler, meter stick, or yardstick to measure an object be sure to line up the edge of the object with the FIRST measurement increment on the ruler. If the ruler has a leader (a space without increments) do not match the edge of the ruler to the edge of the object.

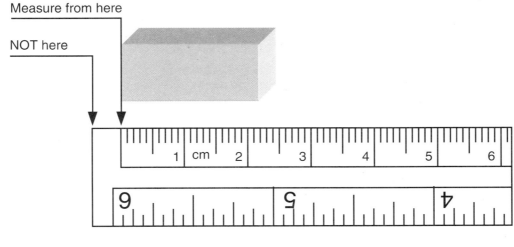

Measure from here

NOT here

EXERCISE 1

LOCATING MEASUREMENTS ON THE ENGLISH RULER

Directions:

1. Rewrite the given fractions as a mixed number whose fraction has a denominator of 16. A review of the fraction section of the previous chapter will help.

2. Example: $3\frac{5}{8} = 3\frac{10}{16}$

3. Locate the measurements on the ruler diagram.

4. Draw an arrow above the picture of the ruler to identify the measurements given below. Write the corresponding letter of the alphabet above the arrow.

5. Check your answers with the answer key at the back of the book when you are finished. Correct all wrong answers.

6. See example. $\boxed{\text{A}}$

A. $\frac{3}{16}$ in	E. $1\frac{3}{4}$ in	I. $3\frac{7}{8}$ in
B. $\frac{7}{16}$ in	F. $2\frac{1}{2}$ in	J. 4 in
C. $\frac{15}{16}$ in	G. $2\frac{13}{16}$ in	K. $4\frac{9}{16}$ in
D. $1\frac{1}{4}$ in	H. $3\frac{1}{8}$ in	L. $5\frac{1}{16}$ in

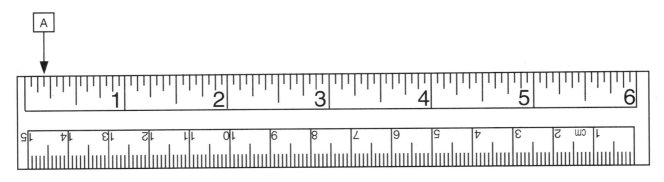

Not to Scale

READING MEASUREMENTS ON THE ENGLISH RULER

Criteria:

1. Answers are to be accurate to $\frac{1}{16}$ of an inch.

2. All fraction answers are to be written in lowest terms.

3. All answers are to be in inches.

Directions:

1. Correctly name the measurements indicated by the arrows on the drawing of the ruler.

2. Write your answers in the spaces that correspond to the matching letter of the alphabet.

3. Check your answers with the answer key in the back of the book.

4. Correct any mistakes.

A = _____   D = _____   G = _____   J = _____

B = _____   E = _____   H = _____   K = _____

C = _____   F = _____   I = _____   L = _____

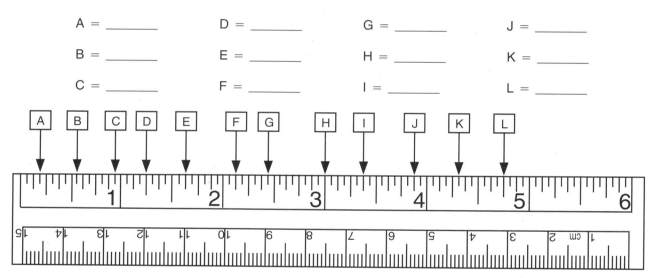

Not to Scale

The Metric Ruler

The basic unit of length in the metric system is the centimeter, abbreviated cm. The centimeter is subdivided into 10 equal parts. Each tenth of a centimeter is equal to one tenth or $\frac{1}{10}$ of a centimeter, which is typically written in decimal format such as;

0.4 cm   0.8 cm   3.2 cm   5.7 cm   15.5 cm

One tenth of a centimeter is equal to one millimeter. Millimeter is usually abbreviated mm.

0.1 cm = 1 mm

0.4 cm = 4 mm   0.6 cm = 6 mm   0.8 cm = 8 mm

One centimeter is equal to 10 millimeters. There are 10 millimeters in one centimeter.

$$1 \text{ cm} = 10 \text{ mm}$$

3 cm = 30 mm   5 cm = 50 mm   7 cm = 70 mm

Each small division on a metric ruler is 0.1 centimeter or 1 millimeter.

EXAMPLES:

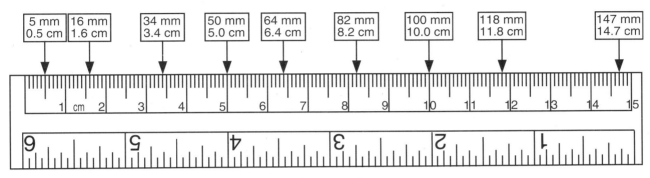

Not to Scale

EXERCISE 3

LOCATING MILLIMETERS ON THE METRIC RULER

Directions:

1. Locate the following measurements on the diagram of a ruler.

2. Draw an arrow above the picture of the ruler to identify the measurements given below. Write the corresponding letter of the alphabet above the arrow.

3. Check your answers with the answer key at the back of the book when you are finished. Correct all wrong answers.

4. See example.

A. 5 mm	E. 58 mm	I. 116 mm
B. 10 mm	F. 71 mm	J. 120 mm
C. 15 mm	G. 100 mm	K. 133 mm
D. 34 mm	H. 108 mm	L. 0 mm

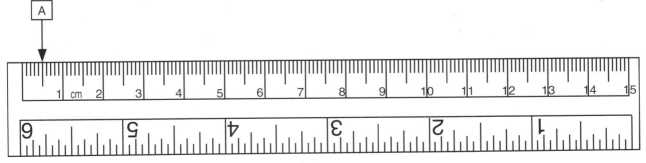

Not to Scale

EXERCISE 4

READING MILLIMETERS ON THE METRIC RULER

Criteria:

1. Answers are to be accurate to the millimeter.

2. All answers are to be in millimeters.

3. All answers are to include the millimeter unit.

Directions:

1. Correctly name the measurements indicated by the arrows on the drawing of the ruler.

2. Write your answers in the spaces that correspond to the matching letter of the alphabet.

3. Check your answers with the answer key in the back of the book.

4. Correct any mistakes.

A = _____	D = _____	G = _____	J = _____
B = _____	E = _____	H = _____	K = _____
C = _____	F = _____	I = _____	L = _____

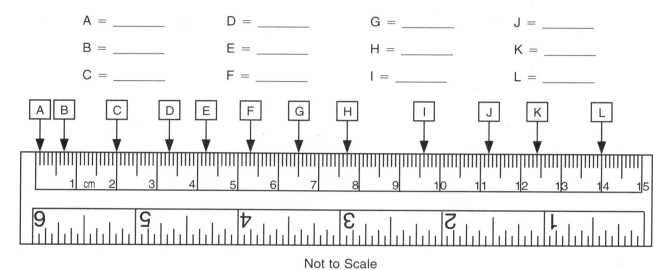

Not to Scale

EXERCISE 5

LOCATING CENTIMETERS ON A METRIC RULER

Directions:

1. Locate the following metric measurements on the diagram of a ruler.
2. Draw an arrow above the picture of the ruler to identify the measurements given below. Write the corresponding letter of the alphabet above the arrow.
3. Check your answers with the answer key at the back of the book when you are finished. Correct all wrong answers.
4. See example. ☐A

A. 0.5 cm	E. 4.8 cm	I. 11.6 cm
B. 1 cm	F. 5.3 cm	J. 12.1 cm
C. 1.5 cm	G. 7.9 cm	K. 13 cm
D. 2.6 cm	H. 10.2 cm	L. 14.4 cm

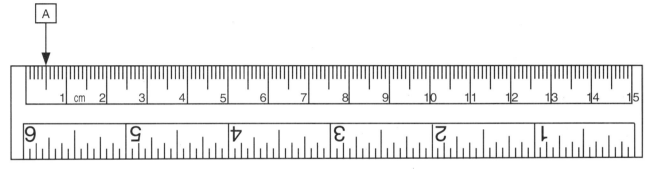

Not to Scale

EXERCISE 6

LOCATING CENTIMETERS ON A METRIC RULER
AND COMPARING CENTIMETERS TO MILLIMETERS

Criteria:

1. All centimeter answers are to be accurate to the tenth's place.

2. All millimeter answers are to be accurate to the one's place.

Directions:

1. Correctly name the measurements indicated by the arrows on the drawing of the ruler.

2. Write your answers in the spaces that correspond to the matching letter of the alphabet.

3. Check your answers with the answer key in the back of the book.

4. Correct any mistakes.

A = _____ cm = _____ mm   G = _____ cm = _____ mm

B = _____ cm = _____ mm   H = _____ cm = _____ mm

C = _____ cm = _____ mm   I = _____ cm = _____ mm

D = _____ cm = _____ mm   J = _____ cm = _____ mm

E = _____ cm = _____ mm   K = _____ cm = _____ mm

F = _____ cm = _____ mm   L = _____ cm = _____ mm

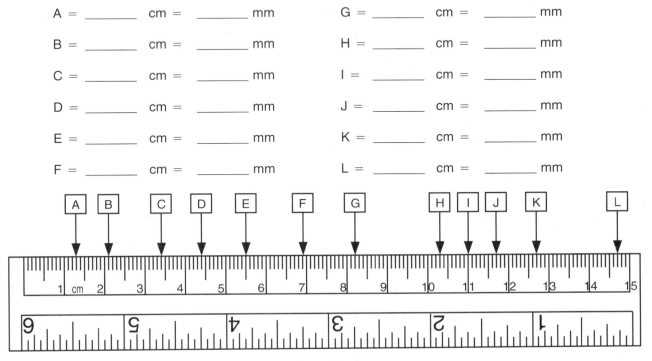

Not to Scale

Solving Mathematical Problems Using Measurements

ADDITION PROBLEMS USING MIXED UNITS

To add mixed units together:

1. Add feet to feet and inches to inches

2. If the results give an inch answer equal to or greater than 12 inches you must convert that portion of the answer to feet and inches. Converting measurements of 12 inches or more into feet or feet and inches is achieved by dividing the number by 12.

EXAMPLE 1: Two pieces of I-beam are welded together. One piece is 5' 4" long and the second piece is 3' 10" long. What is the total length of the I-beam?

```
  5'  4"
+ 3' 10"
  8' 14"
```
} Since 12 inches = 1 foot any dimension equal to or greater than 12" must be converted to feet and inches

Convert 14" into feet and inches: 14" ÷ 12" = 1' 2"

$$\frac{1}{12 \overline{)14}} = 1' 2" + 8' = 9' 2" \text{ total length}$$
$$\frac{-12}{2} \text{ remainder}$$

Answer = 9' 2"

EXAMPLE 2: A 3' 10" piece of fence is added to a 20' 8" existing fence. What is the total length of the fence?

```
 20'  8"
+ 3' 10"
 23' 18"
```
where 18" = 1' 6", added to the 23" gives 24' 6" total fence length

Answer = 24' 6"

EXERCISE 7

ADDING MIXED UNITS

Answers

1. The roof of a building was 12' 7". It was raised by 3' 9". How tall is the roof now?   1. _____

2. Two pieces of trim molding are glued together. One piece is 2' 10" and the other piece is 3' 4". What is the total length of the trim molding?   2. _____

3. What is the total length of a 10' 6" table if a 2' 9" leaf is inserted?   3. _____

4. A carpenter needs 8' 4" of baseboard to complete a project. He has two pieces of baseboard, one measures 5' 8" and the second measures 2' 10". Does he have enough to complete the project?   4. _____

5. Solve for dimensions A and B in the following diagram.   5. A = _____

B = _____

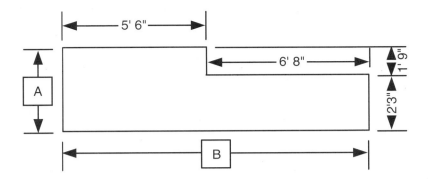

6. The perimeter of an object is the total distance around the object. What is the perimeter of the object in problem 5?

6. _____

Subtraction Problems Using Mixed Units

EXAMPLE: A pattern calls for a 3' 4" piece of metal rod. The rod is now 6' 9". How much must be removed?

To solve this problem subtract feet from feet and inches from inches:

Solution: 6' 9"
          − 3' 4"
          ‾‾‾‾‾‾
            3' 5"

EXAMPLE: An 8' 5" board has a 4' 7" piece cut from one end. What is the length of the remaining piece?

To solve this problem remember that 1 foot is equal to 12 inches. When you borrow one from the feet column add **12** to the inch column, then proceed with the subtraction of feet from feet and inches from inches.

Solution: 8' 5" ⎫ Cannot subtract 7" from 5"
          − 4' 7" ⎬ Borrow 1' from the 8'
                   ⎭ Change 8' to 7' then add 12" to the 5"

              7' 17"
              8' 5"
            − 4' 7"
            ‾‾‾‾‾‾‾‾
    Answer: 3' 10"

EXERCISE 8

SUBTRACTING MIXED UNITS

Answers

1. A year ago a boy was 4' 6" tall. He is now 5' 8" tall. How much did he grow?

1. _____

2. A 16 ft 3 in copper pipe is cut to 12 ft 8 in. How much was cut off?

2. _____

3. A 10 ft 9 in goalpost was raised to 15 ft 4 in. How much was it raised?

3. _____

4. A worker needs a 2' 5" piece of PVC pipe. The pipe is now 8'. How much must the worker cut off of the pipe?

4. _____

5. Solve for dimensions A and B in the following diagram.

5. A = _____

   B = _____

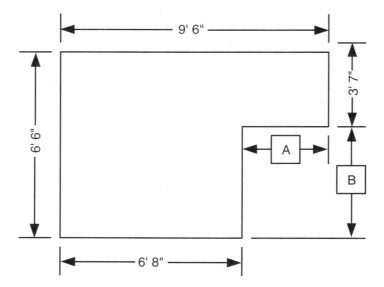

6. How much longer is B than A from problem 5?

6. _____

MULTIPLICATION PROBLEMS

To multiply two or more fractions with same units of measurement:

1. Convert all mixed numbers into improper fraction form (see fraction chapter)

2. Write the problem in linear form

3. Cross cancel where possible (see fraction chapter)

4. Multiply numerators by numerators and denominators by denominators

5. Reduce the answer when possible

EXAMPLE 1: What is the total length of 20 pieces of drill rod each 5¹⁄₁₀" long?

Solution: Convert 5¹⁄₁₀" into an improper fraction:

$$5\frac{1}{10} = \frac{51}{10}$$

Change 20 to a fraction:

$$20 = \frac{20}{1}$$

Then cross cancel and multiply:

$$\overset{2}{\cancel{\frac{20}{1}}} \times \frac{51}{\underset{1}{\cancel{10}}} = 102" = 8'\ 6" \text{ total length of drill rod}$$

Answer = 8' 6"

EXAMPLE 2: How tall is a stack of 12 bricks if each brick is 6¾" high?

Solution: Convert 6¾" into an improper fraction:

$$6 \frac{3}{4} = \frac{27}{4}$$

Change 12 to a fraction:

$$12 = \frac{12}{1}$$

Then cross cancel and multiply:

$$\frac{\overset{3}{\cancel{12}}}{1} \times \frac{27}{\underset{1}{\cancel{4}}} = \frac{81}{1} = 81" \text{ or } 6' \, 9"$$

Answer = 6' 9"

EXERCISE 9

MULTIPLICATION OF UNITS

Answers

1. The volume of a rectangular block of wood is found by multiplying the length by the width by the height. Find the volume of a rectangular block of wood 12¾ in long, 2⅔ in wide, and 2½ in high?

1. _____

2. What is ½ the volume of the block of wood in problem 1?

2. _____

3. What is the approximate volume of concrete needed to fill a form measuring 12⅔ ft long by 6⅜ ft wide by 2 ft high? Volume is found by multiplying length by width by height.

3. _____

4. What is 2½ times the volume of concrete in problem 3?

4. _____

5. Find the volume of the following solid object.

5. _____

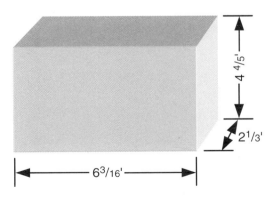

4 ⅘'

2¹/₃'

6³/₁₆'

6. A particular housing contract allows 160 days for completion. If ⅖ of that time is allowed for the rough framing. How many days do the builders have to complete the rough framing of the house?

6. _____

DIVISION PROBLEMS

To divide two or more fractions with the same units of measurement

1. Convert all mixed numbers into improper fraction form (see fraction chapter)

2. Write all whole numbers as fractions by making the whole number the numerator and the one the denominator. **EXAMPLE:** 16" = $^{16}/_1$". Invert all but the first fraction. (To divide one fraction by another, multiply the dividend by the inverse of the divisor.)

3. Write the problem in linear form

4. Cross cancel where possible (see fraction chapter)

5. Multiply numerators times numerators and denominators times denominators

6. Reduce the answer when possible

EXAMPLE 1: A board 20¼" long is to be cut into 9 equal parts. What is the approximate length of each piece?

Solution: Rewrite 9 as a fraction, and since it is the divisor invert the fraction.

$$9 = \frac{9}{1} \quad \text{inverts to} \quad \frac{1}{9}$$

Convert 20¼" into an improper fraction:

$$20\frac{1}{4} = \frac{81}{4}$$

Set up in linear fashion, cross cancel, multiply, and reduce:

$$\frac{\overset{9}{\cancel{81}}}{4} \times \frac{1}{\underset{1}{\cancel{9}}} = \frac{9}{4} = 2\frac{1}{4}$$

EXAMPLE 2: How many 8⅔" pieces can be cut from a 56" length of tubing?

Solution: Convert 8⅔" to an improper fraction, and since it is the divisor invert the fraction.

$$8\frac{2}{3} = \frac{26}{3} \quad \text{inverts to:} \quad \frac{3}{26}$$

Rewrite 56" as a fraction:

$$56 = \frac{56}{1}$$

Set up in linear fashion, cross cancel, multiply, and reduce:

$$\frac{\overset{28}{\cancel{56}}}{1} \times \frac{3}{\underset{13}{\cancel{26}}} = \frac{84}{13} = 6\frac{6}{13}$$

EXERCISE 10

DIVISION OF UNITS

Answers

1. The approximate diameter of a circle is found by dividing the circumference (distance around the circle) by $3\frac{1}{7}$. What is the diameter of a circle whose circumference is $6\frac{3}{16}$"?

1. _____

2. Using the information given in problem 1 find the diameter of a circle whose circumference is $4\frac{1}{8}$'.

2. _____

3. A cubic foot contains approximately $7\frac{1}{2}$ gallons. How many cubic feet are in a 100-gallon tank?

3. _____

4. A $5\frac{5}{8}$-foot length of wire is to be cut into 5 equal parts. How long is each piece (answer in feet)?

4. _____

5. If a storage box is $2\frac{1}{2}$ feet wide and 1 foot deep, how long must it be to hold 35 cubic feet? Volume = length × width × height

5. _____

6. How many whole stars can be cut from the piece of plywood shown below?

6. _____

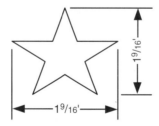

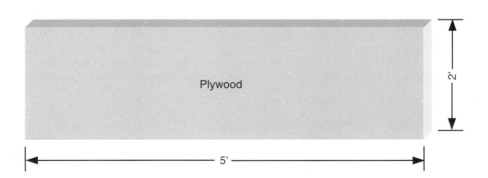

Plywood

MEASUREMENT AND METRIC CONVERSIONS

The Metric system is sometimes preferred in measurement because its units are divided in groups of ten thus making conversions from one metric unit to another extremely easy. To convert from one unit to another in metrics you either multiply or divide by multiples of ten, which can be easily accomplished by moving the decimal to the left or right.

Meter (m) - A basic unit of measurement is the meter. A meter is approximately 39.37 inches long so when people refer to a meter stick it is slightly longer than a yard stick which is 36 inches.

Decimeter (dm) - If you take a meter stick and divide it into ten equal parts you have a decimeter which is 1/10 of a meter. The length of a decimeter is approximately 3.937 inches (almost 4 inches).

Centimeter (cm) - If you divide a meter into one hundred equal parts, each part is a centimeter which is 1/100 of a meter. The length of a centimeter is approximately 0.3937 inches (less than a half inch).

Millimeter (mm) - If you divide a meter into one thousand equal parts, each part is a millimeter which is 1/1000 of a meter. The length of a millimeter is approximately 0.03937 inches (which is approximately the width of a dime).

Decameter (dkm) & Hectometer (hm) - If you lay ten meter sticks end to end you have a decameter. Similarly, if you lay one hundred meter sticks end to end you have a hectometer. Decameters and hectometers are not used very often.

Kilometer (km) - If you lay one thousand meter sticks end to end you have a kilometer which is approximately 0.62 miles (a little over a half mile).

When working with the metric system it is often advantageous to convert one metric unit to another. The prefix on the unit can be very helpful in converting metric units. The mnemonic: "**K**ing **H**enry **D**ied **U**nexpectedly **D**rinking **C**hocolate **M**ilk" is frequently used to help remember the order of units for conversion.

K for king represents the **K** for **K**ilometer, **H** for Henry represents **H** for **H**ectometer, **D** for died represents the **D** for **D**ecameter, **U** for unexpectedly represents the unit of measure being used, for example meter, the second **D** for drinking represents the **D** for **D**ecimeter, the **C** for chocolate represents the **C** for **C**entimeter, and the **M** for milk represents the **M** for **M**illimeter.

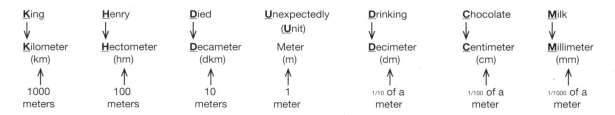

EXAMPLE 1   42 dm = _____ mm

Convert **42 decimeters** to **millimeters**: to convert decimeters to millimeters notice if you start on decimeters you need to move two units to the right to get to millimeters so you do the same with the decimal, that is move the decimal twice to the right. The decimal in the number 42 is after the two. So to move the decimal twice to the right, two zeros must be added to the right of 42 as shown in the answer.2. Locate the following metric measurements on the ruler. Label your answers as in the example.

Kilometer   Hectometer   Decameter   Meter   **Decimeter**   **Centimeter**   **Millimeter**

Answer: 42.dm = <u>4200.</u> mm

EXAMPLE 2   37.9 mm = _____ cm

Convert **37.9 millimeters** to **centimeters**: to convert millimeters to centimeters notice if you start on millimeters you need to move one unit to the left to get to centimeters so you do the same with the decimal, that is move the decimal once to the left.

Kilometer   Hectometer   Decameter   Meter   Decimeter   **Centimeter**   **Millimeter**

Answer: 37.9 mm = <u>3.79 cm</u>

EXAMPLE 3   4.2 km = _____ mm

Convert **4.2 kilometers** to **millimeters**: to convert kilometers to millimeters notice if you start on kilometers you need to move six units to the right to get to millimeters so you do the same with the decimal, that is move the decimal six times to the right.

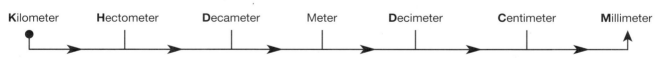

Kilometer   Hectometer   Decameter   Meter   Decimeter   Centimeter   Millimeter

Answer: 4.2 km = <u>4,200,000 mm</u>

EXAMPLE 4   78 m = _____ km

Convert **78 meters** to **kilometers**: to convert meters to kilometers, start on meters, then notice that you need to move three units to the left to get to kilometers so you do the same with the decimal, that is move the decimal three times to the left.

| **K**ilometer | **H**ectometer | **D**ecameter | **M**eter | **D**ecimeter | **C**entimeter | **M**illimeter |

Answer: 78. m = <u>0.078 km</u>

EXAMPLE 5   6.3 m = _____ cm

Convert **6.3 meters** to **centimeters**: to convert meters to centimeters, start on meters, then notice that you need to move two units to the right to get to centimeters so you do the same with the decimal, that is move the decimal twice to the right.

| **K**ilometer | **H**ectometer | **D**ecameter | **M**eter | **D**ecimeter | **C**entimeter | **M**illimeter |

Answer: 6.3 m = <u>630. cm</u>

EXAMPLE 6   1.2 mm = _____ m

Convert **1.2 millimeters** to **meters**: to convert millimeters to meters, start on millimeters, then notice that you need to move three units to the left to get to meters so you do the same with the decimal, that is move the decimal three times to the left.

| **K**ilometer | **H**ectometer | **D**ecameter | **M**eter | **D**ecimeter | **C**entimeter | **M**illimeter |

Answer: 1.2 mm = <u>0.0012 m</u>

Convert each of the following:

1. 18.9 mm = _____ cm

2. 0.72 km = _____ m

3. 5.9 m = _____ dm

4. 0.03 km = _____ mm

5. 173 dm = _____ mm

6. 4.8 cm = _____ mm

7. 11.9 mm = _____ cm

8. 0.06 mm = _____ m

9. 81.9 cm = _____ mm

10. 7,642 m = _____ km

11. 5.8 m = _____ cm

12. 14.2 mm = _____ dkm

13. 46 km = _____ m

14. 70 m = _____ km

15. 27.1 m = _____ mm

16. 3.05 dkm = _____ cm

17. 0.38 km = _____ mm

18. 3 mm = _____ m

19. 0.09 cm = _____ mm

20. 1,937 mm = _____ dm

Metric and English Conversions

Converting:

- Metric measurement units to English (U.S. standard) measurements units and
- English (U.S. standard) measurements units to Metric measurements units

At times there may be a need to convert metric measurement units to English measurement units and also English measurement units to Metric measurement units. Using a table (like the one shown) with conversion facts is very helpful.

Metric to English
1 kilometer (km) ≈ 0.62 miles (mi)
1 meter (m) ≈ 39.37 inches (in)
1 centimeter (cm) ≈ .39 inch (in)

English to Metric
1 mile (mi) ≈ 1.61 kilometers (km)
1 inch (in) ≈ 2.54 centimeters (cm)
1 foot (ft) ≈ 0.3048 meters (m)

(≈ means approximately)

Example 1 (Metric to English)

How many miles are there in 8 kilometers?

a) Start with 8 km and write it as a fraction, then use the Metric to English table.

$$\frac{8 \; km}{1}$$

b) Multiply that by the conversion factor from the table by putting the unit that you want to end up with on top, and the unit that you want to get rid of on the bottom.

$$\frac{8 \; km}{1} \cdot \frac{0.62 \; mi}{1 \; km}$$

c) Then multiply the two fractions together. Notice that the km's divide out leaving you with the desired unit of miles.

$$\frac{8 \; \cancel{km}}{1} \cdot \frac{0.62 \; mi}{1 \; \cancel{km}} \approx 4.96 \; mi$$

Example 2 (Metric to English)

How many inches are there in 14 centimeters?

a) Start with 14 cm and write it as a fraction, then use the Metric to English table.

$$\frac{14\ cm}{1}$$

b) Multiply that by the conversion factor from the table by putting the unit that you want to end up with on top, and the unit that you want to get rid of on the bottom.

$$\frac{14\ cm}{1} \cdot \frac{0.39\ in}{1\ cm}$$

c) Then multiply the two fractions together. Notice that the cm's divide out leaving you with the desired unit of inches.

$$\frac{14\ \cancel{cm}}{1} \cdot \frac{0.39\ in}{1\ \cancel{cm}} \approx 5.46\ in$$

Example 3 (English to Metric)

How many meters are there in 37 feet?

a) Start with 37 feet and write it as a fraction, then use the English to Metric table.

$$\frac{37\ ft}{1}$$

b) Multiply that by the conversion factor from the table by putting the unit that you want to end up with on top, and the unit that you want to get rid of on the bottom.

$$\frac{37\ ft}{1} \cdot \frac{0.3048\ m}{1\ ft}$$

c) Then multiply the two fractions together. Notice that the feet divide out leaving you with the desired unit of meters.

$$\frac{37\ \cancel{ft}}{1} \cdot \frac{0.3048\ m}{1\ \cancel{ft}} \approx 11.2776\ m$$

Example 4 (English to Metric)

How many centimeters are there in 9 inches?

a) Start with 9 in and write it as a fraction, then use the English to Metric table.

$$\frac{9 \ in}{1}$$

b) Multiply that by the conversion factor from the table by putting the unit that you want to end up with on top, and the unit that you want to get rid of on the bottom.

$$\frac{9 \ in}{1} \cdot \frac{2.54 \ cm}{1 \ in}$$

c) Then multiply the two fractions together. Notice that the inches divide out leaving you with the desired unit of centimeters.

$$\frac{9 \ \cancel{in}}{1} \cdot \frac{2.54 \ cm}{1 \ \cancel{in}} \approx 22.86 \ cm$$

Example 5 (Metric to English)

How many meters are there in 25 miles?

a) Start with 25 miles and write it as a fraction, then use the Metric to English table.

$$\frac{25 \ mi}{1}$$

b) Multiply that by the conversion factor from the table by putting the unit that you want to end up with on top, and the unit that you want to get rid of on the bottom.

$$\frac{25 \ mi}{1} \cdot \frac{1.61 \ km}{1 \ mi}$$

c) Then multiply these two fractions by a third fraction that will change km to meters (1 km = 1000 m).

$$\frac{25 \ \cancel{mi}}{1} \cdot \frac{1.61 \ \cancel{km}}{1 \ \cancel{mi}} \cdot \frac{1000 \ m}{1 \ \cancel{km}} \approx 40250 \ m$$

d) Then multiply these three fractions together. Notice that the miles divide out and the km also divide out leaving you with the desired unit of meters.

EXERCISE 12
Metric and English Conversions

Convert each of the following, use the tables below:

Metric to English
1 kilometer (km) ≈ 0.62 miles (mi)
1 meter (m) ≈ 39.37 inches (in)
1 centimeter (cm) ≈ .39 inch (in)

English to Metric
1 mile (mi) ≈ 1.61 kilometers (km)
1 inch (in) ≈ 2.54 centimeters (cm)
1 foot (ft) ≈ 0.3048 meters (m)

1. 16 m = _____ in

2. 50 km = _____ mi

3. 5.9 cm = _____ in

4. 0.4 m = _____ in

5. 12 mi = _____ km

6. 150 ft = _____ m

7. 75 mi = _____ km

8. 30 mi = _____ m

PRE-APPRENTICE TEST

MEASUREMENT AND METRIC CONVERSION

Time: 30 minutes

1. Locate the following English measurements on the ruler. Label your answers as in the example. $\boxed{A}$

A. ¼ in	E. 1¹³⁄₁₆ in	I. 3⅞ in
B. ⁹⁄₁₆ in	F. 2⅛ in	J. 4⅜ in
C. 1⅛ in	G. 2½ in	K. 5 in
D. 1¼ in	H. 3¾ in	L. 5¹⁄₁₆ in

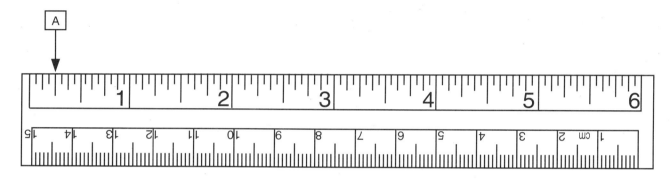

Not to Scale

2. Locate the following metric measurements on the ruler. Label your answers as in the example. $\boxed{A}$

A. 3 mm	E. 4.2 cm	I. 10.7 cm
B. 1 cm	F. 53 mm	J. 121 mm
C. 15 mm	G. 7.9 cm	K. 14.8 cm
D. 2.6 cm	H. 102 mm	L. 0 cm

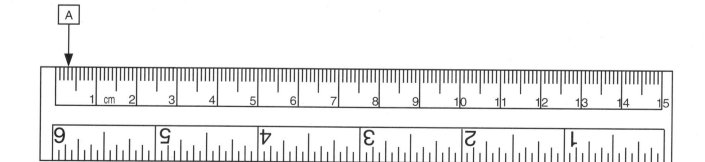

Not to scale

Use the following drawing to answer questions 3 through 9:

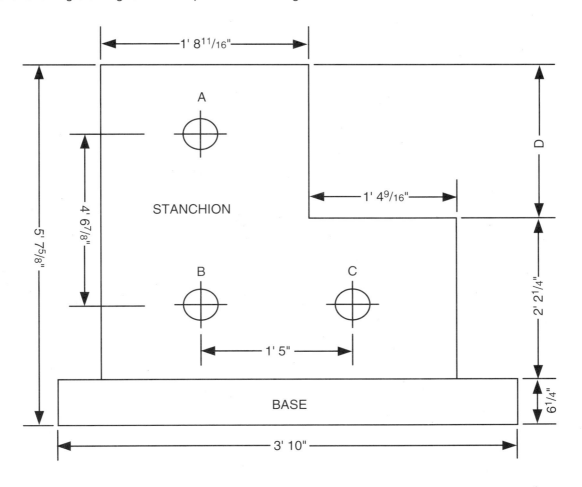

Answers

3. Find the height of the stanchion without the base.　　　3. _____

4. If the stanchion is centered on the base, how much does the base extend
on each side?　　　4. _____

5. Solve for dimension D.　　　5. _____

6. Find the perimeter of the stanchion without the base.　　　6. _____

7. If each hole has a diameter of 2", find the distance between the inside edges
holes A and B.　　　7. _____

8. Find the distance to the outside edges of holes B and C given that both holes
have a diameter of 2".　　　8. _____

9. If the center of hole B is 12 inches above the top of the base, how far is the
center of hole A above the same point?　　　9. _____

Convert each of the following:

10. 449 mm = _____ cm

11. 54 km = _____ m

12. 0.000075 m = _____ cm

13. 1.63 mm = _____ dm

14. 4 cm = _____ mm

15. 9.79 m = _____ mm

Convert each of the following, use the tables below:

Metric to English
1 kilometer (km) ≈ 0.62 miles (mi)
1 meter (m) ≈ 39.37 inches (in)
1 centimeter (cm) ≈ .39 inch (in)

English to Metric
1 mile (mi) ≈ 1.61 kilometers (km)
1 inch (in) ≈ 2.54 centimeters (cm)
1 foot (ft) ≈ 0.3048 meters (m)

16. 32 km = _____ mi

17. 18 cm = _____ in

18. 14.5 ft = _____ m

19. 85 mi = _____ km

20. 5 meters = _____ in

21. 48 in = _____ cm

CHAPTER 5

Ratios, Proportions and Percents

Ratio

A ratio is a comparison of two numbers. Let's say, for example, the daily production of a certain plant is 3,000 usable parts and 150 scrap parts. The ratio of usable parts to scrap parts is 3000 to 150 and can be reduced, as you did with fractions, to give a final answer of 20 to 1. Ratios can be written in any of three forms:

Original set up		Reduced Answer
1. 3000 to 150	=	20 to 1
2. 3000 : 150	=	20 : 1
3. 3000/150	=	20/1

Tip 1. Be careful to write the numbers of a ratio in the order in which they are asked for in the problem.

Tip 2. Ratios should be reduced to lowest terms. Leave any improper fractions in improper fraction form.

Tip 3. Ratios are a comparison of two numbers, the final answer must contain two numbers. Do not rewrite $^{50}/_1$ as 50.

EXAMPLE 1:

A particular alloy is made of 8 parts iron ore to 5 parts aluminum. What is the ratio of aluminum to iron ore?

$$\text{answer} = \tfrac{5}{8}$$

Since the question asks for the ratio of **aluminum** to **iron ore**, the ratio will be written as 5 to 8 with the amount of aluminum written first. The answer also could be written as 5 : 8 or $\tfrac{5}{8}$.

EXAMPLE 2:

The inner radius of a washer is $\tfrac{2}{5}$ inches, the outer radius is $\tfrac{4}{5}$ inches. What is the ratio of the inner radius to the outer radius?

$$\text{answer} = \tfrac{1}{2}$$

The question asks for the ratio of the inner radius to the outer radius, so make a fraction using the inner radius ($\tfrac{2}{5}$) as the numerator and the outer radius ($\tfrac{4}{5}$) as the denominator. Think of the fraction line between the numerator and denominator of the ratio as another way of saying division. The rule for the division of fractions is: invert the second fraction then multiply. Cross cancel wherever possible, and reduce the answer if it is not in lowest terms.

$$\frac{\frac{2}{5}}{\frac{4}{5}} = \frac{2}{5} \div \frac{4}{5} = \frac{2}{5} \times \frac{5}{4} = \frac{1}{2}$$

Two Step Ratio Problems

Some problems will require you to solve for one of the numbers of the ratio.

EXAMPLE 3:

A certain shop employs 50 salaried workers and 575 hourly workers. What is the ratio of salaried workers to the total number of employees at the shop?

1.
$$\begin{array}{r} 575 \quad \text{Hourly} \\ +\,50 \quad \text{Salary} \\ \hline 625 \quad \text{Total Employees} \end{array}$$

2.
$$\frac{\text{Salary}}{\text{Total Employees}} = \frac{50}{625} = \frac{2}{25}$$

Step 1. To find the total number of employees, add the number of salaried workers to the number of hourly workers.

Step 2. Make a ratio with the number of salaried workers as the numerator of the fraction or the first number of the ratio, and the total number of employees as the denominator of the fraction or the second number of the ratio. Reduce the ratio.

EXAMPLE 4:

A recipe for lemonade calls for one part sugar, one part lemon juice and 6 parts water. a) What is the ratio of lemon juice to water? b) What is the ratio of sugar and lemon juice to water? c) What is the ratio of the lemon juice to the lemonade?

Answer a. $\dfrac{1 \text{ Lemon Juice}}{6 \text{ Water}} = \dfrac{1}{6}$

Answer b. $\dfrac{1 + 1}{6} \quad \dfrac{\text{Sugar} + \text{Lemon Juice}}{\text{Water}} = \dfrac{2}{6} = \dfrac{1}{3}$

Answer c. $\dfrac{1}{1 + 1 + 6} \quad \dfrac{\text{Lemon Juice}}{\text{Lemonade}} = \dfrac{1}{8}$

EXERCISE 1

Express the following ratios in the lowest terms:

1. 12 : 18 =

2. 8 to 16 =

3. $^{15}\!/_3$ =

4. $^{7}\!/_8 : {^{9}\!/_{16}}$ =

5. 2.5 to 10 =

6. 3.5 : 5.25 =

7. The larger of two meshed gears makes 240 rpm and the smaller makes 80 rpm. What is the ratio of their speeds in the order they are given? (rpm = revolutions per minute)

8. Marble weighs 168 lb. per cubic foot, granite weighs 170 lb. per cubic foot. What is the ratio of their weights in the order they are given?

9. An alloy is made of 1 part tin to 4 parts copper. A cube made of the alloy weighs 10 lbs.

  a. What is the ratio of tin to copper in the alloy?

  b. How many pounds of tin are in the alloy cube?

  c. How many pounds of copper are in the alloy cube?

  d. Write a ratio comparing the weight of the tin to the total weight of the cube.

Proportion

A proportion is two ratios set equal to each other and can be written in any of three forms:

$$1.\ 3 \text{ to } 4 = 6 \text{ to } 8$$

$$2.\ 3 : 4 = 6 : 8$$

$$3.\ \tfrac{3}{4} = \tfrac{6}{8}$$

Generally, proportions are easier to work with in the third form or fraction form.

Tip 1. Do not reduce the ratios in a proportion.

Tip 2. Do not cross cancel across the equal sign.

EXAMPLE 1:

The ratio of men to women in a certain classroom is 7 to 3. There are 14 men in the class and 6 women. Make a proportion using this data.

$$\frac{7}{3} = \frac{14}{6}$$

Step 1. The numerators of each ratio of the example refers to men in the class.

Step 2. The denominators of each ratio refers to the women in the class.

DO NOT REDUCE THE RATIOS OF A PROPORTION.

Often in proportion problems, you will be asked to solve for a missing term. Identify the unknown quantity with the first letter of the item you are solving for.

EXAMPLE 2:

A van traveling at a rate of 110 miles in 2 hours will travel how many miles in 12 hours?

1. $\dfrac{110 \text{ Miles}}{2 \text{ Hours}} = \dfrac{m}{12 \text{ Hours}}$

2.
$$\begin{array}{r} 110 \\ \times\,12 \\ \hline 220 \\ 1100 \\ \hline 1320 \end{array}$$

3.
$$\begin{array}{r} 660 \text{ Miles} \\ 2\,\overline{)\,1320} \\ 12 \\ \hline 12 \\ 12 \\ \hline 0 \end{array}$$

Step 1. Make a proportion comparing miles to hours. The top number of each ratio shows miles, and the bottom number of each indicates hours.

Step 2. Cross multiply the given terms, 110 miles and 12 hours to get 1320.

Step 3. Divide by the remaining term, 2 hours to get the final answer m = 660 miles.

EXAMPLE 3:

A photograph is to be proportionally enlarged so that it is 32 inches long. The original dimensions are 8" long by 5" wide. How wide will the enlarged photo be?

1. $\dfrac{w}{32 \text{ inches}} = \dfrac{5 \text{ inches}}{8 \text{ inches}}$ 2. $\begin{array}{r} 32 \\ \times\ 5 \\ \hline 160 \end{array}$ 3. $8\overline{)160}\ ^{20 \text{ inches}}$

Step 1. Set up the proportion so that the numerators as well as the denominators of each ratio correspond (top numbers represent widths, bottom numbers represent lengths).

Step 2. Cross multiply the given terms, 32" and 5" to get 160.

Step 3. Divide 160 by the term not used in the cross multiplication, 8", to get the final answer of w = 20".

EXERCISE 2

Solve for the unknown in the following proportions:

1. $\dfrac{6}{7} = \dfrac{12}{x}$ 5. $\dfrac{3}{8} = \dfrac{x}{64}$

2. $\dfrac{3}{5} = \dfrac{x}{15}$ 6. $\dfrac{3\frac{1}{4}}{x} = \dfrac{16.25}{29}$

3. $\dfrac{9}{6} = \dfrac{x}{2}$ 7. $\dfrac{x}{4\frac{2}{3}} = \dfrac{2\frac{1}{6}}{1\frac{1}{18}}$

4. $\dfrac{x}{6.5} = \dfrac{5}{13}$ 8. $\dfrac{1.3}{2} = \dfrac{1.3}{x}$

9. If the two rectangles are sized proportionally, find the missing dimension.

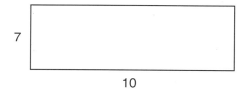 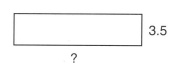

10. A 2 inch pulley on a 3450 rpm motor turns a 4 inch pulley. What is the speed in rpm of the larger pulley if the ratio of their speeds are inversely proportional to their size?

11. If it takes one hour to turn out 560 screws, how many can be made in 8 hours?

12. To the nearest hundredth, what is the resistance of 1500 ft. of copper wire if 225 ft. has .6098 ohms of resistance?

13. If the two triangles are sized proportionally, find the missing dimensions.

 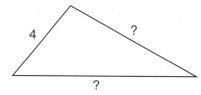

14. A certain shade of purple paint calls for mixing red paint with blue paint in the ratio of 1⅓ to 2. How many gallons of red paint are needed to mix with 7 gallons of blue paint?

PERCENTS

All percents are based on a whole unit which is divided into 100 equal parts. When you talk about a percent of something, your are describing a part of 100. 100% of something is one whole unit. The percent sign (%) means "out of 100" or "per 100".

Percent problems contain 3 pieces of information, for example, 10% of 60 is 6.

1. 10 represents the percent of the problem. You can identify it by the % sign.

2. 60 represents the "whole" or amount your are taking a percent of.

3. 6 represents the "part" or the answer you get when you find the percent of the whole.

EXAMPLE:

Identify the part, whole and percent in the following statement:

12.5% of $500.00 is $62.50.

Step 1. The percent is identified by a % sign, so the percent in the statement is 12.5.

Step 2. The "whole" is the number you are finding a percent of, so the "whole" of the statement is $500.00.

Step 3. The "part" is the result, so the "part" of the statement is $62.50.

Tip 1. A key word to look for to help identify the "whole" of the percent statement is the word "of". Usually the number which corresponds to the word "of" is the "whole".

Tip 2. A key word to look for to help identify the "part" of the percent statement is the word "is". Usually the number which corresponds to the word "is" is the "part".

Tip 3. Do not be fooled into thinking that the "whole" is always larger than the "part", that is not always true.

EXERCISE 3

Identify the percent, whole and part of these percent sentences: Answers

1. 22% of 108 is 23.76.   _____

2. 42 is 44% of 96.   _____

3. 187.5 is 12 1/2% of 1500.   _____

4. 33% of Joe's gross income is deducted for taxes. His deductions
   total $186.45 when his gross is $565.00.   _____

5. Daily production of a shop is 136,000 parts. If 3% of daily production is scrap, then 4080 parts are unusable.

_____

6. A 145 lb. person weighs only 24 pounds on the moon because the moon's gravity is 16.63% of that on earth.

_____

7. 67.2 is 112% of 60.

_____

Solving For the Unknown in a Percent Problem

Many percent problems only give you two of the three pieces of data and require you to solve for the missing third bit of data (part, whole or the percent). They can each be found by using just one formula, so regardless of which one of the three pieces of data you are solving for, the following formula will solve for it.

$$\frac{Part}{Whole} = \frac{\%}{100}$$

Step 1. Substitute the given information into the proper positions in the percent formula.

Step 2. The number under the % sign is always 100, thus eliminating the need to change a percent into decimal form before using it in a calculation.

Step 3. As in proportions, cross multiply the two pieces of given information in the formula, then divide by the remaining number.

Step 4. If you solve for the percent, be sure to write a percent sign to the right of your answer.

EXAMPLE:

What is 20% of 560?

1. $\dfrac{Part}{560} = \dfrac{20}{100}$

2.
```
    560
  ×  20
    000
  11200
  11200
```

3.
```
           112
  100 / 11200
        100
        120
        100
        200
        200
          0
```

Step 1. Substitute the given information into the percent formula.

Step 2. Cross multiply the 560 and 20 to get 11200.

Step 3. Divide by 100, or move the decimal point two places to the left, to obtain the answer of 112.

EXERCISE 4

Directions: Solve for the unknown in the following percent problems.

Answers   Answers

1. 4% of 52 is what?   _____   7. ¼% of 48 is what number?   _____

2. .4% of 52 is what?   _____   8. .375 is what % of .750?   _____

3. 25% of 49 is what?   _____   9. 56% of 1 lb. 4 oz. is what
                                                     amount?   _____

4. What is .04% of 52?   _____
                                                 10. ⅛ is what % of 4?   _____

5. 33 is what % of 45?   _____

6. 22% of 33 is what number? _____

11. A steel bar weighs 37 lbs. It contains 90% iron, .7% carbon, .5% silicon,
    7% chrome, and 1.8% nickel. By weight, give the amount of each alloy to the
    nearest tenth of a pound.   _____

12. The total cost of a tool is $844.25 Only two factors affect the price, material and
    labor. The material cost is $114. To the nearest tenth of a percent, find the percent
    of the total cost attributed to labor.   _____

13. 5% of 55 is what percent of 50% of 50?   _____

14. A gage cost $12.50. The tax is 6% in the state in which the gage was
    purchased. What is the total cost for the gage including tax?   _____

REVIEW PROBLEMS

Ratio

Express the following ratios in lowest terms:

Answers   Answers

1. 6 to 12   _____   6. 16⅓ : 3⅓   _____

2. 8 to 24   _____   7. 25.5 : 15½   _____

3. 25 to 225   _____   8. 12¾ : 4¹⁄₁₆   _____

4. 1.5 : 3   _____   9.   10 ft.
                                            187 ohms   _____

5. 6¼ : 8½   _____   10. 420 revolutions
                                            .5 minutes   _____

Proportion

Solve for the variable x in the following proportions:

Answers

Answers

1. $3 : 5 = 9 : x$ _____

6. 7 to x = 28 to 12 _____

2. $2 : 7 = 8 : x$ _____

7. x to 6 = 4 to 12 _____

3. $30 : 9 = x : 3$ _____

8. $x/12 = 24/6$ _____

4. $x : 24 = 3 : 6$ _____

9. $9/x = 4.5/10$ _____

5. 8 to 12 = 24 to x _____

10. $2.6/x = 9.1/1.75$ _____

Percent

Solve for the unknown in the following percent problems:

1. 16% of 50 is what number? _____

2. 55% of 220 is what number? _____

3. 45 is 60% of what number? _____

4. 419 is 10% more than what number? _____

5. ½ is 25% of what number? _____

6. 18 is what % of 60? _____

7. $107.80 is what percent of $880.00? _____

8. Chris just received a 10% raise. She was making $5.60 an hour. How much does she make now? _____

PRE-APPRENTICE TEST

RATIOS, PROPORTIONS AND PERCENTS

Time: 15 Minutes

Answers

1. 8% of 11 = _____

2. There are 21 pencils and 9 pens in a box, what is the ratio of pencils to pens? _____

3. If a dozen toggle bolts cost $1.44, how much will 5 toggle bolts cost? _____

4. A pattern calls for 5 yards of material plus 5% more to match print. How much material will you need to buy? _____

5. The material used for the above problem normally sells for $4.98 a yard. If the material needed for the above problem is purchased during a 20% off the original price sale, about how much will it cost? _____

6. What is 4% of ¼? _____

7. If, on the average, two out of every 18 cars are red. About how many red cars would you expect to count in a parking lot containing 46 cars? _____

8. A team won 96 games and lost 14. What is the ratio of wins to the total of games played? _____

9. If 48 of the 54 workers in a plant are male, what percent of the workers are female? _____

10. What is the ratio of female workers to the total number of workers in the above problem? _____

11. A paste mix calls for 3 parts powder to 5 parts of water. How much water must be added to 2¼ gallons of powder? _____

12. A package boasts that it contains 25% more. If the original package weighed 12 oz., how much more is in the new package? _____

CHAPTER
6
Directed Numbers

Directed numbers are sometimes known as signed numbers or as negative and positive numbers. The use of directed numbers should already be somewhat familiar to most people as they are used in basic math without definition.

A way to look at directed numbers is to look at a scale such as found on a thermometer.

Here the digits increase on either side of the zero point. One direction from zero is considered above or in a positive ($+$) direction while the other direction is considered below zero or in a negative ($-$) direction. If the temperature is 2 above ($+2$) and increased by 3 ($+3$) these can be readily added together to find the new temperature level.

$$+2 +3 = +5 \text{ or } \begin{array}{r} +2 \\ +3 \\ \hline +5 \end{array}$$

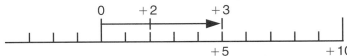

In the same manner, negative numbers can be combined. If the starting temperature is 4 below (-4) and it drops 2 more degrees (-2), these two numbers can be combined to find the new level.

$$-2 -4 = -6 \text{ or } \begin{array}{r} -2 \\ -4 \\ \hline -6 \end{array}$$

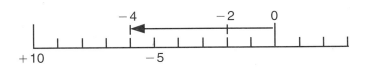

Rules For Addition Of Signed Numbers

Signs Of The Numbers In The Problem		Operation (What To Do To The Numbers)	Sign of The Answer
+	+	Add the numbers	+
−	−	Add the numbers	−
+	−	Subtract the numbers	Keep the sign of the larger number
−	+	Subtract the numbers	Keep the sign of the larger number

EXAMPLE 1: $(+3) + (+2)$

According to the table, when the signs of the numbers are both positive, add the numbers and the sign of the answer is positive.

Answer: $(+3) + (+2) = +5$

The positive sign shown on a number is optional. When no sign is shown in front of a number it is always assumed to be positive. So, the above problem could be stated as: $3 + 2 = 5$.

EXAMPLE 2: $(-4) + (-6)$

According to the table, when the signs of the numbers are both negative, add the numbers and the sign of the answer is negative.

Answer: $(-4) + (-6) = -10$

EXAMPLE 3: $(+8) + (-5)$

According to the table, when the signs of the numbers are not the same, subtract the numbers (yes, subtract the numbers even though this is an addition problem) and the keep the sign of the larger absolute value (the positive form of the number; absolute value of $+8$ is $+8$, the absolute value of -5 is $+5$) from the problem. In this case $+8$ is the larger absolute value in the problem.

Answer: $(+8) + (-5) = 3$

EXAMPLE 4: $(-10) + (+7)$

According to the table, when the signs of the numbers are not the same, subtract the numbers and the keep the sign of the larger absolute value from the problem. In this case -10 is the larger absolute value (the positive form of the number; absolute value of $+8$ is $+8$, the absolute value of -5 is $+5$) in the problem.

Answer: $(-10) + (+7) = -3$

EXERCISE 1

Add values:

_____1. $(-1) + (-6)$ _____10. $(+6) + (+20)$ _____19. $+ (22) + (5) + (2)$

_____2. $(+4) + (+5)$ _____11. $(+13) + (+2)$ _____20. $(-5) + (-8) + (-32)$

_____3. $(-3) + (-7)$ _____12. $(-22) + (-5)$ _____21. $+(2) +(15) +(20)$

_____4. $(-6) + (-9)$ _____13. $(+7) + (+4)$ _____22. $(3.42) + (27)$

_____5. $(-1) + (-13)$ _____14. $(+23) + (+21)$ _____23. $(-6.25) + (-7/8)$

_____6. $(+4) + (+11)$ _____15. $(-3) + (-32)$ _____24. $(-2.625) + (-26.25)$

_____7. $(-2) + (-2)$ _____16. $(-4) + (-27)$ _____25. $(3^5/16) + (2.0625)$

_____8. $(+2) + (+17)$ _____17. $(-3) + (-6) + (-9)$ _____26. $(4/5) + (3/4) + (.023)$

_____9. $(-3) + (-11)$ _____18. $(-3) + (-32)$ _____27. $(3) + (9) + (-18)$

A positive number progressed to the right or in the direction of a positive number. On the other hand, the negative number progressed to the left or in the direction of the negative number.

By simply using the information already learned, combining the numbers having unlike signs can be accomplished.

EXAMPLE: $+6 -4$

Starting with the positive 6 move in a negative direction 4 units arriving at $+2$.
     or
Starting with the negative 4, move in a positive direction 6 units, arriving at $+2$.

This theory can be used to work problems requiring the combination of numbers having unlike signs. However, as with the most theoretical concepts, a simple rule can be applied which states the method of computation more clearly.

THEORY:

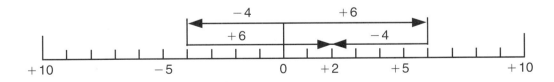

RULE:

In combining numbers having unlike signs, subtract the smaller number from the larger, then give the answer the sign of the larger.

EXAMPLES:

$$
\begin{array}{rrrr}
+8 & -8 & +6 & -3 \\
\underline{-4} & \underline{+4} & \underline{-13} & \underline{+5} \\
+4 & -4 & -7 & +2
\end{array}
$$

Add values:

_____1. $(-1) + (3)$

_____2. $(-6) + (2)$

_____3. $(4) + (-7)$

_____4. $(5) + (-3)$

_____5. $(1) + (-1)$

_____6. $(12) + (-13)$

_____7. $(-5) + (4)$

_____8. $(13) + (-20)$

_____9. $(-12) + (37)$

_____10. $(45) + (-63)$

_____11. $(-33) + (12)$

_____12. $(-6.25) + (4.0)$

_____13. $(6) + (-14)$

_____14. $(8) + (-2\frac{4}{5})$

_____15. $(4.63) + (-12.42)$

_____16. $(-13.625) + (13\frac{3}{5})$

_____17. $(-13.625) + (136.25) + (-.136)$

_____18. $(44\frac{7}{8}) + (-49\frac{2}{5})$

_____19. $(-63.2) + (21\frac{1}{4}) + (-14\frac{2}{5}) + (-3.7)$

_____20. $(-63.2) + (632) + (-6.32) + (.63)$

The combining (or addition) of signed numbers required no special indication. Each number carried the sign of its direction in relation to zero. In subtraction of signed numbers a definite subtraction step is indicated.

EXAMPLE:

$$\begin{array}{r} +8 \\ -(+3) \\ \hline \end{array} \qquad \begin{array}{r} +7 \\ -(-2) \\ \hline \end{array}$$

Both numbers in each example carry a sign, however, a subtraction process is indicated. The only additional step which is necessary beyond simply combining, requires that the sign of the subtrahend (number being subtracted) be changed.

EXAMPLE:

$$\begin{array}{r} +8 = +8 \\ -(+3) = -3 \\ \hline \end{array} \qquad \begin{array}{r} +7 = +7 \\ -(-2) = +2 \\ \hline \end{array}$$

After the change, the numbers are added or combined.

Rules For Subtraction Of Signed Numbers

Step 1. Change the sign of the second number in the problem. If it is positive change it to negative, if it is negative change it to positive.

Step 2. Change the subtraction operation to addition.

Step 3. Solve by applying the rules for addition given previously in the table.

EXAMPLE 1:

$(+6) - (+5)$

$(+6) - (-5)$ Change the sign of the second number

$(+6) + (-5)$ Change the operation to addition

$(+6) + (-5) = 1$ Solve using the rules for addition

EXAMPLE 2: $(-12) - (-16)$
$(-12) - (+16)$ Change the sign of the second number
$(-12) + (+16)$ Change the operation to addition
$(-12) + (+16) = 4$ Solve using the rules for addition

EXAMPLE 3: $(+9) - (-7)$
$(+9) - (+7)$ Change the sign of the second number
$(+9) + (+7)$ Change the operation to addition
$(+9) + (+7) = 16$ Solve using the rules for addition

EXAMPLE 4: $(-6) - (+10)$
$(-6) - (-10)$ Change the sign of the second number
$(-6) + (-10)$ Change the operation to addition
$(-6) + (-10) = -16$ Solve using the rules for addition

EXERCISE 3

Subtract or add as indicated:

_____1. $(-6) - (+2)$ _____11. $(-3) - (+3)$

_____2. $(+7) - (-4)$ _____12. $(+52) - (+37)$

_____3. $(-13) - (+6)$ _____13. $(+14) - (+5)$

_____4. $(+5) - (-7)$ _____14. $(-5) - (+42)$

_____5. $(-14) - (-7)$ _____15. $(+4) -9 - (+3)$

_____6. $(-8) - (+3)$ _____16. $-(+7) +4 - (3)$

_____7. $(-1) - (-1)$ _____17. $(+6.25) +3 - (3.625)$

_____8. $(-16) - (+3)$ _____18. $(-6.25) +3 - (3.625)$

_____9. $(-42) - (-63)$ _____19. $(+4\frac{5}{8}) - (+3.28)$

_____10. $(-4) - (-32)$ _____20. $(-13.63) - (4\frac{3}{5})$

The multiplication of directed numbers differs from conventional multiplication only in the selection of the proper sign for the product. In multiplying only two numbers, two rules cover all possibilities.

1. If the signs are the same, the product is positive.
2. If the signs are different the product is negative.

EXAMPLE:
$$\begin{array}{r} +3 \\ \times\ +2 \\ \hline +6 \end{array} \qquad \begin{array}{r} +3 \\ \times\ -2 \\ \hline -6 \end{array} \qquad \begin{array}{r} -3 \\ \times\ -2 \\ \hline +6 \end{array} \qquad \begin{array}{r} -3 \\ \times\ +2 \\ \hline -6 \end{array}$$

Like signs = positive product
Unlike signs = negative product

The previous rules will not apply if more than two numbers are being multiplied. However, there is a rule to cover every case.

Rules When Multiplying More Than Two Numbers

1. If there are no negative numbers, the product is positive.
2. If there is an even number of negative numbers, the product is positive.
3. If there is an odd number of negative numbers, the product is negative.

EXAMPLES:

$(+4) \times (+2) \times (+3) = +24$ All of the numbers are Positive, so the product is positive.
$(+4) \times (-2) \times (-3) = +24$ An *even* number of negative numbers, so the product is positive.
$(-4) \times (-2) \times (-3) = -24$ An *odd* number of negative numbers, so the product is negative.

The rules for division of signed numbers are the same as the rules for multiplication of signed numbers.

1. If the signs are the same, the answer is positive.
2. If the signs are different, the answer is negative.

EXAMPLE:

$$-2\overline{)\,-6}^{\,+3} \qquad +4\overline{)\,+8}^{\,+2} \qquad -6\overline{)\,+12}^{\,-2} \qquad +5\overline{)\,-10}^{\,-2}$$

Rules For Multiplication and Division of Signed Numbers

Signs Of The Numbers In The Problem		Sign Of The Answer
+	+	+
−	−	+
+	−	−
−	+	−

Put simply, if the signs are the same in the problem, the answer is positive. If the signs in the problem are not the same, the answer is negative.

EXAMPLE 1: $(+7)(+3) = 21$

EXAMPLE 2: $(-5)(-8) = 40$

EXAMPLE 3: $(+3)(-12) = -36$

EXAMPLE 4: $(-10)(+6) = -60$

EXAMPLE 5: $(+6) \div (+2) = 3$

EXAMPLE 6: $(-30) \div (-5) = 6$

EXAMPLE 7: $(+15) \div (-3) = -5$

EXAMPLE 8: $(-60) \div (+5) = -12$

EXERCISE 4

Multiplying values:

_____1. $(+1) \times (+3)$

_____2. $(+7) \times (-5)$

_____3. $(-4) \times (+6)$

_____4. $(-5) \times (-8)$

_____5. $(-14) \times (+8)$

_____6. $(+11) \times (+4)$

_____7. $(-6) \times (-18)$

_____8. $(-9) \times (+9)$

_____9. $(+8) \times (-7)$

_____10. $(-6) \times (-7)$

_____11. $(+13) \times (+5)$

_____12. $(-1.2) \times (+3.5)$

_____13. $(-3\frac{1}{2}) \times (-6.2)$

_____14. $(+\frac{3}{8}) \times (-\frac{1}{4})$

_____15. $(+1) \times (+2) \times (+24)$

_____16. $(+3) \times (+4) \times (-5)$

_____17. $(-6) \times (+2) \times (-9)$

_____18. $(+4.2) \times (+6\frac{1}{2}) \times (-1)$

_____19. $(+.4) \times (-\frac{1}{2}) \times (-3.6)$

_____20. $(+4) \times (-2) \times (-5) \times (+3)$

EXERCISE 5

Dividing values:

_____1. $(+6) \div (+3)$

_____2. $(-4) \div (-2)$

_____3. $(+39) \div (-3)$

_____4. $(+78) \div (-13)$

_____5. $(-42) \div (+6)$

_____6. $(-15) \div (-3)$

_____7. $(+145) \div (-3)$

_____8. $(-450) \div (-5)$

_____9. $(-1.5) \div (+5)$

_____10. $(+20) \div (+0.4)$

_____11. $(-3.2) \div (+8)$

_____12. $(+\frac{4}{5}) \div (-\frac{3}{5})$

_____13. $\dfrac{+14}{-7}$

_____14. $\begin{array}{r} -9 \\ +14 \\ -3 \\ \hline +7 \end{array}$

_____15. $\begin{array}{r} +2 \\ +16 \\ -1 \\ \hline +2 \end{array}$

_____16. $\begin{array}{r} +5 \\ -12 \\ +25 \\ \hline +36 \end{array}$

_____17. $\begin{array}{r} +.25 \\ \hline -1.00 \end{array}$

_____18. $\dfrac{-3.6}{-6.0}$

PRE-APPRENTICE TEST

DIRECTED NUMBERS

Time: 10 Minutes

Directions: Do the indicated operations.   Answers

1. $(6) + (-8) =$

2. $(-9) + (15) =$

3. $(-19) + (-4) =$

4. $(5) - (-3) =$

5. $(29) - (-44) =$

6. $(-3.3) - (-4.2) =$

7. $(4.5) - (+3.8) =$

8. $(450) - (121) + (60) - (-32) =$

9. $(-852) + (-342) - (-124) =$

10. $(5) \times (4) =$

11. $(6) \times (-9) =$

12. $(-12) \times (-44) =$

13. $(-\frac{3}{5}) \times (\frac{5}{20}) =$

14. $(4.25) \times (-3.75) =$

15. $(64) \div (-8) =$

16. $(-32\frac{1}{2}) \div (2.5) =$

17. $(-6.8) \div (-4) =$

18. $(-\frac{1}{8}) \div (-\frac{1}{16}) =$

19. $(7.5) \div (-1\frac{1}{4}) =$

20. $\dfrac{(-6) + 4}{(3)\ (-5)} =$

CHAPTER

7

Order of Operations

Numerous situations in mathematics arise where there is more than one operation used in an expression. Notice the two solutions to the same problem:

Since we want everyone to get the same answer to a specific problem, mathematicians have come up with a set of rules called the **order of operations**. The set of rules that the mathematicians have agreed upon are listed in the box below.

Order of Operations

1) Do all work in **P**arenthesis first
2) Do all work that involves **E**xponents/powers and roots next
3) Do all **M**ultiplication and **D**ivision in order from left to right
4) Do all **A**ddition and **S**ubtraction in order from left to right

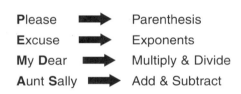

Following the order of operations and doing the multiplication first, the correct answer to the problem above is 17.

A mnemonic that is often used to help people remember is PEMDAS or **_Please Excuse My Dear Aunt Sally_**. The **P** for please represents **P**arenthesis which should always be done first in an expression. The **E** for excuse represents **E**xponents so exponents/powers and roots should be done next, and the **M** & **D** for "my dear" stands for **M**ultiply and **D**ivide which should be done next in the order it appears from left to right. Note, you should "**not**" do all multiplication and then do all division; you must do multiplication or division in the order that it appears from left to right. The last step in the order of operations is **A**ddition and **S**ubtraction, which is represented by "**A**unt **S**ally." The operations of Addition and Subtraction should also be done from left to right. Note, you should "**not**" do all addition and then do all subtraction you must do addition or subtraction in the order that it appears from left to right.

Example 1: $10 - 2 + 3$

$10 - 2 + 3$ do addition and subtraction in order from left to right; subtract 2 from 10

$8 + 3$ do addition and subtraction in order from left to right; add 8 and 3

11 answer

EXAMPLE 2: $6 \div 2(1 + 2)$

$6 \div 2(1 + 2)$ do all work in parenthesis first; add one and two

$6 \div 2(3)$ do multiplication and division in order from left to right; divide 6 by 2

$3(3)$ do multiplication and division in order from left to right; multiply 3 by 3

9 answer

EXAMPLE 3: $6 - 1 \times 0 + 2 \div 2$

$6 - 1 \times 0 + 2 \div 2$ do multiplication and division in order from left to right; $1 \times 0 = 0$; $2 \div 2 = 1$

$6 - 0 + 1$ do addition and subtraction in order from left to right; $6 - 6 = 0$

$6 + 1$ do addition and subtraction in order from left to right; $6 + 1 = 7$

7 answer

The "x" symbol for multiplication is not used in algebra because it gets confused with the letter "x" which is a letter used to represent a number. So 4 x 6 (4 times 6) is often written as 4 • 6 or 4(6). Both a dot and a number written next to a ( ) indicates the operation of multiplication.

Therefore 3 times 9 can be written in the following ways:

$3 \times 9 = 27$ or $3 \bullet 9 = 27$ or $(3)(9) = 27$

Another grouping symbol is a fraction bar. Work on top of the fraction bar must be done first, then work on the bottom of the fraction bar should be completed and the final step is dividing the numerator by denominator. For example: $\dfrac{7 + 5}{8 - 2} = \dfrac{12}{6} = 2$

Exponents (powers) are a way of indicating repeated multiplications. For example: $3 \bullet 3 = 9$ can be written as $3^2 = 9$. Another example illustrating the use of exponents $4 \bullet 4 \bullet 4 = 64$ can be written as $4^3 = 64$.

EXAMPLE 4: $2 - 3^2 + 5(2 + 6)$

$2 - 3^2 + 5(2 + 6)$ do all work in parenthesis first; add 2 and 6

$2 - 3^2 + 5(8)$ do all work with exponents next $3^2 = 9$

$2 - 9 + 5(8)$ do multiplication and division in order from left to right; $5(8) = 40$

$2 - 9 + 40$ do addition and subtraction in order from left to right; $2 - 9 = -7$

$-7 + 40$ do addition and subtraction in order from left to right; $-7 + 40 = 33$

33 answer

EXAMPLE 5: $4 - (6 + 4^2 \div 2)$

$4 - (6 + 4^2 \div 2)$ do all work in parenthesis first; powers first $4^2 = 16$

$\downarrow$

$4 - (6 + 16 \div 2)$ do all work in parenthesis; division $16 \div 2 = 8$

$4 - (6 + 8)$ do all work in parenthesis; add $6 + 8 = 14$

$4 - (14)$ do addition and subtraction in order from left to right; $4 - 14 = -10$

-10 answer

EXAMPLE 6: $2[3 + 2(5 - 2)] + 8$

$2[3 + 2(5 - 2)] + 8$ do all the work inside the parenthesis first; subtract $5 - 2 = 3$

$2[3 + 2(3)] + 8$ do the multiplication inside the brackets; multiply $2(3) = 6$

$2[3 + 6] + 8$ do the addition inside the brackets; add $3 + 6 = 9$

$2[9] + 8$ do the multiplication; multiply $2[9] = 18$

$18 + 8$ finally, solve the addition; add $18 + 8 = 26$

26 answer

EXERCISE 1
ORDER OF OPERATIONS

Simplify each of the following — show all steps:

1. $2 + 3 \times 8$

4. $6 + 9 \div 3 + 2$

7. $10 - (8 - 2) \div 2 + 1$

2. $5 + 4(10 + 2) \div 3 - 7$

5. $12 - 18 \div 3^2 + 6$

8. $8 + 2 \cdot 3^2$

3. $(16 + 2^2) \div 2 \cdot 2$

6. $20 \div 4 \cdot 5$

9. $2 + (3 - 1) \cdot 3^2$

10. $6(4 + 2^2) \div 2$

11. $\dfrac{2 + 3}{4 - 19}$

12. $8 - 3(7 - 4) + 5$

13. $25 - 8 \cdot 2 + 3^2$

14. $5[4 - 3(2^2 + 1)]$

15. $5(-2)^2 - 3 \cdot 0^3 \cdot 5$

16. $(7 - 3^2) + (7 - 3)^2$

17. $6[5 + 2(3 - 8) - 3]$

18. $2 + [4 + 2(10 + 6)]$

19. $7 - (2 \cdot 3 - 11)$

20. $15(13 - 7) \div (8 - 5)$

21. $8 + 4 \div 2 + 1$

22. $3(5 - 7) \div 6 + 3$

23. $6 \cdot 8 \div 4 \cdot 2 + 10$

24. $(4 + 2) \cdot 3 + 2(9)$

25. $30 + (1 - 3)^2 - 4 \cdot 3$

26. $\dfrac{7 + 6(8 - 5)}{4^2 - 6}$

27. $(5 + 3) \div 2 + (5^2 - 3)$

28. $\sqrt{20 - 4} \cdot 8 - 5^3 \div (2 - 7)^2$

29. $\dfrac{5(4 - 1)}{3 \cdot 2 + 5 \cdot 3}$

30. $8 - 6(7 - 2) \div 2 + 1$

ORDER OF OPERATIONS

Time: 15 Minutes

Simplify using the order of operations:

1. $4 + 6 \cdot 8$ _____

2. $24 \div 2 \cdot 6$ _____

3. $5 + 2^3$ _____

4. $6 + 8 \div 2 + 5$ _____

5. $2 + 3(10 + 2) \div 3 - 8$ _____

6. $10 - 3^2 + 5(4 - 6)$ _____

7. $2[5 - 3(3^2 + 2)]$ _____

8. $7 - 3 \times 0 + 9 \div 3$ _____

9. $9 - (6 + 2^3 \div 2)$ _____

10. $\dfrac{8(3) + 2(6)}{5(3) + 3(-7)}$ _____

CHAPTER
8

Algebra

A dictionary definition of algebra is "advanced math." Algebra is simply math with symbols (usually letters) used to represent certain values. Since algebra is nothing more than math, the same operations are used as found in the basic math section.

Adding and subtracting as indicated in algebra are with a plus ($+$) and a minus ($-$) sign. This creates no problem. However, with multiplying and dividing, the methods most commonly use to indicate these operations are not found as in basic math.

Multiplying can be indicated simply by a times sign ($\times$). In algebra, this common multiplication sign is never used. This is because the letter "x" is a common letter used to represent an unknown; and used as a multiplication sign. It would only serve to confuse the problem. Parentheses are commonly used to get around this problem.

$$4 \ (2) \ = \ 8$$

In algebra, it is often necessary to indicate the multiplication of a number and a letter or of two or more letters. In this case, it is not necessary to use any special symbol at all. They are simply written together.

$$ab \ = \ a \ times \ b$$

$$4a \ = \ 4 \ times \ a$$

Division in algebra is always indicated by a fraction. This is accomplished by the rule from section one which stated that in a fraction, the numerator is divided by the denominator.

EQUATIONS

$$3 \ = \ 3$$

This is a math statement of fact. Any number is equal to itself. This is stated in an equation. **An equation is a statement of equality.**

$$x \ = \ 3$$

This is a restatement of the first equation. The only difference is that the letter "x" was used to represent a value.

In the above statements, the equal sign ($=$) dictates that the value on one side must equal the value on the other.

$$3 \ = \ 3$$
$$3 \ = \ 2 + 1$$
$$3 \ = \ 1 + 2$$
$$3 \ = \ 3 \times 1$$
$$3 \ = \ 4 - 1$$

These statements are equations. The values on each side of the equal sign are the same.

By substituting letters in place of numbers in the previous statements, they become recognized as algebra problems.

$$3 = x$$
$$3 = a + 1$$
$$3 = m + 2$$
$$3 = 3c$$
$$3 = z - 1$$

The only requirement when working with equations is that the equality of both sides be maintained.

$$3 = 3$$

Add 2 to both sides of the equation.

$$3 + 2 = 3 + 2$$

$$5 = 5$$

The equation has been maintained. By adding the same value to both sides of the equation, nothing has changed. It is possible to add in this way to any equation without destroying the equality.

Solving Equations

This same idea can be used to find the value of an unknown. In the equation, $A - 1 = 3$, the value of the letter A is not known. In order to see the value of "A," this letter must be isolated on one side of the equal sign. This can be done by adding "1" to both sides of the equation.

$$A - 1 = 3$$
$$A - 1 + 1 = 3 + 1 \text{ (add 1 to both sides)}$$
$$A = 4$$

A value had been subtracted from "A" to make it equal to 3. This value was equal to 1. In order for the value A to be discovered, it was necessary to add the 1 back to it.

To find if 4 is actually the value of the letter A, substitute it for A in the original equation.

$$A - 1 = 3$$
$$4 - 1 = 3$$
$$3 = 3$$

The value has been determined and checked as correct.

EXAMPLE:

$$C - 7.3 = 16.9$$
$$C - 7.3 + 7.3 = 16.9 + 7.3 \text{ (add 7.3)}$$
$$C = 24.2$$

Again, the value which had been subtracted from the unknown value was added to both sides.

In both of the two previous examples, to isolate the letter on one side of the equation, the value which had been taken away was added back to both sides.

In actual practice, this idea can be simplified.

EXAMPLE:

$$z - 9 = 42$$

$$z \boxed{-9 + 9} = 42 + 9$$

The portion in the equation which is within the box becomes zero. Since the operation was designed to accomplish this end, it is usually eliminated in practice.

The problem is done as follows:

$$z - 9 = 42$$
$$z = 42 + 9 \text{ (add 9)}$$
$$z = 51$$

The practical solution can then be explained by the following chart:

Operation Unknown Subjected To:	To Solve:
Subtraction	Add

EXERCISE 1

Solve and check:

_____ 1. $x - 1 = 1$

_____ 2. $n - 4 = 3$

_____ 3. $7 = a - 5$

_____ 4. $y - 4 = 7$

_____ 5. $-3 + n = 2$

_____ 6. $12 = n - 13$

_____ 7. $3 = -10 + a$

_____ 8. $8 = x - 2$

_____ 9. $x - 7 = 14$

_____ 10. $16 = b - 3.2$

_____ 11. $y - 7 = 0$

_____ 12. $-6.4 + h = 7$

_____ 13. $a - 13 = 13$

_____ 14. $24 = c - 3$

_____ 15. $a - 13.25 = 0.015625$

_____ 16. $125 = a - 3$

_____ 17. $-1.3 = -1.3 + x$

_____ 18. $45 = x - 13$

_____ 19. $27.6 = a - 44$

_____ 20. $-67 + x = 33$

By the same reasoning used to prove the reliability of adding to both sides of an equation, other methods of working with equations can be shown.

$$3 = 3$$
$$3 - 1 = 3 - 1 \text{ (subtract 1 from both sides)}$$
$$2 = 2$$

A letter or number can be subtracted from each side of an equation and maintain the equality.

EXAMPLE:

$$x + 2 = 3$$
$$x + 2 - 2 = 3 - 2 \text{ (subtract 2)}$$
$$x = 1$$

It is again possible to simplify the process by the elimination of the part of the second step which has the number being subtracted from itself in order to isolate the unknown.

Expanding the chart shown earlier:

Operation Unknown Subjected To:	To Solve:
Addition	Subtract
Subtraction	Add

EXERCISE 2

Solve and Check:

_____ 1. x + 1 = 4

_____ 2. a + 2 = 6

_____ 3. c + 3 = 7

_____ 4. 9 = 8 + m

_____ 5. 13 = 13 + b

_____ 6. 4 + y = 6

_____ 7. b + 20 = 28

_____ 8. 17 + x = 26

_____ 9. 24 + c = 26

_____ 10. 36 = n + 24

_____ 11. 16 = 4.4 + n

_____ 12. y + 22.25 = 22.27

_____ 13. a + 18 = 21

_____ 14. c + $2\frac{1}{4}$ = 7.875

_____ 15. 19 = 12 + x

_____ 16. 2.3 + k = 4.5

_____ 17. y + $\frac{5}{8}$ = 1.9375

_____ 18. $\frac{3}{5}$ = $\frac{5}{8}$ + x

_____ 19. $\frac{1}{4}$ + m = .3125

_____ 20. .625 = x + $\frac{5}{16}$

The trend seems to show that as long as the same operation is applied to both sides of the equation, the equality will be maintained. It should be possible to multiply or divide both sides by the same numbers.

EXAMPLE:

$$2a = 6$$

In order to isolate the "a" value on one side of the equal sign, it is necessary to divide both sides of the equation by 2. In doing so, the 2a value will become 1a and can be written simply as "a".

$$2a = 6$$

$$\frac{2a}{2} = \frac{6}{2} \quad \text{(divide both sides by 2)}$$

$$a = 3$$

As in addition and subtraction, the process can be simplified.

$$2a = 6$$

$$a = \frac{6}{2} \quad \text{(divide by 2)}$$

$$a = 3$$

Again with the chart being expanded to include this step, it looks as follows:

Operation Unknown Subjected To:	To Solve:
Addition	Subtract
Subtraction	Add
Multiplication	Divide

EXERCISE 3

Solve and Check:

_____ 1. $2x = 4$

_____ 2. $5a = 22$

_____ 3. $36 = 9b$

_____ 4. $43 = 4m$

_____ 5. $7c = 62$

_____ 6. $13k = 65$

_____ 7. $8n = 97$

_____ 8. $14x = 144$

_____ 9. $18y = 108$

_____ 10. $39 = 3m$

_____ 11. $1440 = 16a$

_____ 12. $17b = 51$

_____ 13. $5x = 13.5$

_____ 14. $1.5m = 2.25$

_____ 15. $13c = 5.2$

_____ 16. $.625 = 6.25a$

_____ 17. $45b = 99$

_____ 18. $.35y = 2\frac{5}{8}$

_____ 19. $77 = .7x$

_____ 20. $77 = 77c$

The one major arithmetic process remaining that the unknown may be subjected to is division. The solution for this type of equation is multiplication.

EXAMPLE: $\dfrac{m}{4} = 3$

$\dfrac{4m}{4} = 3\,(4)$ (multiply both sides by 4)

$m = 12$

or simplifying the second step

$\dfrac{m}{4} = 3$

$m = 4\,(3)$

$m = 12$

Operation Unknown Subjected To:	To Solve:
Addition	Subtract
Subtraction	Add
Multiplication	Divide
Division	Multiply

EXERCISE 4

Solve and Check:

_____ 1. $\dfrac{b}{2} = 4$

_____ 2. $\dfrac{x}{5} = 3$

_____ 3. $5 = \dfrac{n}{6}$

_____ 4. $2 = \dfrac{a}{7}$

_____ 5. $\dfrac{n}{5} = 4$

_____ 6. $\dfrac{c}{3} = 12$

_____ 7. $\dfrac{x}{12} = 3$

_____ 8. $\dfrac{x}{4} = 4$

_____ 9. $\dfrac{a}{2} = 4$

_____ 10. $16 = \dfrac{d}{2}$

_____ 11. $\dfrac{x}{5} = 18$

_____ 12. $\dfrac{y}{3} = 9$

_____ 13. $\dfrac{b}{7} = 12$

_____ 14. $\dfrac{y}{10} = \dfrac{3}{5}$

_____ 15. $\dfrac{a}{6} = 13$

_____ 16. $\dfrac{n}{.75} = 4$

_____ 17. $\dfrac{m}{3} = .5$

_____ 18. $\dfrac{c}{17} = 2$

_____ 19. $\dfrac{d}{2} = 6.7$

_____ 20. $2\dfrac{1}{2} = \dfrac{b}{1.6}$

All of the algebra problems that have been presented up to this point have required only one step to solve. Most problems are not that simple. More than one step is usually required for a solution.

EXAMPLE: $2x + 3 = 9$

In this problem the unknown value (x) has first been multiplied by 2. This product has then had 3 added to it. The sum is equal to 9.

The same rules apply for the solution of this problem that applied for the solution of single step problems. In order to isolate to unknown value on one side of the equation, it becomes necessary to undo whatever operations that have been applied to it. Whatever is done to one side of the equation must also be done to the other side in order to keep both sides equal.

$$2x + 3 = 9$$

The number 3 was added to the product last to make it equal 9, therefore, it must be eliminated first.

$$2x = 9 - 3 \text{ (subtract 3)}$$

$$2x = 6$$

Now the problem is to a point that it can be solved in one additional step.

$$x = \dfrac{6}{2} \text{ (divide by 2)}$$

$$x = 3$$

Similarly, the following equation is solved.

$$\dfrac{a}{3} - 7 = 2$$

$$\dfrac{a}{3} = 2 + 7 \text{ (add 7)}$$

$$\dfrac{a}{3} = 9$$

$$a = 9 \text{ (3) (multiply by 3)}$$

$$a = 27$$

Solve and Check:

_____ 1. $2y + 7 = 13$

_____ 2. $4 = 5x - 6$

_____ 3. $4 + \dfrac{c}{3} = 10$

_____ 4. $3m + 8 = 13$

_____ 5. $5x - 6 = 4$

_____ 6. $\dfrac{x}{5} - 6 = 4$

_____ 7. $\dfrac{5}{x} - 6 = 4$

_____ 8. $5c + 25 = 7$

_____ 9. $14 = \dfrac{b}{3} - 8$

_____ 10. $46 = 7n + 11$

_____ 11. $4y - 6 = 8$

_____ 12. $\dfrac{x}{8} + 5 = 13$

_____ 13. $\dfrac{6}{3b} - 5 = 8$

_____ 14. $9c - 8 = 16$

_____ 15. $4 = -12 + \dfrac{3a}{4}$

_____ 16. $\dfrac{6b}{10} + 13 = 22$

_____ 17. $12\dfrac{3}{4} = 8 - 3y$

_____ 18. $6.5 + 3.25d = 1$

_____ 19. $\dfrac{7x}{9} - 6 = 2$

_____ 20. $3x - 2\dfrac{1}{2} = 3.6$

_____ 21. $.625 = 1.25z - .125$

_____ 22. $14y + 4.6 = .88$

In the case of equations involving only letters, the same methods can be used to solve for the desired unknown. In each of the following examples, the unknown being solved for is "x".

EXAMPLE:

$$x + a = c$$
$$x = c - a \text{ (subtract a)}$$

ANSWER: $x = c - a$

The value for "x" is now known. It is the difference of $c - a$.

CHECK:

$$x + a = c$$
$$\underline{c - a + a = c} \text{ (substitute for } -a \text{ in place of x)}$$
$$c = c$$

EXAMPLE:

$$x - a = c$$
$$x = c + a \text{ (add a)}$$

ANSWER: $x = c + a$

CHECK:

$$x - a = c$$
$$c + a - a = c \text{ (substitute } +a \text{ in place of } x)$$
$$c = c$$

EXAMPLE:

$$\frac{x}{a} = c$$
$$x = ac \text{ (multiply by a)}$$

ANSWER:

$$x = ac$$

CHECK:

$$\frac{x}{a} = c$$
$$\frac{ac}{a} = c \text{ (substitute } ac \text{ in place of } x)$$
$$c = c$$

EXAMPLE:

$$ax = c$$
$$x = \frac{c}{a} \text{ (divide by a)}$$

Answer:

$$x = \frac{c}{a}$$

CHECK:

$$ax = c$$
$$a\left(\frac{c}{a}\right) = c \text{ (substitute } \frac{c}{a} \text{ in place of } x)$$
$$c = c$$

EXERCISE 6

Solve and Check for "x":

_____ 1. $a + x = n$

_____ 2. $4x = a$

_____ 3. $c = x - y$

_____ 4. $x - c = y$

_____ 5. $\dfrac{x}{a} = n$

_____ 6. $\dfrac{ax}{c} = y$

_____ 7. $x + 3a = b$

_____ 8. $2x - 4b = 2b$

_____ 9. $\dfrac{ax}{7} + 1 = a$

_____ 10. $\dfrac{a}{x} = b$

_____ 11. $4x = 4$

_____ 12. $ax = 2a$

_____ 13. $x + a - b = c + 2$

_____ 14. $2x = c$

_____ 15. $4b + 6x = b$

_____ 16. $c = x - cy$

_____ 17. $cx = cy$

_____ 18. $ax = \dfrac{ab}{c}$

_____ 19. $\dfrac{a}{b} = \dfrac{x}{c}$

_____ 20. $\dfrac{n}{x} = \dfrac{y}{d}$

Negative Answers

The chance of a negative number appearing as the answer to a problem should not be unexpected. Since a negative number is a definite value, it could well be the value for the unknown.

Many times the final step of the problem is reached and the unknown itself is express as a negative. Because the positive value for the unknown is the most desirable form for it to be in, an additional step might be used.

By multiplying both sides of the equation by -1, the negative sign of the unknown will be changed to positive.

EXAMPLE:

$$12 = 8 - x$$
$$4 = -x \quad \text{(subtract 8)}$$
$$(-1)\,4 = -1\,(-x) \quad \text{(multiply both sides by } -1)$$
$$-4 = x$$

CHECK:

$$12 = 8 - x$$
$$12 = 8 - (-4)$$
$$12 = 8 + 4$$
$$12 = 12$$

EXERCISE 7

Solve and Check:

_____ 1. $2x + 3 = 2$

_____ 2. $\dfrac{x}{2} = 4 + x$

_____ 3. $\dfrac{2x}{3} - 5 = 7x + 2$

_____ 4. $3x + 4 = 5x - 5$

_____ 5. $.7 - 2x = .7x - 2$

_____ 6. $\dfrac{3}{4} + 5y = \dfrac{y}{2} - 7$

_____ 7. $\dfrac{1}{8} + .25y = -4.625$

_____ 8. $12 - 2y = -13$

_____ 9. $-8y + 3 = 41$

_____ 10. $\dfrac{5a}{8} = -\dfrac{3}{5}$

_____ 11. $14x - 5 = 15x + 3$

_____ 12. $\dfrac{5y}{2} - 6 = -8$

_____ 13. $3.75 - 4\dfrac{1}{4}x = 1$

SOLVE FOR X

_____ 14. $ax - 3b = 2b$

_____ 15. $4x - 3y = 8y$

Plotting Points

DEFINITIONS:

1. **Ordered pair** – A pair of numbers expressed inside a parenthesis. The first value is the x coordinate and the second value is the y coordinate. An ordered pair represents one and only one plotted point on a graph.

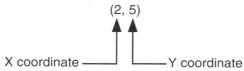

2. **Coordinate axes** – Two perpendicular real number lines used to plot points.

3. **X-axis** - The horizontal number line.

4. **Y-axis** - The vertical number line

5. **Origin** - The point where the x-axis and y-axis intersect. x = 0, y = 0.

6. **Quadrants** – The coordinate axes divide the real number plane into four regions or quadrants.
   A. In quadrant I each point has a positive value for the x coordinate and a positive value for the y coordinate.
   B. In quadrant II each point has a negative value for the x coordinate and a positive value for the y coordinate.
   C. In quadrant III each point has a negative value for the x coordinate and a negative value for the y coordinate.
   D. In quadrant IV each point has a positive value for the x coordinate and a negative value for the y coordinate.

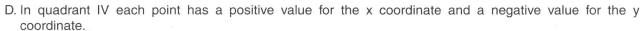

PROCEDURE:

1. Each ordered pair represents one plotted point.

2. The first value of the ordered pair is the x coordinate, the second value of the ordered pair is the y coordinate.

3. Locate the x and y coordinates on the x and y axis. Follow the points along the grid lines until they intersect.

4. Draw a dot at the intersection.

EXAMPLES:

Plot the following points on one graph.

1. (2, 3)
2. (−3, 4)
3. (−2, −6)
4. (5, 0)
5. (6, −6)

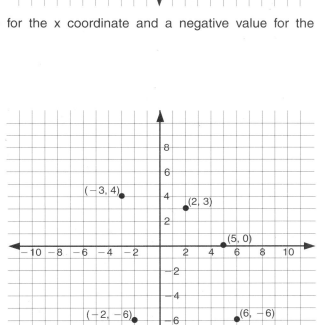

EXERCISE 8

Directions: Plot the following points on graph paper. You may plot them all on one graph.

1. (4, 1)	3. (5, −3)	5. (6,0)	7. (1, −7)	9. (0, 0)
2. (−6, 3)	4. (3, −3)	6. (0, −4)	8. (−5, −4)	10. (−8, −6)

Graphing An Equation

PROCEDURE:

1. Make a table for the x and y coordinates.

2. Select 3 values for the x coordinate. Numbers less than 10 are easier to graph. Include 0 and a negative value to get an even distribution of points.

3. Solve for the corresponding y coordinate in the equation using the rules for algebra.

4. Plot the three points on a graph.

5. Draw a straight line through the plotted points.

EXAMPLES:

1. Draw the graph of $x + y = 8$.

x	y
0	
4	
−1	

Substitute 0 for x, solve for y

$$0 + y = 8$$
$$y = 8 - 0$$
$$y = 8$$

When $x = 0$
    $y = 8$

Ordered pair (0, 8)

Substitute 4 for x, solve for y

$$4 + y = 8$$
$$y = 8 - 4$$
$$y = 4$$

When $x = 4$
    $y = 4$

Ordered pair (4, 4)

Substitute −1 for x, solve for y

$$-1 + y = 8$$
$$y = 8 + 1$$
$$y = 9$$

When $x = -1$
    $y = 9$

Ordered pair (−1, 9)

x	y
0	8
4	4
−1	9

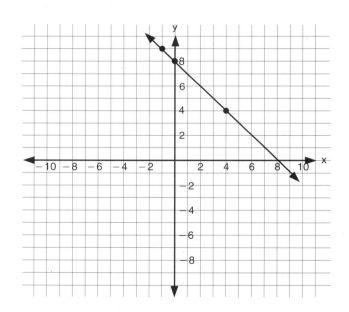

2. Draw the graph of y = 2x.

x	y
0	
4	
−4	

Substitute 0 for x, solve for y

$$y - 2(0)$$
$$y = 0$$

When x = 0
      y = 0

Ordered pair (0, 0)

Substitute 4 for x, solve for y

$$y - 2(4)$$
$$y = 8$$

When x = 4
      y = 4

Ordered pair (4, 8)

Substitute −4 for x, solve for y

$$y - 2(-4)$$
$$y = -8$$

When x = −4
      y = −8

Ordered pair (−4, −8)

x	y
0	0
4	8
−4	−8

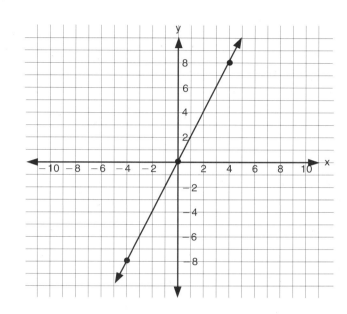

PROCEDURE:

1. Sometimes only one variable is given in an equation.

2. No matter what value is substituted for the missing variable the given variable remains constant.

EXAMPLES:

1. Draw the graph of 2y = 8

x	y
0	4
3	4
−3	4

Solve 2y = 8 for y

$$2y = 8$$
$$y = 4$$

No matter what is substituted for x, y equals 4. At least 3 ordered pairs are required to obtain a straight line graph.

Ordered pair (0, 4)
Ordered pair (3, 4)
Ordered pair (−3, 4)

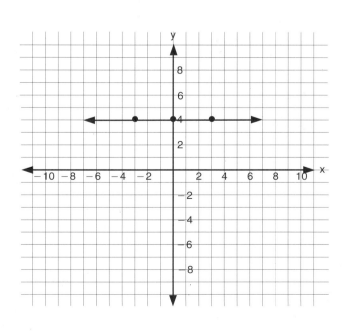

2. Draw the graph of $3x = -12$

x	y
-4	0
-4	4
-4	-2

Solve: $3x = -12$

$3x = -12$
$x = -4$

No matter what is substituted for y, x equals -4. At least 3 ordered pairs are required to obtain a straight line graph.

Ordered pair $(-4, 0)$
Ordered pair $(-4, 4)$
Ordered pair $(-4, -2)$

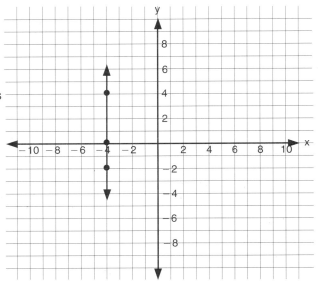

EXERCISE 9

Draw the graph of each of the following equations using graph paper. Each equation should be graphed on its own set of axis.

1. $y = x + 5$

2. $x = y + 3$

3. $x = y - 2$

4. $x + y = 8$

5. $x + y = -4$

6. $y = 5x$

7. $2x = -3y$

8. $7y = 21$

9. $x = 2$

10. $-3x = 9$

Word Problems

One of the biggest problems encountered in shop math and algebra is in the attempt to put the information from a word problem into a workable formula. It is necessary to know the "code" of the word problem.

Up to now, solving problems has required adding, subtracting, multiplying, and dividing. The required information has been shown in signs. In word problems, the signs are no longer there, but have been replaced by words. A few of the words that are used are listed below.

ADD (+)	SUBTRACT (−)	MULTIPLY (×)	DIVIDE (÷)	EQUAL (=)
Sum of	Less than	Product	Quotient	Gives
More than or More	Diminished by	Times	Divide by or Divide	Total
Increased by or Increase	Decreased by	Multiplied by	equally	Result
Greater than	Minus	Of	Per	Altogether
Plus	Subtracted	Twice or Three	Split	Is
Added to	Difference	times, etc.	Out of	
Combined with	Remainder or remains		Separate into parts	
In addition to	How many more		Cut	
	How much less		Shared	
	Reduced by			
	Left			
	Fewer than			

The statement "4 and 7" can be written mathematically by substituting the proper symbol for the word "and".

$$4 \text{ and } 7$$

$$4 + 7$$

Whether the values are represented by numbers or letters has no effect on the substitution for the words representing the operation.

$$x \text{ diminished by } 7$$

$$x - 7$$

EXERCISE 10

Change from a word statement to an algebraic statement.

	Answers		Answers
1. x added to 6	_____	6. $\frac{4}{5}$ of y	_____
2. y diminished by a	_____	7. the sum of 7 and z	_____
3. 5 more than h	_____	8. half of a	_____
4. 4 subtracted from 9	_____	9. the product of t and y	_____
5. 17 divided by c	_____	10. 47 multiplied by y	_____

When problems become more complicated, more than one operation is required in the statement. Care must be taken to be sure that each value is subjected to the proper operation.

EXAMPLE: <u>The product of 4</u> and <u>y is increased by 13</u>

The two important facts in this statement have been underlined.

<u>The product of 4 and y</u>	4y
<u>Increased by 13</u>	+ 13
Putting the two parts of the statement together,	<u>4y + 13</u>

EXERCISE 11

Rewrite: Answers

1. 13 divided by y is decreased by 4   _____

2. The sum of x and the product of 4 and c   _____

3. 4 less than y is divided by a   _____

4. The product of x and z is divided by 2   _____

5. Half of x times c   _____

6. 13 decreased by a number   _____

Answers

7. A number plus 7 _____

8. 33 divided by the difference y less 47 _____

9. Twice m more than 3z _____

10. The sum of a and b minus the product of 5 and c _____

11. ⅓ of y is diminished by 7 _____

12. The difference between x times ⅓ and 7 _____

13. 7 less than the quotient of n divided by p _____

14. 5 less than twice x is divided by 4 _____

The word phrases given in the previous two exercises are samples of parts of typical word problems. In order to have a complete problem it is necessary that a question be asked. The entire question can be rewritten as an equation. Such a question might be, "What number when added to 3 gives 8?"

What number when added to 3 gives 8

Substituting in the problem for the underlined portions the following information is found. The unknown factor in this problem is represented by "what number". This value can be represented by the letter. "x".

x added to 3 gives 8

The phrase "added to 3" can be written " +3".

x + 3 gives 8

"Gives" becomes = .

x + 3 = 8

The question has been rewritten as an algebraic problem. It is in the form of an equation and can be solved for x.

EXERCISE 12

Rewrite the following as equations, solve and check for x or the unknown: Answers

1. x decreased by 4 is 3 _____

2. The difference between y and 7 is equal to four _____

3. The sum of x and y is 13 _____

4. Fifteen is equal to the difference twice x decreased by seven _____

5. If 16 is diminished by an unknown, the difference is 7 _____

6. Twice 5 divided by x is equal to 3 _____

7. If a is subtracted from the product of x and y, the result is equal to z _____

8. When the sum of x and 3 is divided by 4, the value is 3 _____

9. x less than y is equal to z _____

10. The quotient of twice x divided by four is one _____

11. The product of half x divided by 3 is 12 _____

12. The product of x and 3 over 4 is added to half the
    difference of y minus z gives 30 _____

13. Half of x divided by ⅓ equals 12 _____

14. When the sum of x and 8 is divided by 2, the quotient is 14 _____

Word problems increase in difficulty as the values involved are associated with names and things. When this occurs, it is necessary to look past the "extra" words to find those that can be used to form an equation.

EXAMPLE:

John discovered that by **adding seven pieces** of chalk **to the chalk** already **in the box**, the box was full. If **the box held 12 pieces**, how many were in the box to start?

The question supplies the unknown in the problem. The number of pieces in the box to start can be represented by x. By ignoring extra words in the problem, the word problem can be written as follows:

Adding 7 pieces to the chalk in the box	it held 12 pieces
+ 7 + x	= 12

$$7 + x = 12$$
$$x = 12 - 7$$
$$x = 5$$

x = original amount
7 = amount added
12 = amount left

By solving for the letter x, the problem is solved.

EXAMPLE:

After using six bolts, David found he had 12 left. How many did he have to start?

$$x - 6 = 12$$

$$x - 6 = 12$$
$$x = 12 + 6$$
$$x = 18$$

x = original amount
6 = amount used
12 = amount left

Another type of story problem which is quite common is the one which gives two equations. One is for information, the other is the question.

EXAMPLE:

Two trucks delivered a total of eight tons of steel. The first truck carried 14,350 pounds. How much did the second truck deliver?

From the first sentence, the following information is found: together, the first and second truck carried 16,000 pounds. If x is used to represent the first, and y the second, this information can be expressed as follows: $x + y = 16,000$.

The second sentence says that the first truck represented 14,350 pounds of the total amount. x = 14,350

By substituting the value from the second equation into the first, the equation lookes as follows: x = 14,350

$$x + y = 16,000$$
$$14,350 + y = 16,000$$
$$y = 16,000 - 14,350$$
$$y = 1,650$$

EXERCISE 13

Rewrite the following problems on a separate sheet of paper as equations, solve and check: Show your work.

1. Bill has twice as much money as Jim, and ½ as much as Sue. How much does each person have if together they have $120?

2. Brett increases the number of parts ordered by six. This increase makes the total order 3 less than twice the original. How many parts were originally ordered?

3. Corky and John together weigh 102 pounds. If John weighs 66 pounds, how much does Corky weigh?

4. A certain number is increased by 5. The result is 8 more than half the number. What is the number?

5. David wants to buy a bicycle that costs $45. It costs $3 less than twice the money he has now. How much does David have now?

6. There are 50 chairs in the room. All of them are either red or blue. There are 17 more blue chairs than twice the number of red ones. How many red chairs are there?

7. The labor cost of a particular tool is five times the material cost. The total cost of the tool (material and labor) is $1050. How much did the material cost?

8. Three consecutive numbers total 147. What is the lowest of the three.

9. If the number of students in a class is decreased by 6, the remainder is equal to twice the number of boys in the class. If there are 44 students in the class, how many girls are there?

10. This year's model of a certain large appliance has 3 more pounds of plastic than last year's model. The total amount of plastic in this year's model is 36 pounds. How many pounds of plastic in last year's model?

11. A bus headed out from point "A" traveling at 45 mph. Two hours later a car left from the same point traveling on the same road at 55 mph. How many hours before the car catches the bus?

12. The smaller of two numbers is ¾ larger. The sum of the numbers is 28. What are the numbers?

13. The sum of three numbers is 333. The smallest is half the largest and the middle is 22 less than the largest. What are the numbers?

14. The total age of a father and his son is 49 years. The father's age is 6 times his son's age. What is the age of each?

15. The total value of 26 coins is $2.05. If the coins are only dimes and nickels, how many each are there?

Powers and Roots – Algebra

Multiplication can be indicated in the case of a value being multiplied by itself as an exponent. An exponent is a small number that appears to the right of and above the value in question. The exponent tells the number of times the value is multiplied by itself. This number is sometimes referred to as the power by which the value is raised.

4×4 by previous definitions can be written:

$$4 \times 4$$
$$4 \cdot 4$$
$$4 \quad (4)$$

It can also be written by the use of an exponent: $\qquad 4^2$

A value raised to the second power is said to be **squared**. This is because the way to find the area of a square is to multiply the length and width which are equal.

$$3 \times 3 = 3^2$$

When a value is raised to the third power, it is said to be cubed. This is because to find the volume of a cube, the length, width, and height are multiplied. In a cube, these three edges are equal.

$$3 \times 3 \times 3 = 3^3$$

The idea of exponents can be used with all symbols used to represent specific values.

$$a \cdot a = a^2$$

$$a \cdot a \cdot a = a^3$$

$$a \cdot a \cdot a \cdot a = a^4$$

To combine values raised to powers, the exponent becomes the important factor. Just as apples and pears cannot be added or subtracted, terms with unlike exponents cannot be added or subtracted.

$$x^2 + x^2 = 2x^2$$

$$x^2 \text{ and } x^2 \text{ is equal to } 2x^2$$

$$x^2 + x^3 = x^2 + x^3$$

These unlike terms cannot be added.

The multiplication of letters bearing exponents is accomplished by adding exponents.

$$x^2 \cdot x^1 = x^3$$

The lone x or lone number is understood to have an exponent of 1.

EXAMPLE 1: $\qquad x = x^1 \qquad\qquad 3 = 3^1$

If each factor, x^2 and x, is looked at separately, this principle can be easily understood.

$$x^2 = x \cdot x$$

$$x^3 = x \cdot x \cdot x$$

$$x^2 \cdot x^3 = x^5$$

$$x \cdot x \cdot x \cdot x \cdot x = x^5$$

EXAMPLE 2: $\qquad$ $2x \cdot 2x^2$

When the coefficients are multiplied and the exponents are added together.

$2x \cdot 2x^2 = 2 \cdot 2 \cdot x \cdot x^2 = 4x^3$

$3m^2n \cdot 4mn = 3 \cdot 4 \cdot m^2 \cdot m \cdot n \cdot n = 12m^3n^2$

$3 (3^3) (3^5) = 3 \cdot 3^3 \cdot 3^5 = 3^9$

EXERCISE 14

Multiply:

Answers: $\qquad\qquad\qquad\qquad$ Answers:

1. $x^2 \cdot x^4$ _____

11. $-xy^2 (6yz^2) (-10az)$ _____

2. $a^6 \cdot a^3$ _____

12. $-2 (7y) (abx)$ _____

3. $c^2 \cdot c \cdot c^3$ _____

13. $3ay (4y^2z) (6bz)$ _____

4. $5(5^2) (5^4)$ _____

14. $-mn^2 (-am^2n^3) (ab)$ _____

5. $xy^2 (x^2y^6) (x^3y^7)$ _____

15. $x^2 (y^2)$ _____

6. $x^3y^4 (xy^2)$ _____

16. $7x (4mxy)$ _____

7. $ab^2c^4 (a^3b^5c^6)$ _____

17. $6ax^3y (7a^2xy^3) (3)$ _____

8. $-6x (4xy)$ _____

18. $y^7z^8 (6xy^5) (-8x^6y^4z^7)$ _____

9. $2a^2b (3b^3c)$ _____

19. $6a^6b^3c (9a^2x) (cx)$ _____

10. $3ab (2a^2) (3bc^3)$ _____

20. $3wx^3yz (9a^6x) (cx)$ _____

In division, the exponents are subtracted instead of added as in multiplication.

EXAMPLE 1: $\qquad$ $x^3 \div x^2 = x^1 = x$

EXAMPLE 2: $\qquad$ $\dfrac{2x}{4x^2} = \dfrac{\cancel{2}x}{\cancel{2} \cdot 2 \cdot \cancel{x} \cdot x} = \dfrac{1}{2x} = .5x^{-1}$

EXAMPLE 3: $\qquad$ $6a^2b^3c \div 2a^4bc = \dfrac{3b^2}{a^2} = 3b^2a^{-2}$

EXAMPLE 4: $\qquad$ $9ab^2 \div 3b = 3ab$

Answers: Answers:

1. $\dfrac{8a^2b}{4ab}$ _____

11. $\dfrac{-27m^2nx^5}{9m^5x^3}$ _____

2. $18xy \div 9x$ _____

12. $\dfrac{52a^5xy^4}{13xyz}$ _____

3. $20x^3z^2 \div -10xz$ _____

4. $24bc \div 8bc$ _____

13. $\dfrac{16a^8b^7c^3d^5}{-4a^5b^7cd^7}$ _____

5. $(-6x^5y) \div (2x)$ _____

14. $13x^2y^{13}z^8 \div 39xy^{12}z$ _____

6. $15xyz \div (-3xz)$ _____

15. $80am^4z^7 \div 15a^3m^2z^2$ _____

7. $25ab^2c^3 \div (-4n)$ _____

16. $24bm^4z^7 \div 8a^6y^3z$ _____

8. $36m^4n \div 9m$ _____

17. $\dfrac{a^7b^6m^9y^5z^8}{-4b^5y^3z^3}$ _____

9. $12a^2bc^7 \div 3a^3b^2c$ _____

18. $3z^3y^4x^8 \div 2x^2y^5z^7$ _____

10. $144x^8y \div 18y^2z$ _____

Roots

It has been explained how an exponent dictates the power to which a number can be raised. The opposite may well be as important in any given problem. The requirement of such a problem would be to find what number multiplied by itself is equal to a certain value.

EXAMPLE 1: What number multiplied by itself gives 16? The answer is 4 since $4 \times 4 = 16$.

The above question could be indicated by a radical sign. $\sqrt{16}$

The question in the example can be rephrased as follows:

$$\sqrt{16}$$

$$\sqrt{16} = \sqrt{4 \times 4} = 4$$

$$\sqrt{25} = \sqrt{5 \times 5} = 5$$

$$\sqrt{4y^2} = \sqrt{2(2)y(y)} = 2y$$

The entire number under the radical need not be brought out from underneath. At times, it becomes necessary to find the square root of only part of a given number.

EXAMPLE 2: $\sqrt{2x^2}$

In this case, the square root of x can easily be found, but since there is no perfect square for the number, it can be left under the radical.

$$\sqrt{2x^2} = \sqrt{2x(x)} = x\sqrt{2}$$

$$\sqrt{24} = \sqrt{2 \cdot 2 \cdot 2 \cdot 3} = \sqrt{2 \cdot 3} = 2\sqrt{6}$$

NOTE: Reduce 24 to prime numbers.

The number which was found to be multiplied by itself to give the number under the radical is called the square root.

Roots other than the square root can be found. Just as a number can be raised to the third power (cubed), fourth power, etc., roots such as the cube root, fourth root, etc., can be found.

If a root other than the square root is desired, it will be indicated by an index number in front of the radical.

EXAMPLE 3:

$$\sqrt[3]{8} = \sqrt[3]{(2)(2)(2)} = 2$$

$$\sqrt[3]{x^3} = \sqrt[3]{x \cdot x \cdot x} = x$$

$$\sqrt[4]{16} = \sqrt[4]{2 \cdot 2 \cdot 2 \cdot 2} = 2$$

The index can go to any desired number.

The roots of fractions can be found by the same principle as given previously. In taking the roots of a fraction, the roots of both the numerator and denominator must be found.

EXERCISE 16

_____1. $\sqrt{4}$

_____2. $\sqrt{x^2y^4}$

_____3. $\sqrt[3]{125}$

_____4. $\sqrt{36a^2b^4}$

_____5. $\sqrt[4]{256x^8}$

_____6. $\sqrt[3]{y^{15}}$

_____7. $\sqrt{\dfrac{64}{81}}$

_____8. $\sqrt[5]{32a^7}$

_____9. $\sqrt[5]{32a^6}$

_____10. $\sqrt[3]{\dfrac{27x^3}{125x^3}}$

_____11. $\sqrt{32x^4}$

_____12. $\sqrt{\dfrac{9a^2}{16y^2}}$

Factoring

Naming the parts of an algebraic expressions:

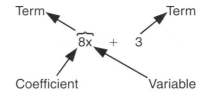

This particular expression has two terms : 8x and 3, one variable : x, and one coefficient : 8. A cooefficient is the number which appears with a variable. An expression with two terms is called a binomial.

EXAMPLES:

Name the terms, variables and coefficients in the following binomial expressions.

	Terms	Variables	Coefficients
2y + 4	2y, 4	y	2
18m − 9	18m, 9	m	18
7x + 14y	7x 14y	x, y	7, 14

Steps To Factor An Expression

1. Determine the largest number and/or letter which divides evenly into each term of the expression. This is called the greatest commmon factor of the expression or GCF.

2. Divide each term of the expression by the GCF.

3. Rewrite the expression as follows:

     a. Write the quotients from step 2 in place of the original terms in the expression.

     b. Enclose the new expression in parenthesis.

     c. Place the GCF outside of the parenthesis.

EXAMPLES:

Factor the following expressions:

> factor 4m + 8
> GCF = 4
> answer: 4 (m + 2)

Step 1. The greatest common factor for the terms 4m and 8 is 4.

Step 2. Divide each term by the GCF and rewrite the expression using the quotients. Enclose in parenthesis.
    (m + 2)

Step 3. Write the GCF outside the parenthesis 4 (m + 2)

EXAMPLES:

factor $36m^2 + 9m$
GCF = 9m
answer: $9m(4m + 1)$

factor $6m^3 - 36m^2 - 12m$
GCF = 6m
answer: $6m(m^2 - 6m - 2)$

EXERCISE 17

Factor the following completely:

1. $9m + 6$

2. $12x + 4$

3. $36y - 6$

4. $24z - 8$

5. $20p^2 + 15p$

6. $7r^2 - 14r$

7. $26a^2 + 39a$

8. $51b^2 - 34b$

9. $13e^2 + e$

10. $44p^3 + 66p^2 - 33p$

Factoring Using The Foil Method

The foil method is used to multiply two binomial expressions.

Identify the term positions:

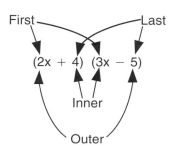

To multiply $(2x + 4)(3x + 5)$, do the following steps in the order in which they are given.

Step 1. Multiply the First terms of each binomial   F

$$(2x)(3x) = 6x^2$$

Step 2. Multiply the Outer terms of each binomial   O

$$(2x)(-5) = -10x$$

Step 3. Multiply the Inner terms of each binomial   I

$$(4)(3x) = 12x$$

Step 4. Multiply the Last terms of each binomial   L

$$(4)(-5) = -20$$

Step 5. Write the products in descending order of exponents and include the appropriate signs

$$6x^2 - 10x + 12x - 20$$

Combine

Step 6. Combine the like terms together to get a trinomial (a three-term expression)

$$\text{Answer} = 6x^2 + 2x - 20$$

Use the letters F O I L as a guide to be sure that each of the terms of the binomials are multiplied by all of the other terms.

EXAMPLES:

1. Multiply $(5x - 2)(2x + 1)$

    F $(5x)(2x) = 10x^2$

    O $(5x)(1) = 5x$

    I $(-2)(2x) = -4x$

    L $(-2)(1) = -2$

    $10x^2 + 5x - 4x - 2$

    Combine

    $\text{Answer} = 10x^2 + x - 2$

2. Multiply $(6m - 3)(4m - 5)$

    F $(6m)(4m) = 24m^2$

    O $(6m)(-5) = -30m$

    I $(-3)(4m) = -12m$

    L $(-3)(-5) = 15$

    $24m^2 - 30m - 12m + 15$

    Combine

    $\text{Answer} = 24m^2 - 42m + 15$

3. Multiply $(3x - 4y)(x + y)$

    If the coefficient is not shown it is assumed to be one

    F $(3x)(x) = 3x^2$

    O $(3x)(y) = 3xy$

    I $(-4y)(x) = -4xy$

    L $(-4y)(y) = -4y^2$

    $3x^2 + 3xy - 4xy - 4y^2$

    Combine

    $3x^2 - xy - 4y^2$

Use F O I L to multiply the following binomials:

Answers: Answers:

1. $(4m + 5)(3m + 4)$ _____   11. $(x + y)(x + y)$ _____

2. $(x + 7)(4x - 2)$ _____   12. $(2m - h)(3m + 2h)$ _____

3. $(3p + 2)(4p - 1)$ _____   13. $(3e + 2f)(e - f)$ _____

4. $(2d + 6)(d - 1)$ _____   14. $(3c - 2d)(4c - d)$ _____

5. $(4x - 3)(3x + 1)$ _____   15. $(4a - 2m)(a + 9m)$ _____

6. $(2t - 3)(3t - 5)$ _____   16. $(r + s)(3r - s)$ _____

7. $(3h + 6)(h - 8)$ _____   17. $(2x - y)(x - 2y)$ _____

8. $(5w - 2)(2w - 5)$ _____   18. $(r + s)(r - s)$ _____

9. $(3c + 4)(c - 2)$ _____   19. $(4j + k)(j + 3k)$ _____

10. $(5b + 2)(2b + 1)$ _____   20. $(y - z)(y + z)$ _____

Using FOIL to Factor A Trinomial Into Two Binomials

A trinomial is an algebraic expression containing 3 terms.

$$x^2 + 10x + 25 \text{ for example}$$

A trinomial can often be factored into two binomials using trial and error and F O I L.

EXAMPLE 1:

factor $x^2 + 10x + 25$

answer = $(x + 5)(x + 5)$

Step 1. The first term of each binomial must be x in order to give the first term of x^2 in the trinomial.

$$(x \quad)(x \quad)$$

Step 2. The last terms of each binomial must give 25 when multiplied together. The possible combinations to consider are: 5, 5 and 1, 25

$$(\qquad 5) (\qquad 5)$$

$$(\qquad 25) (\qquad 1)$$

*(**HINT:** When the coefficient of the first term of the trinomial is "one", then the last terms of the answer will be the combination of numbers which gives the last term of the trinomial when multiplied, and gives the middle term of the trinomial when combined)*

So, the correct combination is 5, 5. When multiplied, 5 times 5, gives 25 (the last term of the trinomial) and when combined, 5 + 5, gives 10 (the middle term of the trinomial)

$$(x \qquad 5) (x \qquad 5)$$

Step 3. The operation sign of each binomial is determined as follows:

Problem:	Answer:
Trinomial Signs	Binomial Signs
+ +	+ +
− +	− −

$$\left. \begin{array}{c} - \; - \\ + \; - \end{array} \right\}$$ The terms of the binomial will have opposite signs

So, $x^2 + 10 + 25 = (x + 5) (x + 5)$

Step 4. Check the answer using F O I L.

$$(x + 5) (x + 5)$$

(x) (x) = x^2	F
(x) (5) = 5x	O
(5) (x) = 5x	I
(5) (5) = 25	L

$$x^2 + 5x + 5x + 25$$

$$x^2 + 10x + 25$$

Yes, we end up with the original trinomial.

EXAMPLE 2:

factor $m^2 - 2m - 8$

answer (m + 2) (m − 4) or (m − 4) (m + 2)

Step 1. The first term of each binomial must be "m".

$$(m \qquad) (m \qquad)$$

Step 2. The last terms must be a combination who's product is −8, and combined, gives −2. (But remember, this applies only when the coefficient of the first term of the trinomial is one.)

$$(\qquad + 2) (\qquad - 4)$$
or
$$(\qquad - 4) (\qquad + 2)$$

Step 3. $(m + 2)(m - 4)$ or $(m - 4)(m + 2)$

Step 4. Use F O I L to check your answers.

$$(m + 2)(m - 4)$$

$$(m)(m) = m^2 \qquad F$$
$$(m)(-4) = -4m \qquad O$$
$$(2)(m) = 2m \qquad I$$
$$(2)(-4) = -8 \qquad L$$

$$m^2 - 4m + 2m - 8$$

$$m^2 - 2m - 8$$

We will leave it up to the student to check
$(m - 4)(m + 2)$ using F O I L

EXAMPLE 3:

$$\text{factor } 2m^2 + 5m + 2$$

Notice that the coefficient of the first term is not "one".

$$\text{answer } (2m + 1)(m + 2)$$

Step 1. The product of the first terms of the answer must be "2m".

$$(2m \quad)(m \quad)$$

Step 2. The possible combinations for the last terms are: 2, 1 and 1, 2. Use trial and error to determine which combination will work.

try $(2m + 2)(m + 1)$

$$(2m)(m) = 2m^2 \qquad F$$
$$(2m)(1) = 2m \qquad O$$
$$(2)(m) = 2m \qquad I$$
$$(2)(1) = 2 \qquad L$$

$$2m^2 + 2m + 2m + 2$$

$$2m^2 + 4m + 2$$

No, this combination does not work

try $(2m + 1)(m + 2)$

$$(2m)(m) = 2m^2 \qquad F$$
$$(2m)(2) = 4m \qquad O$$
$$(1)(m) = m \qquad I$$
$$(1)(2) = 2 \qquad L$$

$$2m^2 + 4m + m + 2$$

$$2m^2 + 5m + 2$$

Yes, this combination does work

With practice, you will become proficient at determining the correct binomial combinations with few trial and error steps.

Factor the following trinomials into binomials.

Answers: Answers:

1. $x^2 + 2x + 1$ _____   10. $5s^2 - 7s - 6$ _____

2. $m^2 + 5m + 6$ _____   11. $3n^2 - 4n + 1$ _____

3. $p^2 + 7p + 10$ _____   12. $5t^2 - 22t - 15$ _____

4. $y^2 + y + (-2)$ _____   13. $2c^2 - 5c + 3$ _____

5. $a^2 - a - 2$ _____   14. $g^2 + 5g + 6$ _____

6. $z^2 - 4z + 3$ _____   15. $d^2 - 3d - 4$ _____

7. $2b^2 + 5b + 3$ _____   16. $2e^2 - e - 6$ _____

8. $3f^2 + 10f + 3$ _____   17. $5k^2 + 3k - 2$ _____

9. $2r^2 + r - 1$ _____   18. $7a^2 - 23a + 6$ _____

Number and Letter Sequences

To solve a number or letter sequence problem:

Step 1. Look at the sequence and determine the pattern or patterns of the numbers or letters in the sequence.

Step 2. Once you have "broken the code" decide which number or letter would occur next in the sequence pattern. Some tests ask for the next two or three figures, so be sure you know what the test is asking for before you begin.

EXAMPLES:

Find the next number or letter in the following sequences:

1.   2 − 4 − 6 − 8 − 10 − _____

answer: this example contains just one pattern; counting by two's, so the next number would be 12.

2.   7 − 8 − 22 − 9 − 10 − 21 − 11 − 12 − _____

answer: there are two patterns in this example; counting by ones in groups of two (7, 8) (9, 10) (11, 12) and counting backwards from 22 by ones (22, 21), so the next number would be 20.

3.   a − e − i − o _____

answer: there is one pattern in this sequence; listing the vowels, so the next letter would be "u".

4.   6 − 12 − 24 − 48 − 96 − _____

answer: this sequence contains one pattern: multiplying by two to get the next number, so 96 x 2 = 192.

Sequences

EXERCISE 20

Directions: Find the next number or letter in the following sequences, then write the letter of the correct answer next to the problem number. Time yourself 15 minutes.

_____ 1.   2 − 4 − 1 − 6 − 8 − 2 − 10 − 12 − 3 −

   a. 4   b. 5   c. 16   d. 14   e. none of these

_____ 2.   6 − 20 − 8 − 18 − 10 − 16 − 12 − 14 −

   a. 14   b. 12   c. 5   d. 16   e. none of these

_____ 3.   9 − 10 − 11 − 1 − 12 − 13 − 14 − 2 − 15 − 16 −

   a. 3   b. 17   c. 14   d 15   e. none of these

_____ 4.   ½ − 1 − 1.5 − 2 − 2½ − 3 −

   a. 4.5   b. 3.5   c. 3¼   d. 5   e. none of these

_____ 5.   a − z − b − y − c − x −

   a. e   b. w   c. f   d. d   e. none of these

_____ 6. $\frac{16}{64}$ − $\frac{8}{32}$ − $\frac{4}{16}$ − $\frac{2}{8}$ −

   a. ⅙   b. 2/4   c. ¼   d. ½   e. none of these

_____ 7.   .25 − ½ − ¾ − 1 − 1¼ − 1½ − 1.75 −

   a. 1¾   b. 2   c. 2.25   d. 2/1   e. none of these

_____ 8.   a − c − e − g − i − k −

   a. l   b. m   c. n   d. o   e. none of these

_____ 9.   104 − 98 − 102 − 99 − 100 − 100 − 98 −

   a. 96   b. 98   c. 101   d. 100   e. none of these

_____ 10. 42 − 41 − 60 − 40 − 39 − 61 − 38 −

       a. 37   b. 62   c. 36   d. 60   e. none of these

_____ 11. 1 − 5 − 7 − 3 − 9 − 11 − 5 − 13 − 15 −

       a. 11   b. 15   c. 17   d. 7   e. none of these

_____ 12. 1 − 5 − 3 − 10 − 9 − 20 − 27 − 40 −

       a. 75   b. 81   c. 36   d. 45   e. none of these

_____ 13. 3.125 − 1 − 3.25 − 2 − 3.375 − 3 −

       a. 3.75   b. 4.25   c. $2\frac{1}{2}$ d. 3.5   e. none of these

_____ 14. a − b − d − g − k − p −

       a. t   b. s   c. v   d. w   e. none of these

_____ 15. 25 − 100 − 300 − 600 − 600 −

       a. 0   b. 1200   c. 600   d 300   e. none of these

_____ 16. 16 − 18 − 7 − 20 − 22 − 9 − 24 − 26 − 11 −

       a. 12   b. 16   c. 13   d. 29   e. none of these

_____ 17. d − c − o − a − g −

       a. f   b. t   c. i   d. a   e. none of these

_____ 18. 2 − 10 − 2 − 10 − 4 − 10 − 12 − 10 − 48 − 10 −

       a. 192   b. 144   c. 240   d. 230   e. none of these

_____ 19. 1a − 1b − 2d − 6g

       a. 24c   b. 24h   c. 24   d. 361   e. none of these

_____ 20. 6 − 20 − 12 − 18 − 24 − 16 − 48 − 14 −

       a. 64   b. 96   c. 12   d. 86   e. none of these

_____ 21. 3 − t − 6 − r − 9 − p − 12 −

       a. n   b. m   c. o   d. 15   e. none of these

_____ 22. 65 − 2 − 52 − 4 − 39 − 6 − 26 − 8 −

       a. 16   b. 18   c. 15   d. 13   e. none of these

_____ 23. k − 3 − j − 4 − i − 6 − h − 9 − g −

       a. f   b. 13   c. 18   d. 16   e. none of these

_____ 24. 21 − 24 − 25 − 28 − 29 −

       a. 30   b. 28   c. 33   d. 32   e. none of these

_____ .25. 17 − 28 − 20 − 25 − 24 − 21 − 29 − 19 −

       a. 35   b. 33   c. 30   d. 28   e. none of these

PRE-APPRENTICE TEST

ALGEBRA, FACTORING AND SEQUENCES

Time: 28 Minutes

Solve for the unknown: Answers

1. $-67 + x = 33$ 1._____

2. $y + 22.25 = 22.27$ 2._____

3. $1440 = 16a$ 3._____

4. $2\frac{1}{2} = b/1.6$ 4._____

5. $a/2 = \frac{1}{2}$ 5._____

6. $x/4 = 4/x$ 6._____

7. $5/x - 6 = 4$ 7._____

8. $ax/c = y$ for x 8._____

9. $n/x = y/d$ for x 9._____

10. $3(x + 2) = x + 20$ 10._____

Directions: Multiply, factor or find the next number in the sequence problems.   Answers

11. Factor $9m + 3$ 11._____

12. Factor $6a^2 - 2a$ 12._____

13. Factor $2c^2 - c - 6$ 13._____

14. Multiply $(x - y)(x + y)$ 14._____

15. $3 - 5 - 9 - 15 - 23 -$ 15._____

16. Factor $2z^2 + z - 3$ 16._____

17. Multiply $(2m + 1)(m - 2)$ 17._____

18. $5 - 10 - 20 - 35 - 55 -$ 18._____

19. Factor $3m^3 + 9m^2 - 18m$ 19._____

20. Multiply $(3b - 2)(b - 2)$ 20._____

21. $7 - 8 - 9 - 11 - 13 - 16 - 19 -$ 21._____

22. Multiply $(5k + 1)(k - 3)$ 22._____

23. $12 - 14 - 13 - 15 - 14 - 16 -$ 23._____

24. $1 - 20 - 2 - 19 - 3 - 18 -$ 24._____

25. Factor $7t^2 - 17t + 6$ 25._____

Graph the following equations. Each equation should be graphed on its own set of axes.

26. $-x + y = -4$

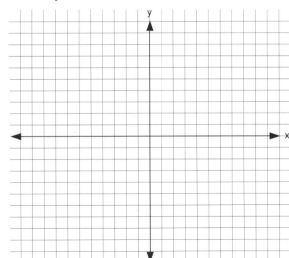

29. $2x = -8y$

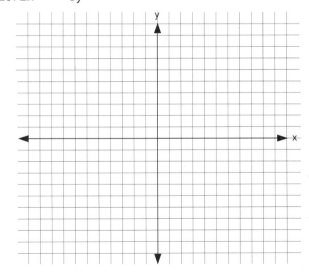

27. $y = -5$

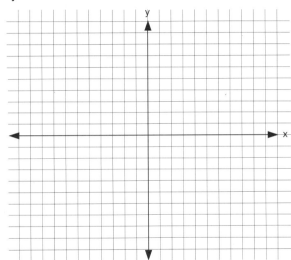

30. $12x = -60$

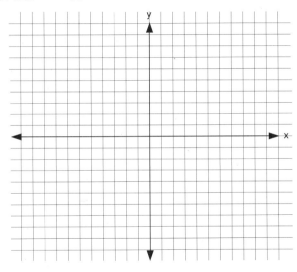

28. $-16 = x - 19$

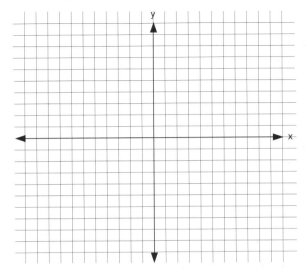

30. $6x = 36y$

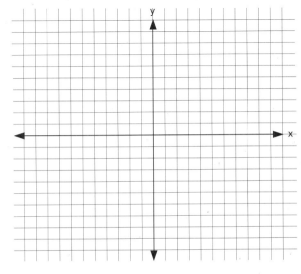

CHAPTER 9

Geometry

Geometry (plane) is a study of points, lines, triangles, circles, polygons, quadrilaterals and other common figures which are lying in a plane. A plane is a flat surface such that a straight edge would touch the surface at all points.

The blueprint and drawings that a tradesperson would use is a good example of a plane. In the drawing the skilled tradesperson utilizes points, lines and angles; along with the corresponding dimensions to describe an object.

The tradesperson must be able to interpret the angles and lines, and through basic geometric rules they are able to determine the operations they must perform.

Before we start our study of geometry, we must first learn the following rules.

Definitions

1. Point – A point is only a position. The point itself has no dimensions.

2. Line – Can be described as the visible path of a moving point. (A pencil point leaves evidence of its path after it passes. This is a line.)

    a. Only one straight line can be drawn between two points.

    b. A straight line is the shortest distance between two points.

3. Parallel lines – Lines which are the same distance apart regardless of how far extended. (They will never intersect.)

    a. Through a given point, only one line can be drawn parallel to a given line.

4. Angle – Formed by two lines that meet at a point. The angle is represented by the rotation of one line from the other.

EXAMPLE:

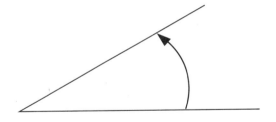

a. Degree – A degree is ⅟₃₆₀ part of a circle. It may be further broken down into 60 equal parts called minutes. Each minute may be further broken down into 60 equal parts called seconds.

b. Right angle – The angle formed by rotation of one line from another by 90°. The two lines of this angle are said to be perpendicular to each other. It is equal to one fourth revolution.

c. Straight angle – Form the angle formed by a rotation of one line from another by 180° or one half rotation. The legs form a straight line.

d. Acute angle – Any angle less than 90°.

e. Obtuse angle – Any angle greater than 90° and less than 180°.

1. Adjacent angle – Two angles with a common vertex and a common side.

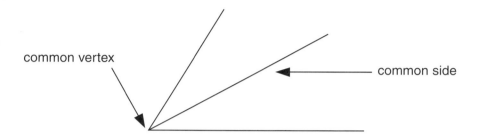

common vertex

common side

2. Complimentary angles – Two angles whose sum is 90°.

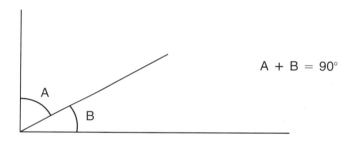

A + B = 90°

3. Supplementary angles – Two angles whose sum is 180°.

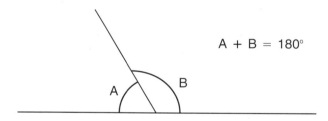

A + B = 180°

4. Intersecting lines – The opposite ∠'s formed are equal and the adjacent angles are supplementary.

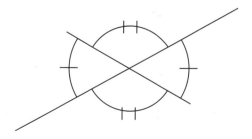

5. Corresponding angles – When two parallel lines are intersected by a third line, corresponding angles are formed. These corresponding angles are equal.

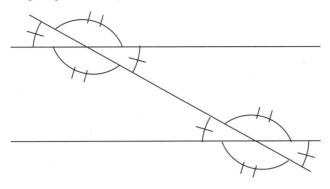

4 sets of corresponding angles are formed. By using definition #8, the relationship between any of the ∠'s can be determined.

6. Right triangle – Is a polygon of three sides where one angle is a right angle.

    a. Hypotenuse – Is that side of the right triangle opposite the right angle.

    b. Adjacent sides – Are the two lines that form the angle.

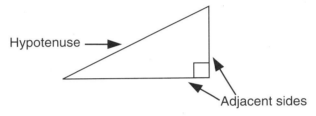

Objects Enclosed By Straight Lines

In order to enclose an object, a minimum of three straight lines are needed. The maximum number of lines is unlimited.

Polygon – An enclosed figure made up of three or more straight lines.

Regular Polygon – A polygon having all sides and all angles equal.

Perimeter – Of a polygon is the sum of all the sides of the polygon, the total distance around.

Number of Sides	Name	Polygon	Regular Polygon	Total No. of degrees in included angles (No. Sides − 2) (180°)
3	Triangle			180°
4	Quadrangle			360°
5	Pentagon			540°

Number of Sides	Name	Polygon	Regular Polygon	Total No. of degrees in included angles (No. Sides − 2) (180°)
6	Hexagon			720°
8	Octagon			1080°

Samples of polygons having any given number of sides could have been included in the chart. To save space, only those which commonly used in the various trades are shown.

Designations of Points, Lines, Angles, etc.

In order that points and lines can be more easily identified, points are usually designated by letters.

EXAMPLE:

When these points are connected, the lines can be identified by the letters of the points which limit them.

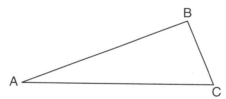

These lines are identified as AB, BC, and AC, together they form the triangle ABC (ABC).

Angles can be identified by the letter designation of the point where the sides of the angle come together.

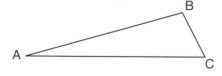

These angles can be identified as angle A, angle B, and angle C. There are times when it is impossible to completely identify a specific angle in this way. It is then necessary to use the line designations in the abbreviated form to identify the angle.

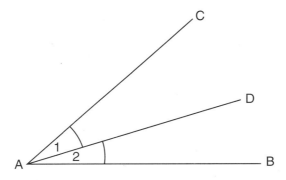

If angle 2 is the angle in question, simply designating it angle A is not enough as this can be confused as angle 1, angle 2, or both.

Angle 2 is bounded by both sides AD and AB with A being the point of intersection (vertex). Angle 2 could then be described as the angle having sides, BA and AD.

This can be shortened to read angle BAD. The angle reads starting from point B, to vertex A, to point D. It does not matter which outer point is read first. The governing factor is the vertex point being read in the middle.

Symbols

In describing and writing rules and explanations for geometry problems, much time can be saved if some method of coding or symbols could be used in place of a word or words. Some of the symbols that can be used to simplify statements are as follows:

Angle	∠
Degree	○
Equal	=
Minute	'
Second	''
Parallel	//
Perpendicular	⊥
Right Angle	⌐
Right Triangle	◺
Triangle	△
Circle	⊙

Angles and Degrees

Considering the fact that one degree equals 60 minutes, and also that one minute equals 60 seconds, certain addition and subtraction problems can be done with two or more angles.

EXAMPLE 1:

$$28° \ 37' \ 16''$$
$$43° \ 22' \ 54''$$
$$+ \ 8° \ 15' \ \ 7''$$
$$\overline{80° \ 15' \ 17''}$$

Steps:

1. As in addition, start at the right and add the seconds.

$$16''$$
$$54''$$
$$+ 7''$$
$$\overline{77''}$$

77" is equal to 1' 17". Write the seconds under the seconds in the problem and carry the 1' to the minutes.

2. Add the minutes (including the one carried from the addition of the seconds).

$$1'$$
$$37'$$
$$22'$$
$$+ 15'$$
$$\overline{75'}$$

75' is equal to 1° 15'. Write the minutes under the minutes in the problem and carry the 1° to the degrees.

3. Add the degrees (including the one carried).

The sum is 80° 15' 17".

$$1°$$
$$28°$$
$$43°$$
$$+ 8°$$
$$\overline{80°}$$

EXAMPLE 2:   Subtract: $46° \ 27' \ 15''$
$23° \ 42' \ 54''$

In a problem where it is necessary to subtract a smaller number from a larger one, borrowing is the rule to be followed. In this case the seconds to be subtracted are greater than those being subtracted from. It becomes necessary to borrow from the minutes.

$$26' \ 75''$$
$$46° \ \cancel{27'} \ \cancel{15''}$$
$$23° \ 42' \ 54''$$
$$\overline{ \ 21''}$$

If the minutes to be subtracted are greater than those being subtracted from, one must again borrow, but this time 1° must be borrowed.

$$45° \ 86'$$
$$\cancel{46°} \ \cancel{26'} \ 75''$$
$$23° \ 42' \ 54''$$
$$\overline{22° \ 44' \ 21''}$$

The degrees can be subtracted.

EXERCISE 1

Add or subtract as indicated:

1.   22° 43' 15"
    + 46° 25' 29"

6.   27° 37' 47"
    − 26° 38' 48"

2.   15° 15' 15"
      45° 45' 45"
    + 30° 30' 30"

7.   27° 37' 47"
    + 26° 33' 48"

3.   28° 14' 34"
    − 7° 29' 15"

8.   49° 6' 28"
    − 47° 36' 47"

4.   14° 49' 23"
    − 13° 49' 34"

9.   24° 19' 53"
      36° 25' 16"
    + 5° 9' 48"

5.   22° 43' 55"
      44° 27' 6"
    + 83° 55' 9"

10.   16° 37' 28"
    − 7° 43' 54"

EXERCISE 2

1.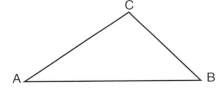

  ∠ A = 38° 17'
  ∠ B = 45°
  ∠ C = _____

2.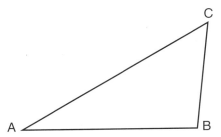

  ∠ A = 29° 28' 27"

  ∠ B = 96°

  ∠ C = _____

3.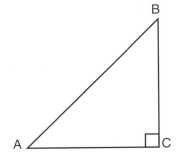

  ∠ CAB = 45°

  ∠ B = _____

4.

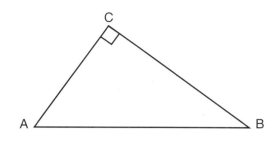

∠ B = 37° 56' 48"

∠ A = _____

5.

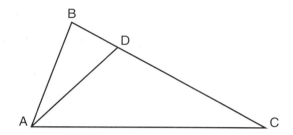

∠ B = 79°

∠ C = 33°

∠ BAD = 26°

∠ ABD = _____

∠ ADC = _____

∠ BAC = _____

6.

∠ A = 3°

∠ B = 2°

∠ C = _____

7.

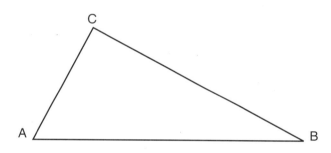

∠ C = 89°

∠ A = 65°

∠ B = _____

8.

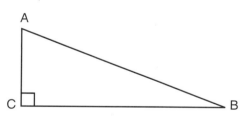

∠ B = 19°

∠ A = _____

9.

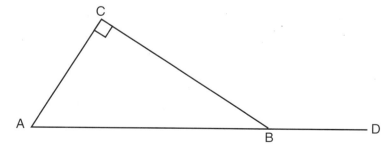

∠ CBD = 144°

∠ A = _____

10.

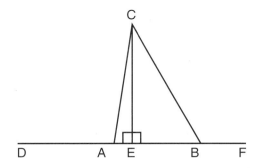

∠ CBF = 121°
∠ ACE = 10°
∠ CAD = _____
∠ ECB = _____
∠ ACB = _____

11.

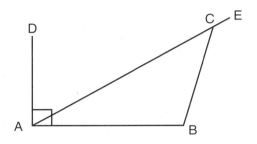

∠ DAE = 60°
∠ BCE = 135°
∠ B = _____

12.

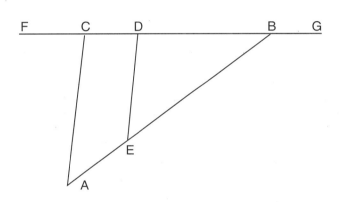

AC & DE are parallel
∠ EDB = 96°
∠ CBA = 37°
∠ ACF = _____

13.

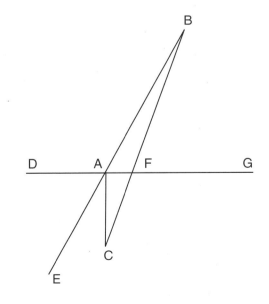

∠ DAE = 64°
∠ CAF = 90°
∠ BFG = 71°
∠ B = _____
∠ C = _____

14.

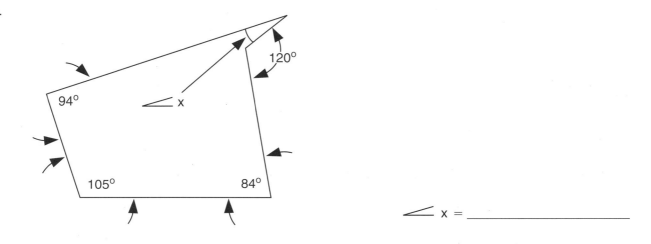

∠ x = _____

Circle Definitions

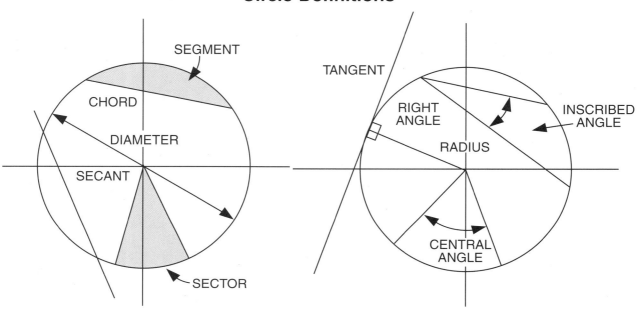

Geometric Propositions

A proposition is a statement which can be proven to be true by the use of rules and definitions. Previously proven statements utilizing previously stated rules and definitions are propositions.

Stated in this section are additional propositions that will be needed to continue with the additional exercises found at the end of this chapter.

Proposition 1

If two or more lines that are in the same plane are perpendicular to the same line, they are parallel to each other.

UV ⊥ ST

XW ⊥ ST

then,

UV // XW

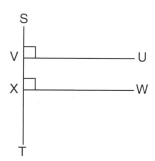

Proposition 2

If two angles have their corresponding sides parallel, they are equal.

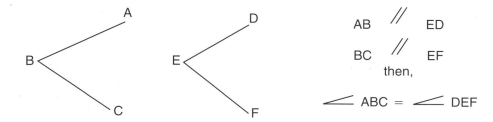

Proposition 3

If 2 angles have their corresponding sides perpendicular, they are equal.

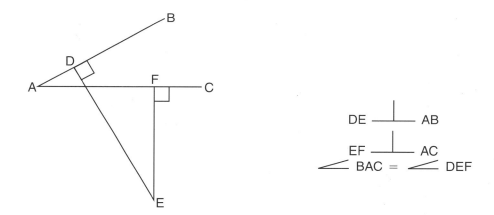

Proposition 4

An exterior angle of a triangle is equal to the sum of the two interior angles at the other vertices.

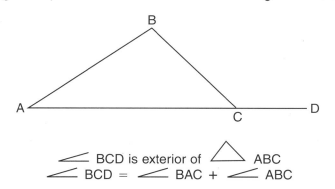

Proposition 5

In an isosceles triangle, the angles opposite the equal sides are equal.

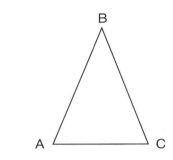

$\triangle$ ABC is isosceles

AB = CB

$\angle$ BAC = $\angle$ BCA

Proposition 6 (Pythagorean theorem)

The square of the hypotenuse is equal to the sum of the squares of the two legs.

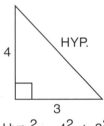

$Hyp.^2 = 4^2 + 3^2$

$Hyp.^2 = 16 + 9$

$Hyp.^2 = 25$

$Hyp. = \sqrt{25} = 5$

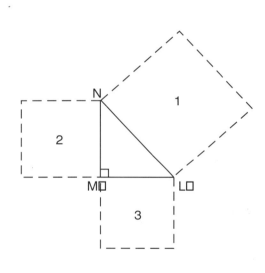

In rt. $\triangle$ LMN large square
#1 = square #2 + square #3

or

$NL^2 = NM^2 + ML^2$

$(NL)(NL) = (NM)(NM) + (ML)(ML)$

$NL = \sqrt{(NM)^2 + (ML)^2}$

$NM = \sqrt{(NL)^2 - (ML)^2}$

$ML = \sqrt{(NL)^2 - (MN)^2}$

Proposition 7

The circumference of a circle is equal to the products of the diameter and pi.

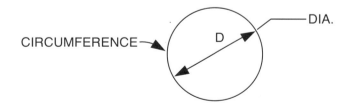

$C = \pi D$

$D = \dfrac{C}{\pi}$

Proposition 8

Area of a circle is equal to product of π and the radius squared.

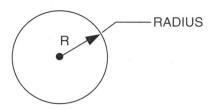

$$\text{Area} = \pi \times R^2$$

Proposition 9

An inscribed angle is measured by ½ its intercepted arc.

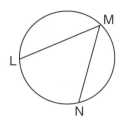

M is a point on the circumference
∠ LMN is an inscribed angle
∠ LMN = 1/2 LN (in degrees)

EXERCISE 3

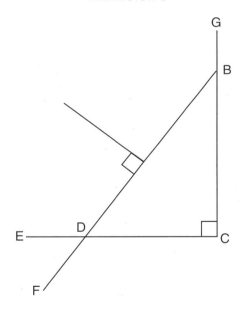

1. ∠ BDC in right △ BCD if ∠ DBC = 38° _____

2. ∠ BDE = _____

3. ∠ EDF = _____

4. ∠ DBG = _____

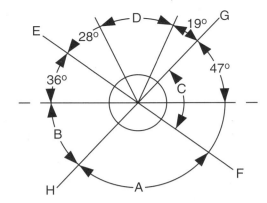

Given that: EF and GH are straight lines passing through the center of the circle.

1. Determine D. _____

2. Determine A. _____

3. Determine C. _____

4. Determine B. _____

5. What is the complement of D? _____

6. What is the supplement of A? _____

7. What is the complement of C? _____

8. What is the complement of B? _____

GEOMETRY

Time – 6 minutes

TRUE OR FALSE   **Answers**

1. A right angle is 75°.   _____

2. The shortest distance between two points in not necessarily a straight line.   _____

3. A segment of a line is a part of a line.   _____

4. Parallel lines meet at a point called the vertex.   _____

5. A degree is ⅟₃₆₀ part of a circle.   _____

6. A polygon is a plane figure enclosed by 2 or more straight lines.   _____

7. A quadrilateral is a polygon having 4 sides.   _____

8. A right triangle is a 3-sided polygon having one angle equal to 90°.   _____

9. An acute angle is more than 90°.   _____

10. The perimeter of a polygon is the total distance around.   _____

11.

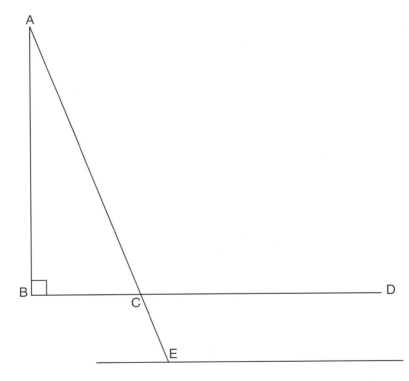

∠ BAC = 20°

∠ ACD = _____

∠ DCE = _____

∠ ACD = _____

12.

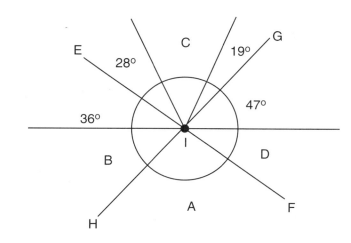

Given that:
EF and GH are straight lines
and Point I is the center of
the circle

∠ C = _____

∠ A = _____

∠ B = _____

∠ D = _____

13.

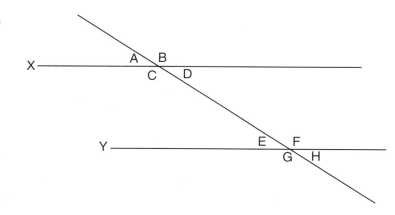

X // Y

∠ A = 30°

∠ B = _____

∠ C = _____

∠ D = _____

∠ E = _____

∠ F = _____

∠ G = _____

∠ H = _____

14.

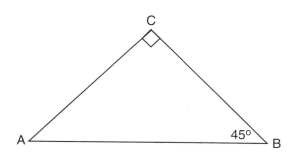

Line CB = 10" _____

∠ CAB = _____

Line CA = _____

CHAPTER
10

Graphic Math

Area

Area is a two-dimensional measurement, for example, the area of a rectangle is found by multiplying the two dimensions length and width.

$$\text{Length} \times \text{Width} = \text{Area}$$

width

length

Area units are **squared length units**, for example, in^2, mi^2, ft^2, cm^2, m^2, etc. The reason for this lies in the calculation of area. To find the area of a 12 ft $\times$ 8 ft wall, the formula calls for multiplication of the length times the width. The numerical part of the calculation is $12 \times 8 = 96$, but the unit of each dimension must also be multiplied. In this problem, the unit calculation is ft $\times$ ft $= ft^2$. When no exponent is shown on a number, variables or units are multiplied, the exponents are added, so, another way to look at the unit calculation would be:

$$ft^1 \times ft^1 = ft^{1+1} = ft^2$$

The unit calculation does not need to be done separate from the number calculation, the problem above was to demonstrate a point. Keep in mind that the units must be the same (ft $\times$ ft or in $\times$ in, etc.) before they can be multiplied together. Be sure to convert all given unlike units to like units before proceeding with the calculation.

To calculate how many square inches are in a square foot, recall that there are 12 inches in one foot, then square both sides of the equality.

$$(1 \text{ ft})^2 = (12 \text{ in})^2$$

$$(1 \text{ ft}) (1 \text{ ft}) = (12 \text{ in}) (12 \text{ in})$$

$$1 \text{ ft}^2 = 144 \text{ in}^2$$

To calculate the number of square feet in a square yard, recall that there are 3 feet in one yard. Now square both sides of the equality.

$$(1 \text{ yd})^2 = (3 \text{ ft})^2$$

$$(1 \text{ yd}) (1 \text{ yd}) = (3 \text{ ft}) (3 \text{ ft})$$

$$1 \text{ yd}^2 = 9 \text{ ft}^2$$

Basic Area Formulas

Square $A = s^2$

where: A = Area
        s = side length

Rectangle $A = lw$

where: A = Area
        L = length
        W = width

Triangle $A = \frac{1}{2} bh$

where: A = Area
        B = base length
        H = height

Circle $A = \pi r^2$

where: A = Area
        π = 3.14
        r = radius

and: $r = \dfrac{d}{2}$

EXAMPLE 1:

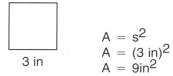

3 in

$A = s^2$
$A = (3 \text{ in})^2$
$A = 9 \text{in}^2$

EXAMPLE 2:

2 ft

3 ft

$A = lw$
$A = (3 \text{ ft})(2 \text{ ft})$
$A = 6 \text{ ft}^2$

EXAMPLE 3:

5 cm

$A = \frac{1}{2} bh$
$A = \frac{1}{2} (5 \text{ cm})(4 \text{ cm})$
$A = \frac{1}{2} (20 \text{ cm}^2)$
$A = 10 \text{ cm}^2$

EXAMPLE 4:

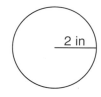

2 in

$A = \pi r^2$
$A = (3.14)(2 \text{ in})^2$
$A = (3.14)(4 \text{ in}^2)$
$A = 12.56 \text{ in}^2$

EXAMPLE 5:

6 cm

$r = \dfrac{d}{2}$

$r = \dfrac{6 \text{ cm}}{2}$

$r = 3 \text{ cm}$

$A = \pi r^2$
$A = (3.14)(3 \text{ cm})^2$
$A = (3.14)(9 \text{ cm}^2)$
$A = 28.26 \text{ cm}^2$

Trapezoid $A = \dfrac{h(c + b)}{2}$

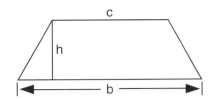

where: A = Area
         h = height
         c = top length
         b = base length

EXAMPLE 6:

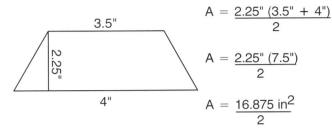

$A = \dfrac{h(c + b)}{2}$

$A = \dfrac{2.25"\,(3.5" + 4")}{2}$

$A = \dfrac{2.25"\,(7.5")}{2}$

$A = \dfrac{16.875 \text{ in}^2}{2}$

$A = 8.4375 \text{ in}^2$
or
$A = 8.44 \text{ in}^2$

EXERCISE 1

Find the area of the following:

_____ 1.

 9 in

_____ 2.

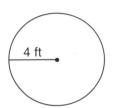 4 ft

_____ 3.

 1"

_____ 4.

 3 yd

8 yd

_____ 5.

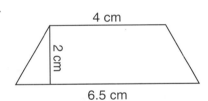

4 cm
2 cm
6.5 cm

_____ 6.

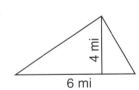

4 mi
6 mi

_____ 7. Find the area of the rectangle which is 8' × 5'.

_____ 8. What is the total area of three 9' × 12' walls if there are no windows or doors?

_____ 9. How many cars can park in a 60 ft × 20 ft lot if one car requires 24 ft^2? (this figure includes driving lane space)

_____ 10. Find the cross-sectional area of the shaded object.

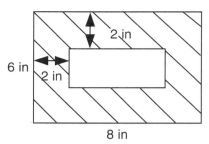

_____ 11. How many square feet of paper are needed to cover a 9" × 6" × 3" box?

_____ 12. The 4 walls of a room each measure 10 ft × 8 ft. A 4 ft × 5 ft window is located in one wall. A gallon of paint covers 1200 square feet. Not including the floors or ceilings, how many rooms, with these dimensions, can a gallon of paint cover?

_____ 13. A floor measuring 18 ft × 10 ft is to be tiled using 3 in × 3 in tiles. How many tiles are needed?

_____ 14. What is the surface area of the counter top minus the hole for the sink basin, shown here, to the nearest square foot?

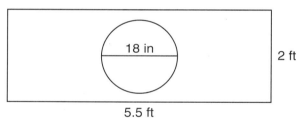

_____ 15. How many square feet of nylon are needed to make the kite?

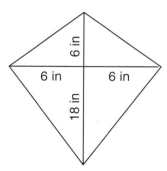

Perimeter

Perimeter is a measure of the distance around an object. Perimeter is measured in distance units such as: feet, inches, meters, miles, kilometers, etc.

Perimeter Formulas

Square P = 4s

where: P = Perimeter
        s = side length

Rectangle P = 2L + 2w

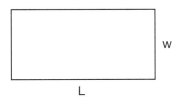

where: P = Perimeter
        L = length
        w = width

Circle The distance around a circle is called the circumference. The formula to solve for the circumference of a circle is:

$$C = 2\pi r$$

where: C = Circumference
        π = 3.14
        r = radius

or

C = πd
where: C = Circumference
        π = 3.14
        d = diameter

EXAMPLE 1:

65 ft

P = 4s
P = 4 (65 ft)
P = 260 ft

EXAMPLE 2:

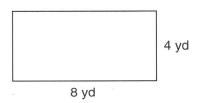

4 yd

8 yd

P = 2L + 2w
P = 2 (8 yd) + 2 (4 yd)
P = 16 yd + 8 yd
P = 24 yd

EXAMPLE 3:

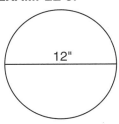

12"

C = πd
C = 3.14 (12")
C = 37.68"

Triangle P = a + b + c

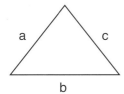

where: P = Perimeter
a = length of side a
b = length of side b
c = length of side c

EXAMPLE 4:

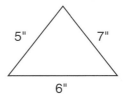

P = a + b + c
P = 5 in + 6 in + 7 in
P = 18 in

EXERCISE 2

1. Find the perimeter of the following:

_____ a.

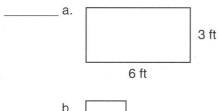

_____ c.

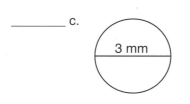

_____ b.

_____ d.

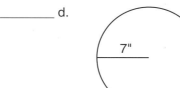

_____ 2. The perimeter of a rectangle is 40 cm. Find the width if the length is 15 cm.

_____ 3. Calculate how much edging will be needed for a circular pool with a radius of 8 feet.

_____ 4. A rectangular yard is to be fenced using two kinds of fencing. The lengths will have heavy-duty fence, costing $4.00 a foot. The widths will have standard fencing at $2.00 a foot. If the yard measures 40 ft × 24 ft, what is the total cost of the fencing?

_____ 5. The length of one side of a triangle is twice the length of the second side. The third side is 2 mm shorter than the second side. If the perimeter of the triangle is 34 mm, find the length of the three sides.

_____ 6. A square and a rectangle have the same perimeter. The length of the rectangle is 6 cm more than the width. If each side of the square is 12 cm, find the length of the sides of the rectangle.

_____ 7. Find the perimeter of the sail.

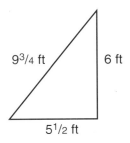

$9^3/4$ ft   6 ft

$5^1/2$ ft

Volume

Volume is a 3-dimensional measurement, for example, the volume of a rectangle can be found by multiplying length $\times$ width $\times$ height. Volume of solid objects is measured in cubic length units, such as, in, ft, cm, and mi.

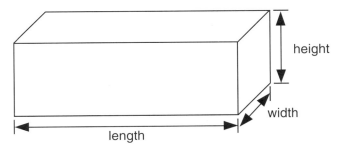

height

width

length

Gallon, pint, quart, liter, and kiloliter are examples of fluid units (notice these units are not cubed). Before you multiply to find the volume, be sure that all units are alike.

To calculate the number of cubic inches in a cubic foot, recall the fact that there are 12 inches in one foot, then cube (or raise to the third power) both sides of the equality.

$$(1 \text{ ft})^3 = (12 \text{ inches})^3$$

$$(1 \text{ ft}) (1 \text{ ft}) (1 \text{ ft}) = (12 \text{ in}) (12 \text{ in}) (12 \text{ in})$$

$$1 \text{ ft}^3 = 1728 \text{ in}^3$$

To calculate the number of cubic feet in one cubic yard, recall that there are 3 feet in one yard, then cube each side of equality.

$$(1 \text{ yd})^3 = (3 \text{ feet})^3$$

$$(1 \text{ yd}) (1 \text{ yd}) (1 \text{ yd}) = (3 \text{ ft}) (3 \text{ ft}) (3 \text{ ft})$$

$$1 \text{ yd}^3 = 27 \text{ ft}^3$$

Volume Formulas:

Square $V = s^3$

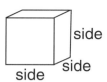

where: V = volume
             s = side length

EXAMPLE 1:

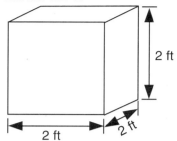

$V = s^3$
$V = (2 \text{ ft})^3$
$V = (2 \text{ ft}) (2 \text{ ft}) (2 \text{ ft})$
$V = 8 \text{ ft}^3$

Rectangle $V = lwh$

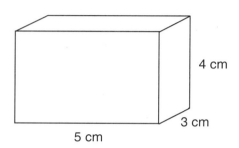

where: V = Volume
             l = length
             w = width
             h = height

EXAMPLE 2:

$V = lwh$
$V = (5\text{cm}) (3 \text{ cm}) (4 \text{ cm})$
$V = 60 \text{ cm}^3$

EXERCISE 3

Find the volume of the following objects:

_____ 1.

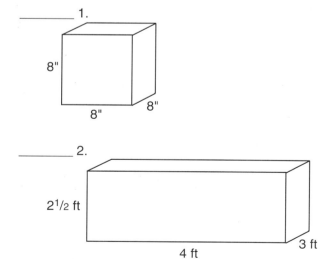

_____ 3.

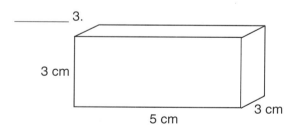

_____ 2.

_____ 4.

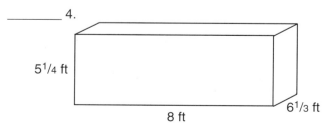

_____ 5. If 3 bags of cement mix makes 2 cubic feet, how many bags will be needed for a 270 in × 16 in × 4 in sidewalk?

_____ 6. There are 231 cubic inches in one liquid gallon. How many cubic inches are in 10 gallons?

_____ 7. A brick mold has the dimensions 8" × 4" × 2". How many cubic inches of clay will be needed to make 200 bricks?

_____ 8. The volume of a shipping crate is 432 in^3. If the width and height are both 6 in., what is the length of the crate?

_____ 9. A vase measuring ⅓ ft by ⅓ ft by ½ ft is to be shipped in the crate in problem 8. Will the vase fit into the crate?

_____ 10. The inside dimensions of a rectangular candle mold are 8 in by 4 in by 4 in. How many cubic inches of candle wax are needed to fill the mold?

_____ 11. Candle wax is sold in 4 in × 2 in × 2 in blocks. How many are needed for the candle mold in problem 10?

_____ 12. Find the volume, in cubic inches, of a rectangle whose measurements are 2½ ft by 18 in by 6 in.

GRAPHIC MATH

Time: 15 Minutes

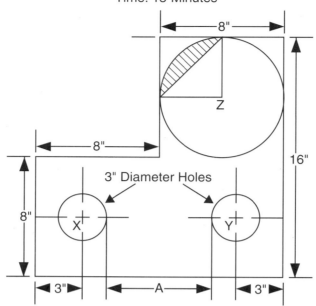

Use above drawing for questions 1-6.

Answers

1. What is the center-to-center distance between circles x and y?
    a. 7 in
    b. 9 in
    c. 10 in
    d. none

    1. _____

2. Find dimension A.
    a. 7 in
    b. 9 in
    c. 10 in
    d. none

    2. _____

3. Find the area of circle z to the nearest tenth (use π = 3.14).
    a. 50.2 sq in
    b. 254.3 sq in
    c. 12.6 sq in
    d. none

    3. _____

4. Find the perimeter of circle x.
    a. 18.84 in
    b. 9.42 in
    c. 4.71 in
    d. none

    4. _____

5. Find the area of the shaded portion of circle z (use π = 3.14).
    a. 1.72 sq in
    b. 1.57 sq in
    c. 42.24 sq in
    d. none

    5. _____

6. Find the perimeter around the outer border of the drawing in feet to the nearest tenth.
    a. 4.7 feet
    b. 5.3 feet
    c. 64.0 feet
    d. none

    6. _____

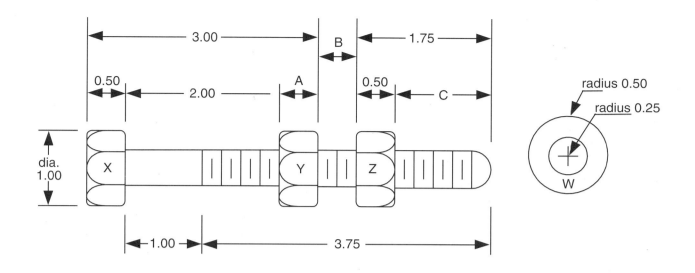

Use above drawing for questions 7 - 14. X is a bolt, Y and Z are nuts, and W is a washer. Circle the correct answers.

7. Solve for dimension A.
   a. 1.00
   b. 0.50
   c. 0.75
   d. 2.25
   e. none

8. Solve for dimension B.
   a. 0.25
   b. 1.50
   c. 0.75
   d. 0.50
   e. none

9. Solve for dimension C.
   a. 1.00
   b. 0.25
   c. 0.75
   d. 0.50
   e. none

10. Find the diameter of the bolt shaft if it is ½ the diameter of the bolt head.
    a. 0.05
    b. 0.50
    c. 5.00
    d. 0.75
    e. none

11. Solve for the area of the washer.
    a. 0.785
    b. 0.835
    c. 0.589
    d. 0.625
    e. none

12. Solve for the circumference of the bolt head.
    a. 1.57
    b. 0.785
    c. 0.625
    d. 6.28
    e. none

13. Solve for the circumference of the washer hole.
    a. 1.57
    b. 3.14
    c. 0.785
    d. 0.625
    e. none

14. If the washer is ⅛ inch thick, what would be the height of a stack of 13 washers?
    a. 1⅔
    b. 1⅝
    c. 1⅜
    d. ⁸⁄₁₃
    e. none

CHAPTER

11

Spatial Skills

The art of blueprint reading is the ability to visualize a three dimensional object from lines on a plane surface. Without this ability, the lines on a print are without meaning since they do in fact represent a three dimensional object.

Prints and sketches are the plans that a tradesperson is required to use in their everyday assignments. It is therefore necessary to sharpen, spatial skills in order to correctly read blueprints.

Orthographic Projection

The term orthographic projection is one used to describe the most common method of drawing views of an object on a print. This method is one which incorporated views taken 90° from the adjacent views. In orthographic projection there are six main points to view, namely: front, top, bottom, back, right side, and left side.

It is not necessary to draw all six views of an object to adequately describe its shape. However, it it always necessary to draw at least two views to show the length, width, and depth. As the object in question becomes more complicated, more views become necessary. Most objects require three views to be completely described.

Consider a rectangular box:

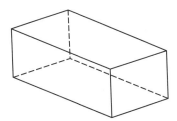

The same rectangular box can have its sides labeled as follows:

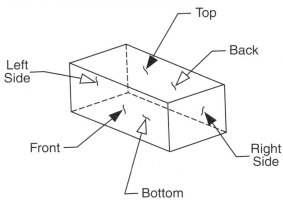

As it sets, all sides are seen in their true size and shape. The top and right side appear on this paper as parallelograms. In fact, the back, left side, and bottom views are not visible at all.

The principle of orthographic projection is to take these six views of the object and put them on one plane in proper relationships to one another. This relationship can best be described by unfolding the surfaces of this solid until they lie on one plane.

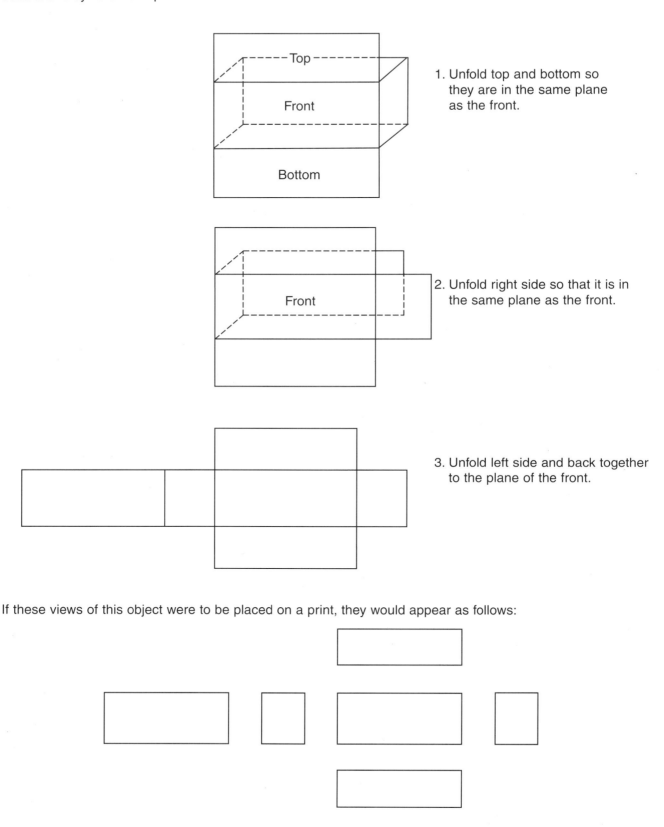

1. Unfold top and bottom so they are in the same plane as the front.

2. Unfold right side so that it is in the same plane as the front.

3. Unfold left side and back together to the plane of the front.

If these views of this object were to be placed on a print, they would appear as follows:

Unfortunately, all objects that are drawn on prints are not as simple as the one we have just shown. It becomes necessary to use this idea of the rectangular box to show how orthographic projection works on other objects.

Take the following object as an example:

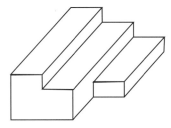

It becomes necessary to visualize this object inside a box.

As the object is viewed from each side, the lines visible are projected to the side of the box. The projection of the front view would be accomplished as follows.

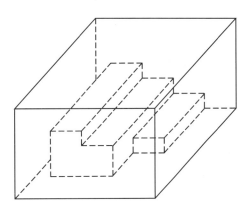
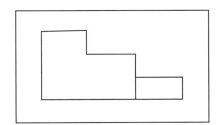

If all the object lines (lines showing all visible edges in a view) were projected to the front surface, the front view of an orthographic projection is seen.

In the same way, the top and right views can be done by viewing the object from the top and right sides and projecting all visible edges to the plane of the box. With these three projections made, the box would look as follows:

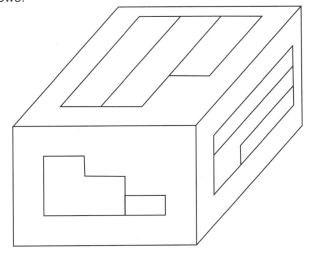

EXAMPLE 1:

An orthographic drawing is a method used to draw a 3-dimensional object on a 2-dimensional sheet of paper. The orthographic drawing can be visualized by unfolding the box created previously and laying it out flat to show the Front, Top, Right, Back, Left, and Bottom views of the object. The dotted lines indicate hidden lines, or lines not visable from that point of the view. The dashed lines are projection lines used by the draftsperson to line up the views of the object (in this case the Right and Top views). Typically the projection lines are not shown on the final drawing.

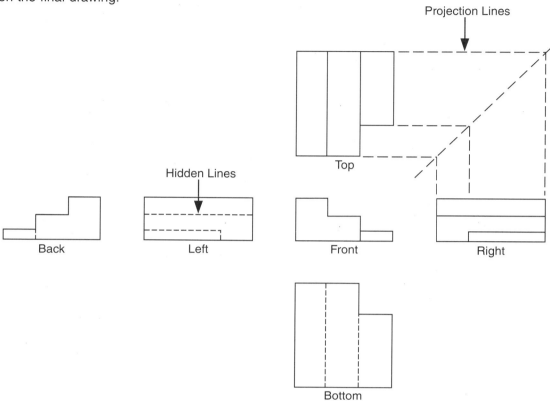

Only 3 views are necessary to give a clear idea of the 3-dimensional object being represented in the orthographic drawing. Standard practice is to use the Front, Top, and Right side views of the object. The Front view is the first view drawn and is used as the guide for the Top and Right side views. The draftsperson decides which side of the object is to be called the Front view (typically it is the side showing the most detail or the most complicated side) from which all other views are based.

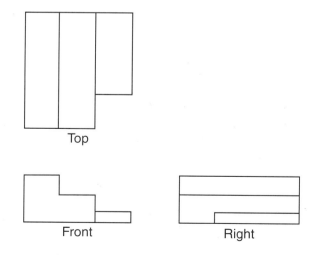

EXAMPLE 2:

One view alone does not give enough information to accurately predict what the object will look like in 3-dimensions. In the examples below the front view by itself does not give the viewer a true perspective of the object, additional information is needed. The front view shows the height and width of the object but does NOT indicate the depth (thickness) of the object. Also, the front view does not tell us if surfaces A, B, C, and D protrude or recede. And if surfaces A, B, C, and D protrude then how far? There is just not enough information given in one view alone.

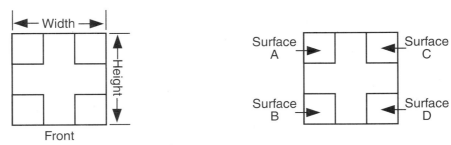

Using projection lines to align the features from the front view to the top view, let's see if the two views (front and top) in the drawing below give enough information to visualize the object.

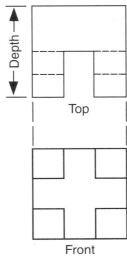

The top view in the drawing above gives the third dimension depth, and the hidden lines are helpful in visualizing the surfaces A, B, C, and D but more information is needed. Let's include the right side view using projection lines to transfer features from the top view to the right view.

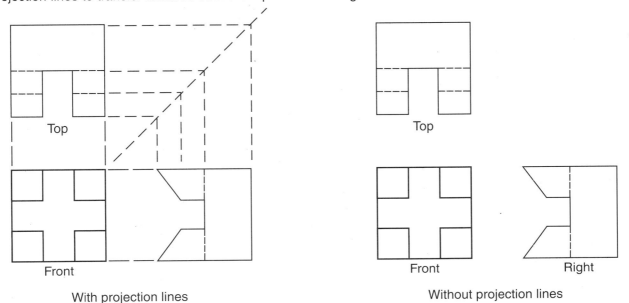

With projection lines   Without projection lines

With all three views the viewer has the information needed to visualize the object in 3-dimensions.

One more aid might be to sketch a 3D picture of the object using the information given.

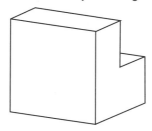

It can be seen here that the step is hidden and must be shown in the front view.

EXERCISE 1

Fill in the missing line or lines in each drawing. All missing lines in each problem are in the same view.

1.

2.

3.

4.

5.

6.

7.

8.

9.

10.

11.

12.

Still another problem that develops is one which requires the drawing of three views of an object from the object itself or a pictorial representation.

In the following exercise, pick as the front view the one that best shows the shape of the part. The other two views picked will be the top and right side. Draw a sketch of each of the three views on a separate sheet of paper.

1.

2.

3.

4.

5.

6.

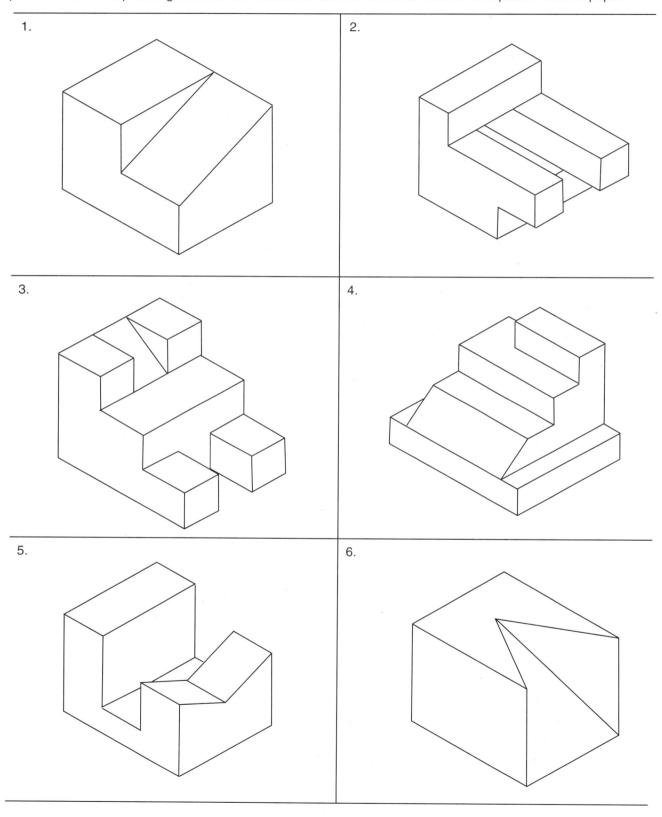

EXERCISE 3

In the following problems, one or more lines have been omitted. Complete each sketch with the necessary lines.

Instructions: Make a three view orthographic drawing of the object shown. Each square represents ¼".

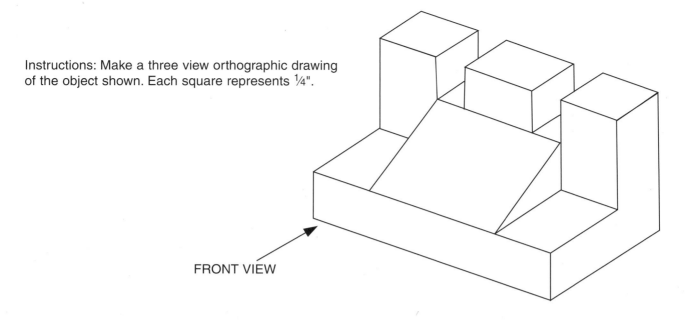

FRONT VIEW

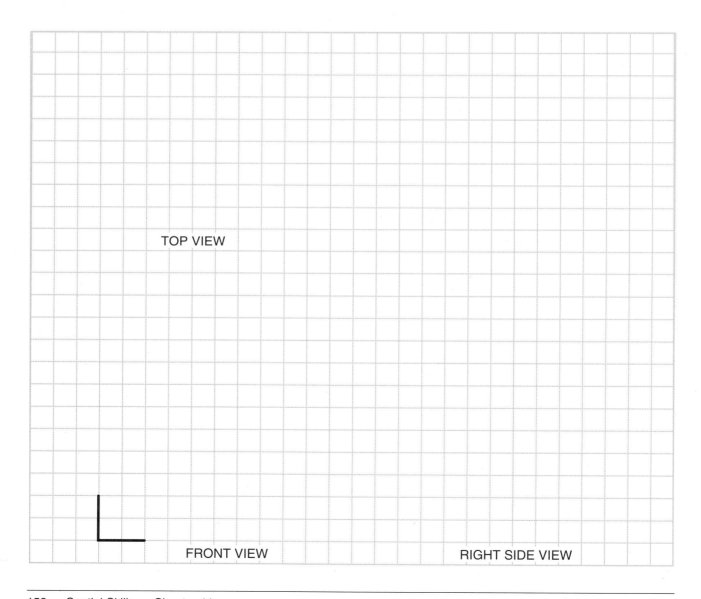

TOP VIEW

FRONT VIEW

RIGHT SIDE VIEW

EXERCISE 5

Identification of Numbered Points

Place the appropriate numbers in the circles on the orthographic drawings.

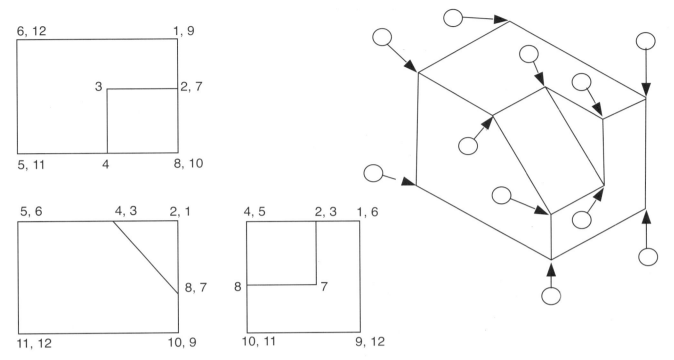

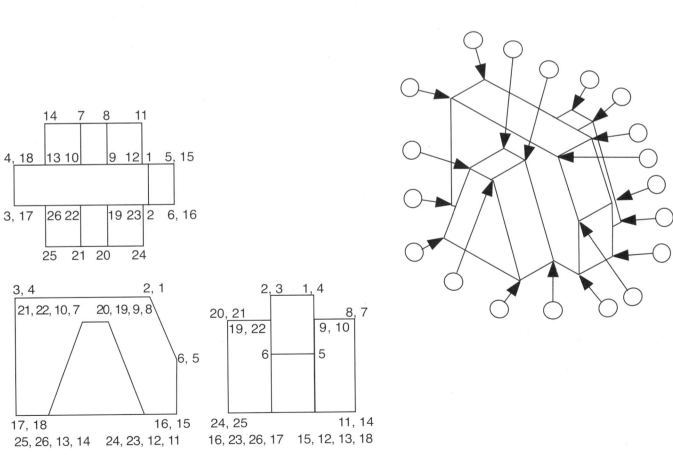

EXERCISE 6

Surface Identification

Place letters in the circles attached to the surfaces of the picture to correspond to the letters attached to the views.

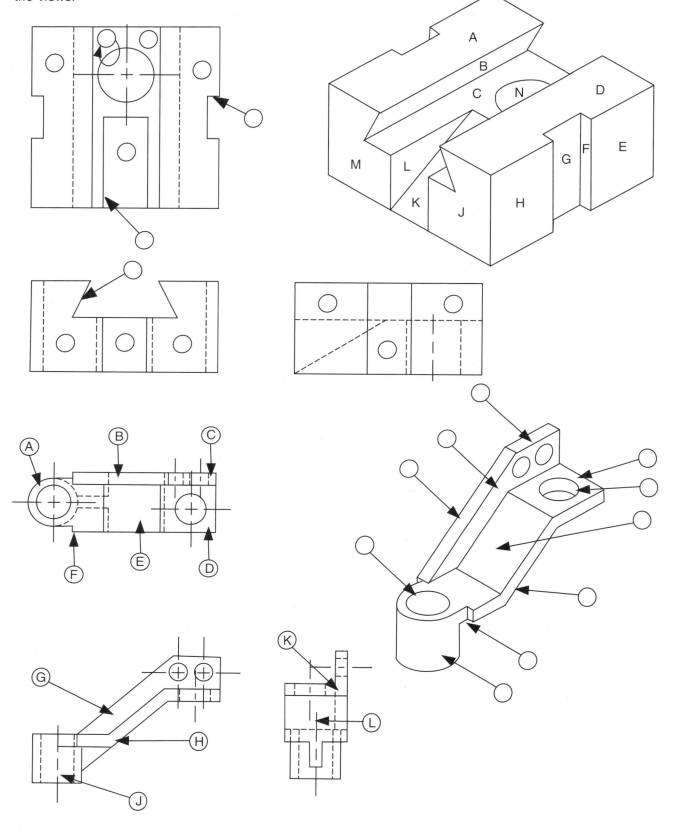

Circle the letter of the drawing which best matches the pieces in the numbered square.

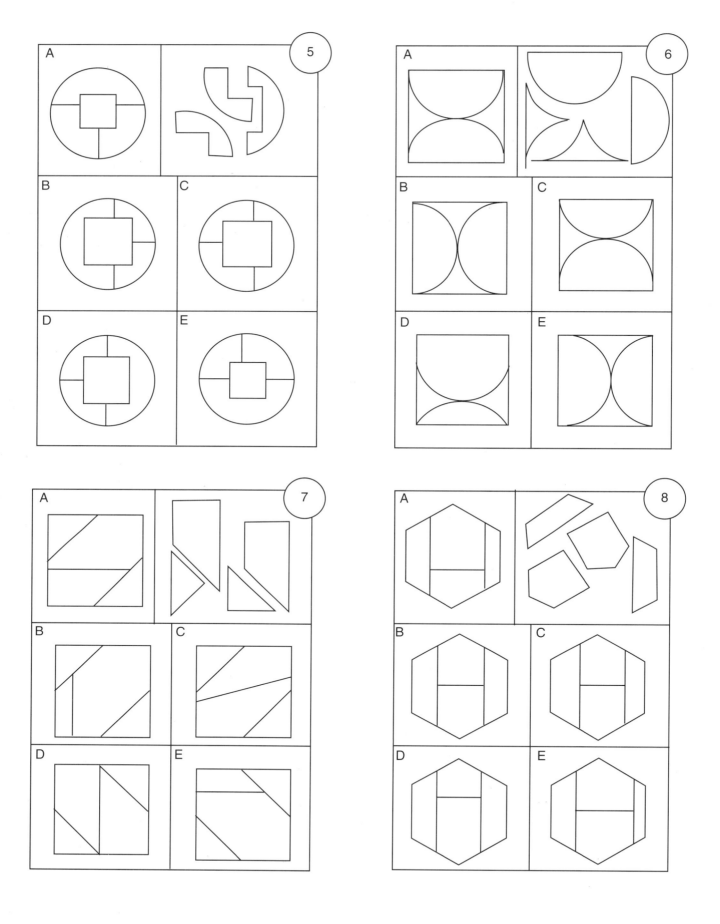

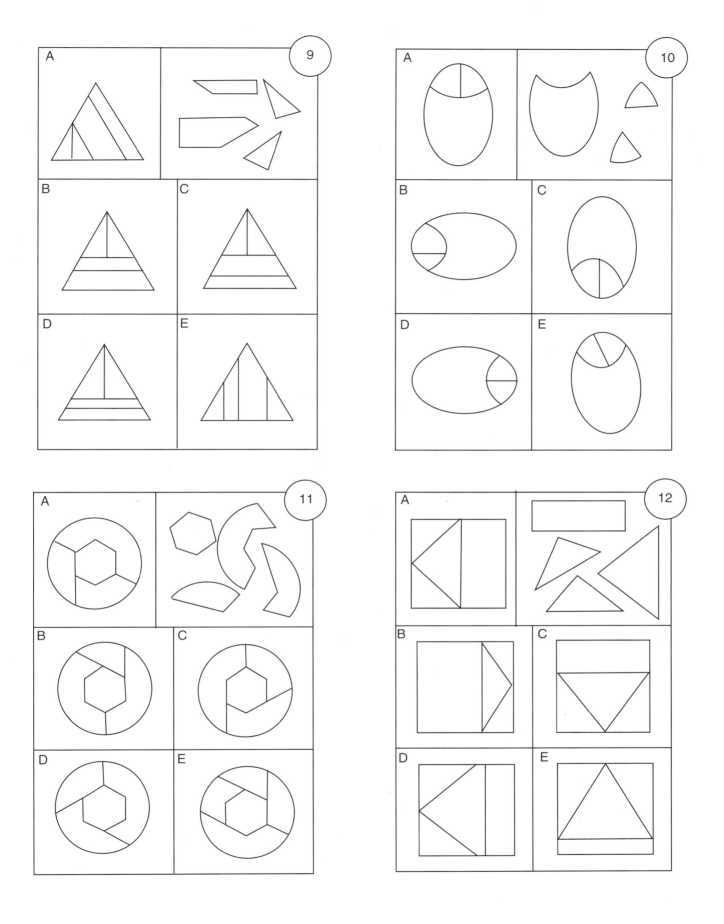

Rotated/Flipped & Same Object/Different Object

Part Y.   Rotated/Flipped - The first object in the row is to be compared with the five numbered objects in the same row. Each numbered object is one question on the test. There are only two answer possibilities:

answer a. if the numbered object is a rotated (up to 360 degrees rotation) version of the first unnumbered object in the row.

answer b. if the numbered object is flipped over (and could also be rotated) version of the first unnumbered object in the row.

EXAMPLE 1:

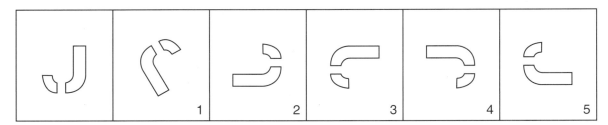

answers: 1a   2b   3b   4a   5a

Part Z.   Same Object/Different Object - The first unnumbered object in the row is to be compared with the five numbered objects which follow in the row. Each numbered object is one test question. There are only two possible answer choices:

answer a. if the numbered object is the same object as the first unnumbered object in the row. The object may be rotated.

answer b. if the numbered object is a different object when compared to the first unnumbered object in the row.

EXAMPLE 2:

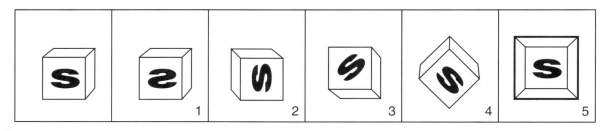

answers: 1b   2a   3b   4a   5b

TIMED TEST - 12 Minutes for Forms Y & Z

Form Y   For each object answer either, "A" if rotated or "B" if flipped over.

⌐	Ⅎ	⅃	Ⅎ	Ⅎ	F
	1	2	3	4	5
4	4	4	4	4	4
6	7	8	9	10	
٩	٩	P	P	٩	P
11	12	13	14	15	
9	6	∂	6	e	∂
16	17	18	19	20	
G	G	G	G	G	G
21	22	23	24	25	
7	⌐	7	7	7	7
26	27	28	29	30	
&	&	&	&	&	&
31	32	33	34	35	

36	37	38	39	40
41	42	43	44	45
46	47	48	49	50
51	52	53	54	55
56	57	58	59	60
61	62	63	64	65
66	67	68	69	70

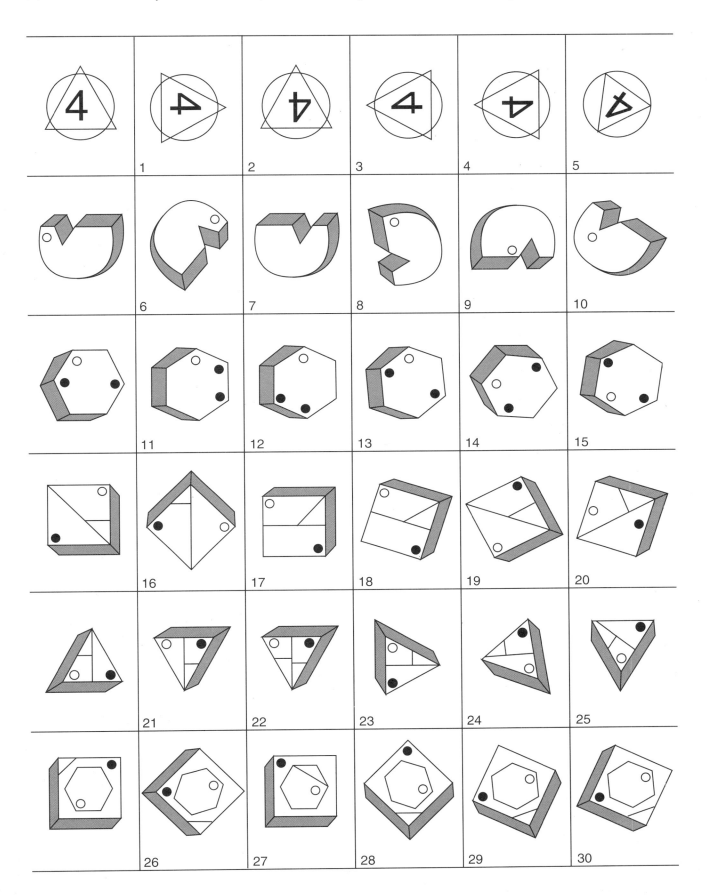

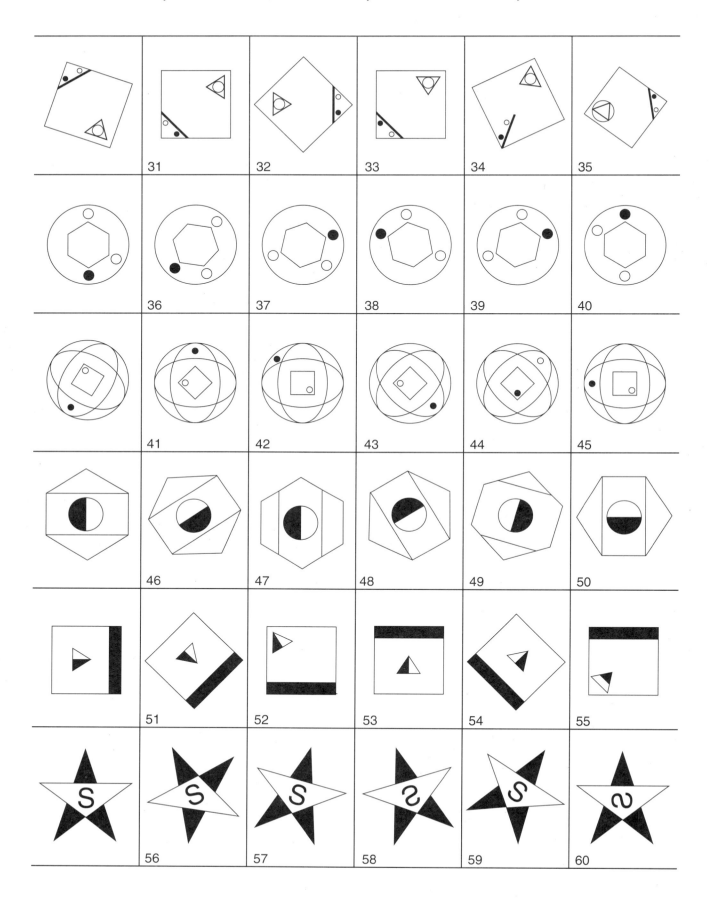

Cube Unfolding & Cube Folding Test

Time allowed is 14 minutes to complete parts A, B, C, and D of the test. Dotted lines indicate fold lines.

Part A.   Cube Unfolding

The first numbered cube in the row is folded. Compare it to the four lettered unfolded cubes in the row. Circle the letter of the unfolded cube which matches the numbered cube.

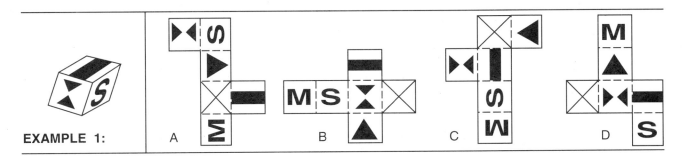

EXAMPLE 1:

Part B.   Cube Folding

The first numbered cube in the row is unfolded. The four folded cubes which follow in the row are lettered. Circle the letter of the folded cube which corresponds to the numbered cube.

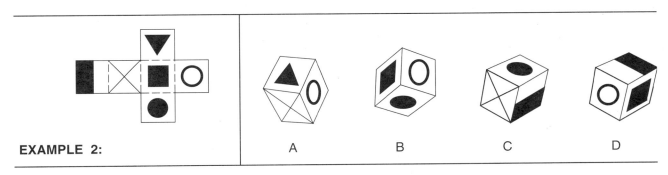

EXAMPLE 2:

Answers: Example 1 = D   Example 2 = B

Hint 1: Note where the point of a triangle lines up with the shape in the adjacent side, and where the base of a triangle lines up.

Hint 2: Note where a solid line meets the shapes in adjacent sides.

Hint 3: Note letter or number orientation.

Hint 4: Concentrate only on the visible faces of the cubes, don't be concerned with what may be on the non-visible faces.

Part A Directions - Circle the letter for the object that best matches the assembled cube.

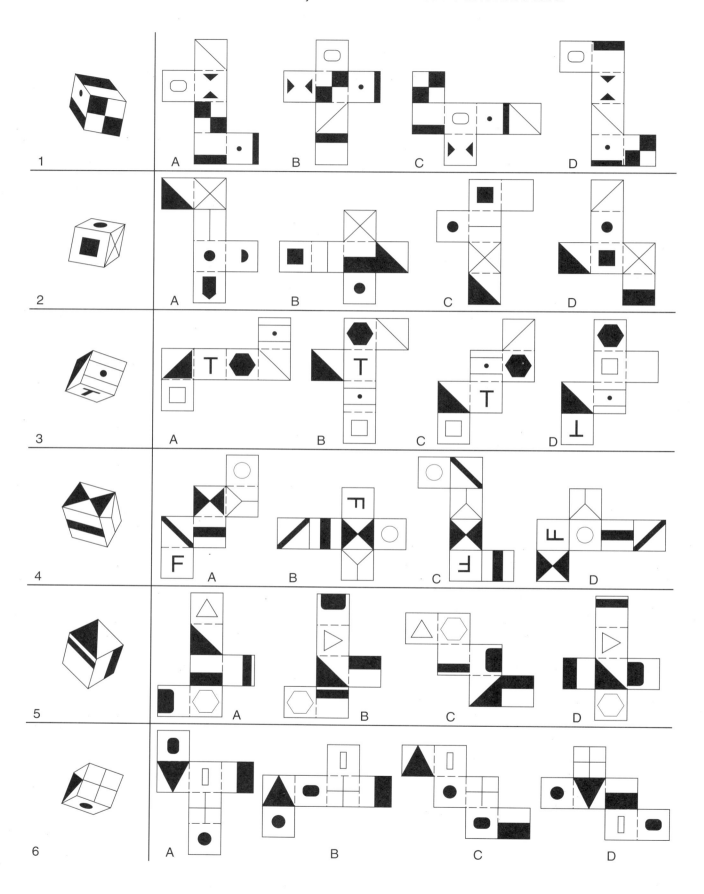

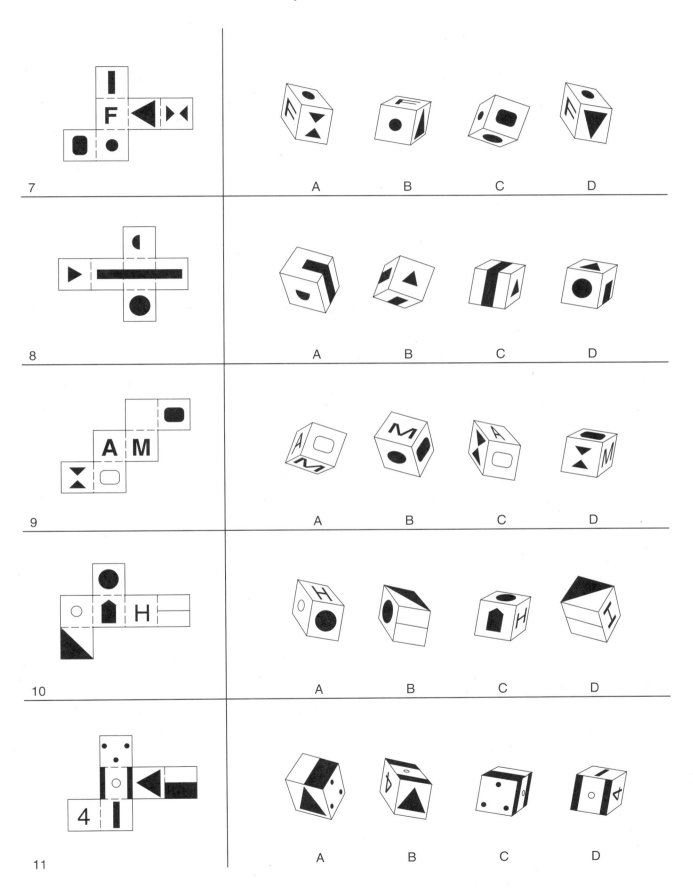

7   A   B   C   D

8   A   B   C   D

9   A   B   C   D

10   A   B   C   D

11   A   B   C   D

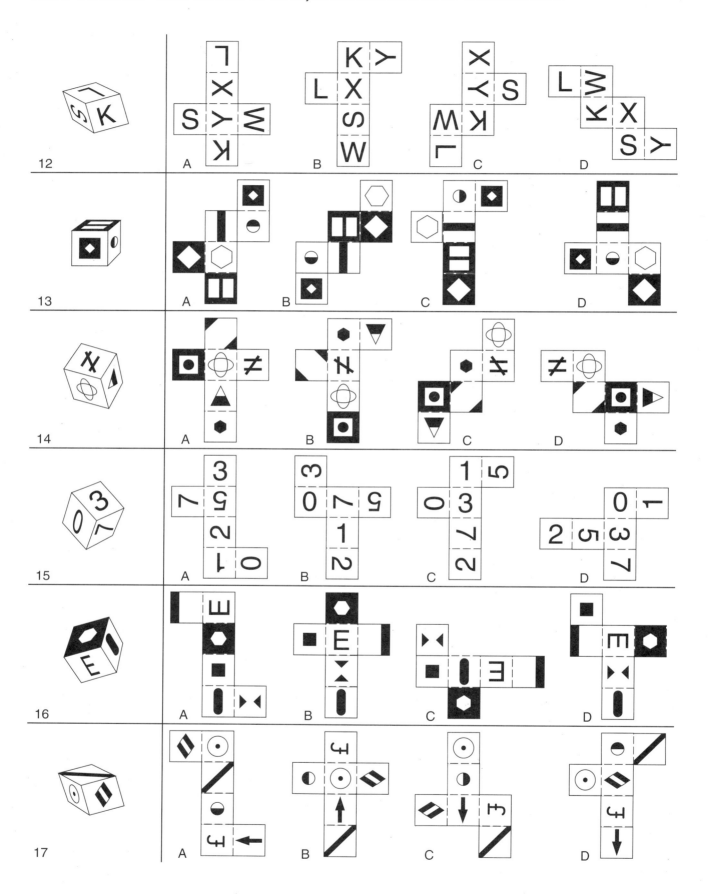

Part D Directions - Circle the letter for the object that best matches the unfolded cube.

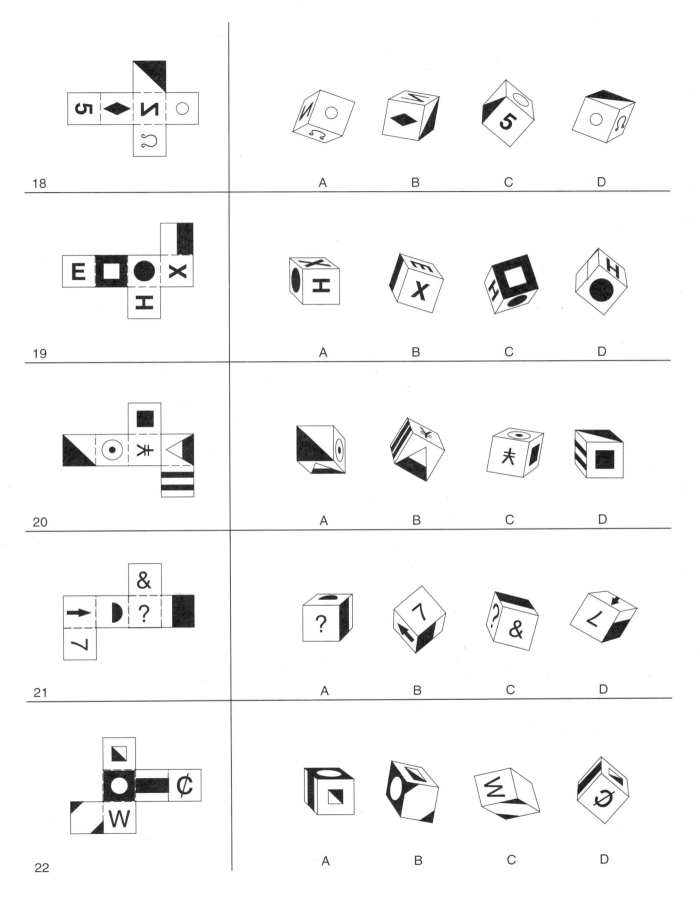

18   A   B   C   D

19   A   B   C   D

20   A   B   C   D

21   A   B   C   D

22   A   B   C   D

12

Basic Electricity

Definitions

Current (I) – The motion of charged particles in a conductor. Current is a means of transmitting energy. Current is measured in amps where 1 amp is equal to 6.25×10^{18} electrons passing a point in the circuit in one second. The abbreviation used to represent current is the letter I.

Direct Current (dc) – When charged particles flow in only one direction in a conductor.

Alternating Current (ac) – When the charged particles change their flow direction in a conductor.

Electromotive Force (E) – Current flows in a circuit because of the difference in the potential in different parts of the circuit just as water flows in a river due to the difference in elevation at different points of the river bed. Raising the electrical potential in the source which results in a greater potential difference is called the emf or electromotive force. Emf is also abbreviated as E.

Voltage (V) – The lowering of the potential energy in a circuit as electricity is used in a load is called voltage drop. The volt is the unit for both emf and voltage drop. 1 volt is equal to 1 joule of work per coulomb. The volt is abbreviated as V.

Resistance (R) – The opposition of the flow of current in a circuit. Opposing forces include temperature, length of the conductor, cross-sectional area of the conductor, and the material of which the conductor is composed. The unit of resistance is measured in ohms (Ω). The abbreviation for resistance is R.

Conductor – Any material that allows electrical current to flow through it. Wires made of metals are commonly used.

Non-conductor – Any material that is a poor conductor of electrical current. Glass, wood, and most non-metallic substances are non-conductors. Non-conductive materials are used as insulating material in electrical circuits; for example the protective coating on an electrical wire.

Semi-conductor – Substances which conduct current in one direction, for example Silicon and Germanium. Semi-conductive materials are commonly used in circuit board components such as diodes, and transistors.

Circuit – The path that the electrical current follows as it travels through wires.

Closed Circuit – One in which electricity can flow through a circuit or continuous path of conductive material.

Open Circuit – One in which electricity cannot flow due to a break or opening of a switch in the circuit.

Load – Any device which requires electrical energy to function. Light bulbs, bells, electric stove, space heater, iron, etc.

Source – The electrical supply or power source. Batteries (for dc power) and generators (for ac power) are two common electrical sources.

EXAMPLE 1: Current will flow in which circuit?

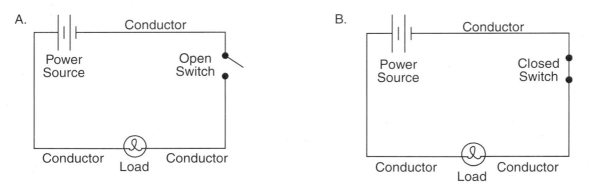

Correct answer is circuit B. In circuit A the switch is open. Current cannot flow in an open circuit. In circuit B there is a closed path for the current to travel from the battery through the bulb, and back to the battery.

Direct Current

Direct current is the flow of charged particles (electrons) through a conductor (wire) in one direction. The source of power for a dc circuit is often a battery. The battery uses chemical reactions to give energy to the electrons. When charged, the electrons have potential energy (the potential to do work). The potential difference between the energized electrons at the negative pole and the low energy of the electrons at the positive pole causes the electrons to flow from the high energy point (the negative pole) to the low energy point (the positive pole) when the two poles are connected with a conductor. The energized electrons inside the battery collect at the negative pole, and since like charges repel, the electrons repel each other and push towards the positive pole. The current moves in one direction from the negative pole towards the positive pole. Some of the electron energy is lost to the loads in the circuit and resistance.

1. **Current** – The rate of flow of electrons through a conductor. It is the number of electrons passing a point in the circuit during a certain time period. However the number of electrons is so large (about 10^{18} electrons per second) that a more practical unit is used. One coulomb is equal to 6.25×10^{18} electrons. One coulomb of charged electrons passing a point in one second is called an ampere, abbreviated amp, or A.

$$1 \text{ coulomb} = 6.25 \times 10^{18} \text{ electrons}$$

$$1 \text{ amp (A)} = \frac{1 \text{ coulomb (C)}}{1 \text{ second (s)}}$$

2. **Voltage** – The amount of electrical power supplied by the source. The raising of potential energy in a source is called electromotive force (emf). The lowering of potential energy as it is used to power a load is called a voltage drop. Both are measured in volts abbreviated V. Examples include a 12 volt battery and standard household 110 volt or 220 volt outlets.

$$1 \text{ joule} = \text{work produced in moving 1 coulomb of charge from one point to another}$$

$$1 \text{ volt (V)} = \frac{1 \text{ joule (J)}}{1 \text{ coulomb (C)}}$$

3. **Resistance** – The opposition to the flow of electricity. Substances with few free electrons tend to have greater opposition to current flow. The Ohm is the abbreviation for resistance. The Greek letter Ω is the unit for resistance. The resistance of a wire is determined by several variables:

    A. **Temperature** – As the temperature of a wire increases, the resistance also increases. This is why high power wires are not insulated, the insulation holds in heat. Insulators are required at the point the wire attaches to the tower. Birds are not electrocuted when landing on a non-insulated wire because they are not grounded. Only if a body part such as a wing touches the tower will the circuit close to allow energy to flow through the animal.

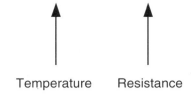

Temperature   Resistance

B. **Length** – As the length of the wire increases, so does the resistance. If a wire is doubled in length the resistance doubles also. This is why high power tools cannot operate on long extension cords. To operate the cord has to have a wider radius.

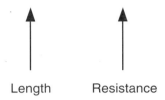

Length   Resistance

C. **Cross-sectional area** – As the cross-sectional area of the wire increases, the resistance of the wire decreases. Doubling the cross-sectional area reduces resistance by half. Think of a hose as a wire and the water flowing through the hose as electric current. Water will flow more easily through a larger hose (fire hose) than through a smaller hose (garden hose). Cross-sectional area is found by: Area $= \pi r^2$

Cross-sectional area   Resistance

D. **Material** – as the number of free electrons in a material increases, the resistance to the flow of electrical current decreases. Some materials make better conductors of electricity than others. Gold and silver are very good conductors of electricity but cost and material softness rule them out for use as household wiring. Copper and aluminum are also good conductors of electricity.

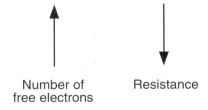

Number of   Resistance
free electrons

EXAMPLE 2: Which bare copper wire has more resistance to electrical current?

A.   Cross-section view   B.   Cross-section view

Correct answer is B. Wire A has a greater cross-sectional area than wire B.

EXAMPLE 3: Which bare aluminum wire has more resistance to electrical current?

A. ▬▬▬▬▬▬▬▬▬▬   B. ▬▬▬▬▬▬▬

Correct answer is A. Wire B is shorter than wire A.

Series Circuits

Series Circuit - An electrical circuit with only one path for the current to flow. Current flows through all parts of the circuit. Removing any one feature from the circuit will open the circuit stopping the flow of electricity.

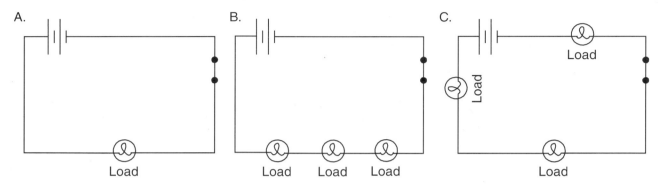

EXAMPLE 4: If bulb B burns out in the following circuit which bulbs will remain lit?

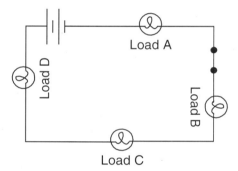

Correct answer is None. This is an example of a series circuit, and if any part of the circuit fails current cannot flow through the circuit. All 4 bulbs will go out if the circuit is opened.

Parallel Circuits

Parallel Circuit – An electrical circuit with more than one path for the current to flow. Current flows through all parts of the circuit. The current is divided among the loops of the circuit. The current from the source divides to flow through each loop, so the sum of the current in each loop is equal to the current from the source. How the current divides into each loop depends upon the resistance of each loop.

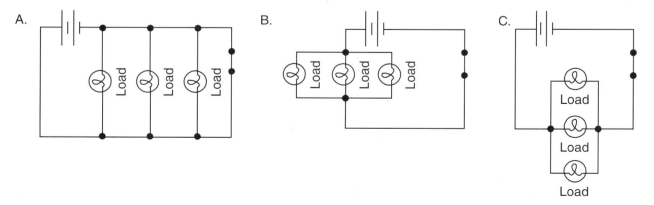

EXAMPLE 5: Which wire carries more current; A, B, or C?

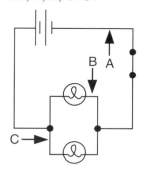

Correct answer is A. In a parallel circuit the current from the source divides to flow through each loop.

EXAMPLE 6: If bulb A burns out, which bulbs will remain lit?

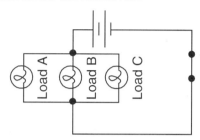

Correct answer bulbs B and C will remain lit. In a parallel circuit the power from the source is divided and flows through each loop.

EXAMPLE 7: If bulb A burns out, which bulbs will remain lit?

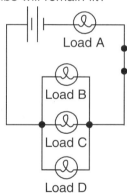

Correct answer is none. Bulb A is in series with the remaining circuit. When the current through bulb A stops it opens the circuit.

Ohm's Law and dc Circuits

Ohm's law reveals a correlation between current, voltage, and resistance when current flows through a circuit. Ohm's law applies to all dc circuits and those ac circuits containing only resistance. The correlation is represented in the Ohm's law equation:

$$I = \frac{V}{R} \qquad \text{or} \qquad I = \frac{E}{R}$$

where: I = current measured in amps   where: E = emf measured in volts
          V = voltage measured in volts
          R = resistance measured in ohms

$$amp = \frac{V}{\Omega} \qquad\qquad \Omega = \frac{V}{amp} \qquad\qquad V = amps \times \Omega$$

EXAMPLE 8: A radio is operating on a 110 volt outlet. It creates 20.0 Ω of resistance. How much current does it draw?

Given:

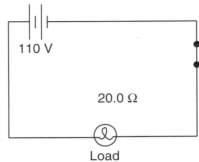

$V = 110\ V$
$R = 20.0\ \Omega$
$I = ?$

Substitute and solve:

$I = \dfrac{V}{R}$ state Ohm's law

$I = \dfrac{110\ V}{20.0\ \Omega}$ substitute given information

$I = 5.5\ V/\Omega$ divide

$I = 5.5\ amp$ answer

EXAMPLE 9: An LED draws 0.25 amps in a 1.50 volt dc circuit. How much resistance does it generate?

Given:

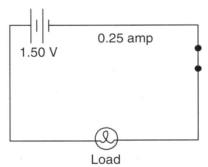

$V = 1.50\ V$
$I = 0.25\ amp$
$R = ?$

Substitute and solve:

$R = \dfrac{V}{I}$ state Ohm's law

$R = \dfrac{1.50\ V}{0.25\ amp}$ substitute given information

$R = 6.00\ V/amp$ divide

$R = 6.00\ \Omega$ answer

ELECTRICAL

TIME 6 Minutes

_____ 1. Which non-insulated copper wire offers less resistance?

    a. A
    b. B
    c. Equal

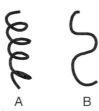

A   B

_____ 2. Which material is a better conductor of electricity?

    a. Penny
    b. Glass Bottle
    c. Wooden Dowel
    d. Cotton String

_____ 3. If switches 2 and 3 are opened which bulbs will remain lit?

    a. A, B
    b. B, C
    c. A, C
    d. None

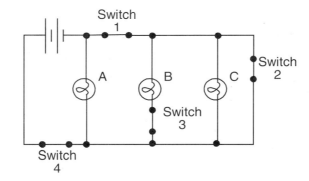

_____ 4. If bulb C burns out, name all of the bulbs that will remain lit.

    a. A, E
    b. A, B, E
    c. A, B, D, E
    d. None

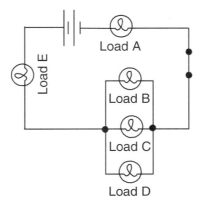

_____ 5. Which wire carries more current?

a. A
b. B
c. C
d. Equal

_____ 6. If bulbs C and E burn out, name all of the bulbs that will remain lit.

a. A, D, and F
b. A, B, D, and F
c. A, B, and G
d. None of the above

_____ 7. A space heater operating on a 220 volt line has a resistance of 16.00 Ω. What current does it draw?

a. 13.75 A
b. 3520 A
c. 0.07 A
d. 236 A

_____ 8. An iron on a 110 volt circuit uses 5 amps. What is the resistance generated by the iron?

a. 550 Ω
b. 0.45 Ω
c. 12 Ω
d. 22 Ω

_____ 9. The office coffeepot draws 3 amps and has a resistance of 12 Ω. Will it operate on a 12 volt source?

a. yes
b. no

CHAPTER
13 Mechanical Comprehension

This chapter is divided into two sections; natural physics and mechanical physics. Both topics fit in the apprenticeship test category of mechanical comprehension.

Natural Physics

You don't have to be a scientist to observe and wonder about the world around you. Your natural curiosity and an inquisitive mind are the only tools needed to learn about the physics of nature. You won't have to look very hard to recognize patterns in the natural world. The changing seasons, the ocean tides, the patterns made by the stars in the night sky, the effects of gravity, the cycle of life and death, and the east to west movement of the sun across the sky are just a few examples of natural patterns. Once a pattern is recognized the next step is to ask why, and seek a logical explanation. It is a simple case of cause and effect. For example: the orbit of the moon around the earth (cause) and the cycles of tides (effect). If the cause always has the same effect you have established a theory. If the theory is tested many times over a long period of time and always has the same effect then the theory becomes a law. We have several laws of physics. The study of our physical world is an old science. It is the study of the physical laws of nature.

This chapter is by no means a complete study of physics for that would require an entire volume of texts; instead, this chapter is a physics primer. In order to answer the typical apprentice mechanical test question you must have a working understanding of the basic laws of physics. Typically, the questions involve a picture or diagram without any values or numbers. Even though mathematical calculations are often not required, you may need to know the formulas to arrive at the correct conclusion. Also, you must be able to quickly identify which physical law (formula) applies to a particular diagram. Once you have learned the physics concepts described in this chapter and are able to apply them to a variety of situations, you will be successful on the mechanical comprehension test.

Forces and Motion

DEFINITIONS:

Scalar Quantity — any quantity that can be written as a number with the appropriate unit such as 15 feet, 8 blocks, 95 miles, 16 pounds, etc. Scalar quantities show magnitude only.

Vector Quantity — quantities which include direction as well as magnitude (size) such as 15 feet north, 8 blocks west, 95 miles south, 16 pounds perpendicular to the floor, etc. Vector quantities show magnitude and direction.

Displacement — the change in position of an object due to motion. Displacement includes both the distance the object moved as well as the direction. Displacement is a vector quantity.

Force (F) — a push or pull that tends to cause motion. Force units include pounds and Newtons.

An arrow is used to represent a vector or force quantity. The length of the arrow, drawn to scale, represents the magnitude of the force and the arrow direction represents the direction of the force.

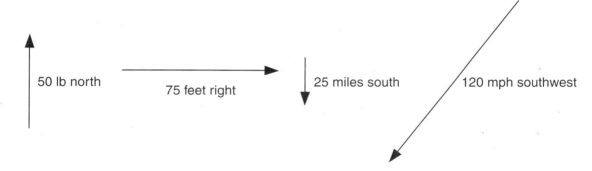

When more than one force acts upon an object, and all of the forces act in the same direction, the forces are to be added together to obtain the resultant force on the object. The resultant vector (R) is the sum of the set of vectors acting on the object in the same direction.

EXAMPLE 1: What is the resultant force and direction of the wagon (ignoring friction)?

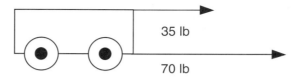

Answer: The two forces acting on the wagon combine to give a resultant force of 105 lb to the right.

When two forces act upon an object, and the forces are in the opposite directions, the forces are to be subtracted to obtain the resultant force on the object. The resultant vector (R) is the difference of the vectors acting on the object.

EXAMPLE 2: What is the resultant force and direction of the wagon (ignoring friction)?

Answer: The resultant force acting on the wagon is 5 lb to the left, so the wagon will roll to the left.

To find the resultant force and direction of an object with multiple forces acting upon the object, add all forces going in the same direction, then subtract the sum of the forces acting in the opposite direction.

EXAMPLE 3: What is the resultant force and direction of the wagon (ignoring friction)?

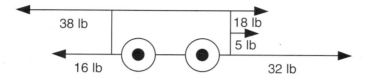

Answer: The sum of the forces acting to the right is 55 lb and the sum of the forces acting to the left is 54 lb, giving a resultant force of one pound and direction to the right.

The length of the resultant vector can be used to estimate forces acting at right angles to each other.

EXAMPLE 4: What is the resultant direction of the wagon (ignoring friction)?

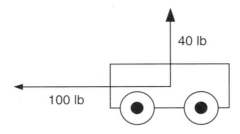

Answer: The resultant motion will not be in either the direction of the 40 lb force or the 100 lb force, but will be somewhere in between. Although the 100 lb force is the dominant force, the 40 lb force will have an effect on the result. To determine the result, complete a parallelogram using the two vector forces as the two adjacent sides. The diagonal from the point of origin is the resultant vector (R). This vector will give the magnitude of the resultant force which can be determined by scaling. It also shows the direction of the resultant force. A protractor can used to measure the angle of R, and a scale to measure the length of R. Or, approximate R to be to the left and slightly upward at a force slightly greater than 100 lb (estimated by comparing the length of R to the length of the 100 lb vector).

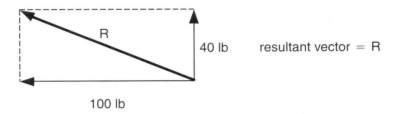

EXAMPLE 5: An airplane is traveling east at 150 mph. The wind is from the southwest at 30 mph. What is the approximate resultant airspeed and direction?

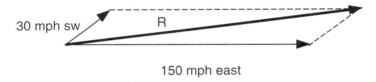

Answer: Use a protractor to measure the angle of R, and a ruler to scale the length of R. Or, approximate the resultant vector to be northeast at slightly greater than 150 mph.

Force and motion vectors can also be used to calculate the tension in cables and other machine parts. A force vector can be drawn to represent a cable holding a 2000 lb weight.

In the diagram above the downward force created by the 2000 lb weight is equalized by an upward pull of the cable. When there is no motion in the system the two forces are in balance. The vectors cancel each other out. Whenever a force is applied and no motion is generated then there must be an equal and opposite force. When you set a 5 lb bag of groceries on the table the table pushes back with equal force, otherwise the table would collapse. When you sit in a chair the chair pushes back with an equal and opposite force otherwise you would end up on the floor.

What happens if another force is added to the cable diagram?

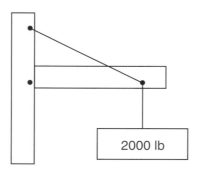

As the weight is pushed the cable is no longer pulling directly upward against the weight, the tension in the cable increases to maintain stability. Use the parallelogram to prove this.

Draw a vector equal in length but opposite in direction to the weight vector. This vector represents the force necessary to support the weight. (dotted line)

Draw a line at 90° from the tip of the vector added in the last step to the angled cable. This line is the same length as the upward support (4000).

The tension in the cable can now be estimated to be greater than 4000 lb. The angled cable is longer than the 4000 lb suport line. As the angle of the second cable increases so does the tension in the cable.

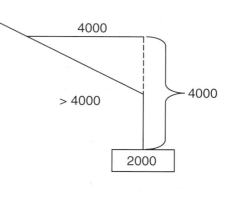

EXAMPLE 6: Which wagon, A or B, will require more effort to move the 200 lb cannon ball?

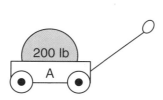

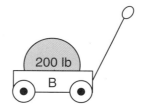

Answer: B — The wagon handle is at a greater angle than wagon A.

Speed

Speed is the distance an object travels in a certain amount of time. Consider the speedometer on the dashboard of an automobile it measures speed in miles per hour or kilometers per hour. The speed of a boat in water is typically measured in knots, 1 knot = 1 nautical mile per hour. Speed is a scalar quantity since it indicates magnitude only, not direction. Any moving object has a speed. Speed is found by dividing the total distance traveled by the amount of time it took to move that distance.

Speed

$$\text{speed} = \frac{\text{distance}}{\text{time}} \qquad\qquad s = \frac{d}{t}$$

EXAMPLE 1: Assuming each car stays in its lane, which car must go faster in order for both cars to cross the finish line at the same time?

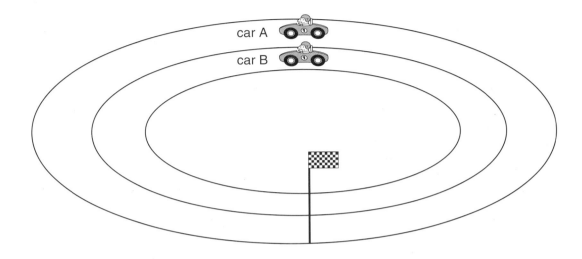

Given:

    time = time is the constant for both cars. They both start at the same time and it is stated that the cars are to cross the finish line at the same time. Use any value, but use the same value for both cars.

    distance = car A must travel further than car B because it is on the outside track. Use any values, but use a longer distance for car A.

    speed = calculate for the speed of both cars

Substitute and solve:

$$\text{speed}_{car}A = \frac{d}{t} \qquad\quad \text{state the formula for speed} \qquad\quad \text{speed}_{car}B = \frac{d}{t}$$

$$s_{car}A = \frac{.26 \text{ mi}}{.002 \text{ hr}} \qquad\quad \text{substitute given information and divide} \qquad\quad s_{car}B = \frac{.25 \text{ mi}}{.002 \text{ hr}}$$

$$s_{car}A = 130 \text{ mph} \qquad\quad \text{answer} \qquad\qquad\qquad\qquad s_{car}B = 125 \text{ mph}$$

Answer: Car A must travel faster because it must travel a greater distance in the same amount of time as car B.

EXAMPLE 2: Which point on the spinning disk is moving faster?

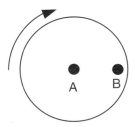

Answer: Point B is moving faster; it covers a greater distance than point A in one revolution of the disk.

Law of Inertia

The Law of Inertia

An object in motion tends to stay in motion with the same velocity (constant speed) and in the same direction) unless acted upon by another force, and an object at rest tends to stay at rest unless it is acted upon by another force.

The amount of force needed to slow down or stop a moving object will be determined to a great extent by the mass of the object. It would take a greater force to stop a fully loaded car hauler moving at 65 mph than a compact car moving at the same speed. Other factors will have an impact on the motion of an object. If you remove your foot from the accelerator of your car it will slow down due to friction between the tires and the road, wind resistance, and the friction between moving parts. The amount of force needed to change the direction of a moving object is also a factor of force. The direction of a ball on a pool table will be easier to change than the direction of a bowling ball on the same pool table. The amount of force needed to start an object at rest in motion will also depend upon the mass of the object and the environment it is in. A crate on ice will be easier to push than the same crate on grass.

EXAMPLE 1: A boy spins a ball tied to a string in a counterclockwise direction. Which picture shows the path of the ball if he releases the string?

a. A
b. B
c. Neither

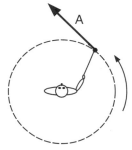
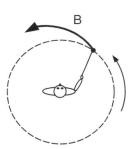

Answer: A

EXAMPLE 2: A car traveling north is moving too fast to complete a left turn and runs off the road. The car will run off which side of the road?

a. Right shoulder
b. Left shoulder
c. Neither

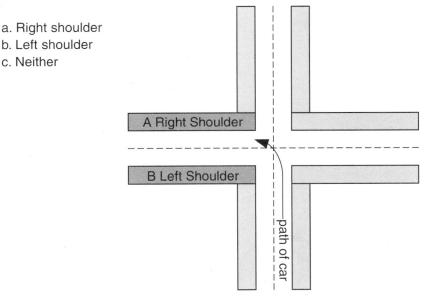

Answer: A — The car's inertia tries to keep the car moving forward, but the force of the wheels turned to the left pull the car onto the right shoulder.

Gravity

Gravity is a fundamental force of nature. Gravity is a force that exists between two or more objects. The force of gravity is proportional to the product of the masses of the objects and inversely proportional to the square of the distance between their respective centers. In other words, the greater the mass of an object the greater the gravitational pull that it exerts on another object, and the greater the distance between the objects the weaker the gravitational pull. All objects have a gravitational force relative to the mass of the object. However, the gravitational force exerted by your body for example is negligible when in the presence of the Earth's gravitational force. In a vacuum such as outer space where there are no celestial bodies overpowering the gravitational pull of a human, the weaker force is more discernable.

The gravitational pull exerted between two objects increases directly proportional to the masses of the objects.

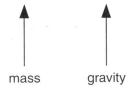

mass   gravity

EXAMPLE 1: A golf ball hit with equal force on the moon as on Earth will:

a. Travel farther on Earth
b. Travel farther on the moon
c. Travel equal distance

Answer: B — The moon's mass is about one sixth the mass of the Earth, so its gravitational pull will also be one-sixth the gravitational pull on Earth. On the moon the ball will be able to travel further before gravity finally pulls it down to the surface.

The gravitational pull between two objects is inversely proportional to the square of the distance between the centers of each object.

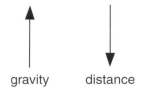

gravity   distance

EXAMPLE 2: The Earth's atmospheric particles will be denser at which point in the diagram?

a. A
b. B
c. C

Answer: A — Earth's atmosphere is held in place by the gravitational pull of Earth. Earth's atmosphere is not empty; it consists of particles of Nitrogen, Oxygen, water vapor and various other particles and elements. The air particles closest to the Earth's surface are held tighter than those further away from the center of the Earth. Just as water pressure increases with depth, air pressure is greatest at the Earth's surface. We live at the bottom of the atmospheric ocean surrounding the Earth. Mountain air becomes thinner in higher elevations.

Weight and Mass

The terms mass and weight are often used interchangeably; however, there is a difference between the two terms. Weight is a measurement of the gravitational pull on an object, whereas mass is the amount of matter contained in an object. The weight of an object varies with the location of the object, so weight is relative to location. Why does weight change, because gravity changes from one place to another. Gravity on Earth is stronger than the gravity on Pluto, but not as strong as the gravity on the sun. And since there is no gravity in outer space objects are said to be weightless. You don't have to travel into space to see how gravity affects weight; gravity varies from one location to another right here on Earth. The further you are from the center of the Earth the less gravitational pull on your body. You weigh slightly less in higher elevations. Your weight depends on many things, including your actual mass, the mass of the celestial body you are on, and how far away you are from the center of that celestial body.

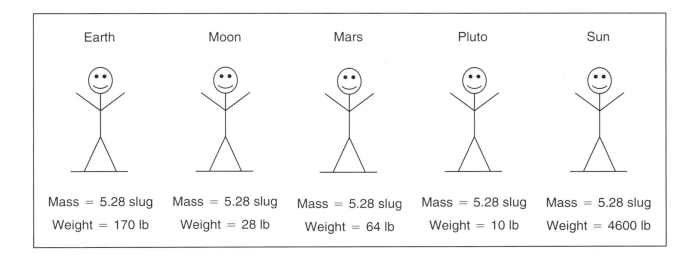

Earth	Moon	Mars	Pluto	Sun
Mass = 5.28 slug	Mass = 5.28 slug	Mass = 5.28 slug	Mass = 5.28 slug	Mass = 5.28 slug
Weight = 170 lb	Weight = 28 lb	Weight = 64 lb	Weight = 10 lb	Weight = 4600 lb

The tool used to measure weight is a spring scale. The gravity pulling on the object compresses a spring inside the scale causing the dial on the scale to move. The greater the spring compresses the greater the reading on the scale. The weight of an object will fluctuate depending upon where the object is located. Weight in the English system of measurement is measured in pounds, ounces, or tons. The unit Newtons represents weight in the metric system.

Spring scale measures weight

Balance Beam measures mass

The mass of an object is the amount of matter the object has. Mass is a measure of the object's resistance to acceleration. Compare a 1-foot square Styrofoam cube to a stone cube of the same size. The Styrofoam cube would be easier to move (accelerate) than the stone cube. The Styrofoam cube has fewer particles per square inch than the stone cube. It has less mass than the stone cube of equal size. Mass is measured with a scale. The scale compares the mass of the object in question to the mass of a known object. The scale used in a doctor's office compares your mass to the mass of the metal weights on a balance beam. Mass is not relative to location. Your mass would be the same on the moon as on Earth. As long as you contain the same amount of matter your mass will be constant regardless of your location. Mass is measured in slugs in the English system and grams or kilograms in the metric system.

A kilogram (kg) is a metric quantity of **mass** and a Newton (N) is a metric quantity of **force**. One kilogram (kg) = 2.205 pounds of mass and 4.45 Newtons (N) = 1 pound of force.

Center of Gravity

The center of gravity of any object is that point at which all of the weight can be considered to be concentrated, or centered.

An object of uniform shape has its center of gravity at its middle or center. Holding the object near its center of gravity makes it easier to lift and carry the object, and is safer because it will help prevent back injuries. For example, it is easier for one person to carry an 8 foot 2" x 4" at the middle of the board rather than at the end.

Objects of irregular shape, like a hammer, do not have their weight evenly distributed. The center of gravity is located nearer the heavier end of asymmetrical shaped objects. You have probably used each of these tools at some time. If you had to balance each item with one hand where would you hold the item?

Chances are that you have just identified the center of gravity for each of these tools.

EXAMPLE 1: Which object would be easier to tip over?

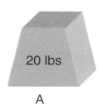 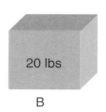 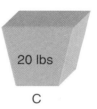

Answer: C — The center of gravity is higher on object C, thus it would be easier to tip over.

EXAMPLE 2: Which picture shows how the 3 dimensional wooden shapes with lead plugs will stand on a flat surface?

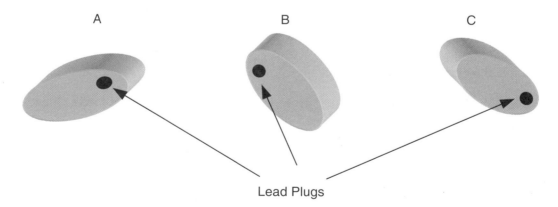

Lead Plugs

Answer: C

EXAMPLE 3: At what point will the clothesline most likely need a support pole as the wet clothes are evenly distributed on the line?

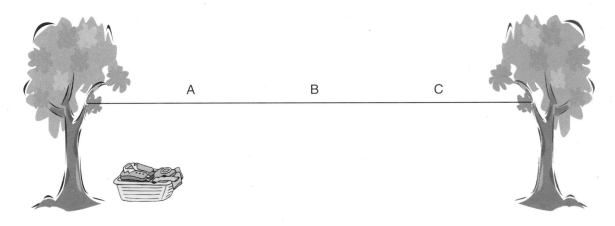

Answer: B

Density

Density
$D = \dfrac{W}{V}$

Where: D = Density   W = Weight   V = Volume

Density is defined as the weight of an object per given unit of volume. For example the volume of a bucket of sand would be greater than the volume of the same bucket filled with ping pong balls. The pail of sand has a greater weight because the molecules of sand are more compact, denser. The pail of ping pong balls weighs less because there are fewer molecules per square inch so it is less dense. Density is a property of all matter and since different substances have different densities the density of the substance is often used as one way to identify an unknown substance. We can use the property of density as a comparison factor. Using water as a standard we can compare the densities of equal volumes of other substances to the density of water.

EXAMPLE 1: Which is denser, a gallon of water, a gallon of oil, or a gallon of sand?

1 gallon water   1 gallon oil   1 gallon sand

Answer: The gallon of sand. There are equal amounts of each substance, but to determine which is denser we need to consider their weights. Without knowing the actual weights we can compare their weights; which is the lightest, heaviest, and in between. To do this imagine what happens when you place each item into water. You know that oil floats on water because you have seen the rainbow colored oil slicks on mud puddles at gas stations, and you know that sand will sink when placed in water when you think of a lake or ocean with a sandy bottom. So, by comparison, oil is lighter than water, and sand is heavier than water. Thus, the gallon of sand is the denser material.

General Rule of Density

Whenever you have equal amounts of substances and wish to know which weighs more, compare them to water.

EXAMPLE 2: Which is denser:
a. wooden croquet ball
b. pool table eight ball

A   B

Answer: Imagine placing both objects into a bucket of water. The wooden croquet ball would tend to float while the pool ball would sink. Thus, the pool ball is denser.

Law of Acceleration

Acceleration is the change in the velocity of an object over a given time. Acceleration can be an increase, as a car speeds up for example, or a decrease in speed, as a car slows down or brakes.

Law of Acceleration

$$a = \frac{\Delta v}{\Delta t}$$

---

*The Greek letter delta Δ is read as "change in"

Where: a = acceleration Δv = change in velocity Δt = change in time

EXAMPLE 1: On the graph below, which line shows the greater acceleration in the 10 minute time interval, the car or the airplane?

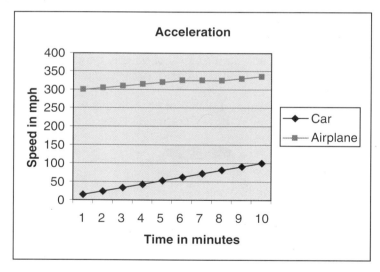

Answer: The car has a greater change in velocity (Δv approximately 15 mph to 105 mph) when compared to the airplane (Δv approximately 300 mph to 345mph) in the same time period, so the acceleration of the car is greater than the plane's acceleration.

Acceleration can also be considered in terms of the mass of the object where the mass of an object multiplied by the acceleration of the object equals the force acting on the object.

Law of Acceleration
F = ma

Where: F = force   m = mass   a = acceleration

EXAMPLE 2: Which object will require a greater force to set it into motion?

A   B   C

Answer: A. The truck has a greater mass than the car or motorcycle, so it will require a greater force to set it in motion. According to the formula as mass increases (holding acceleration constant) the force required also increases.

The formula can be rewritten to solve for acceleration. Acceleration is equal to mass divided by force. So, the greater the mass of the object, the greater the acceleration when force is constant.

$$a = \frac{F}{m}$$

EXAMPLE 3: Which ball has the greater acceleration on a flat plane after a 5 lb push?

Answer: A. The mass of the foam ball is less than the mass of the steel ball. As mass increases acceleration decreases.

Law of Action and Reaction

Law of Action and Reaction
For every force applied by object X to another object Y (action), there is a force exerted by object Y on object X (reaction) which has the same magnitude but is opposite in direction.

When a cannon ball is shot from a cannon (action), the recoil on the cannon (reaction) is strong enough to roll the cannon backwards several feet. The same is true of a bullet shot from a gun (action) the gun recoil (reaction) is felt by the shooter. The action of the tires of an accelerating auto produces a reaction force from the road pushing against the tires.

A simple formula can be used to symbolize the law of action and reaction:

$$F_1 = -F_2$$

Where: F_1 represents the action force F_2 represents the reaction force

EXAMPLE 1: In order for a car to accelerate a force must be applied to it. The force moving the car forward is the tires on the road. We can call the force of the tires on the road the action force. What is the reaction force?

Answer: The reaction force is the road below the tires pushing back on the tires with equal force.

Momentum

Momentum

Momentum is a measure of the effect an object would have in a collision if that object's motion is stopped in a certain amount of time. Momentum can be calculated by multiplying the mass of the object by the velocity of the object.

$$p = mv$$

Where: p = the momentum of the object   m = the mass of the object   v = the velocity of the object

Momentum units are slug ft/s in the English system (slug is the English mass unit), and kg m/s in the metric system. Momentum is a vector quantity (has both magnitude and direction) where the direction is the same as the velocity.

EXAMPLE 2: Which wrecking ball would do more damage to the building in a head-on collision at 40 mph, the 200 lb ball or the 2000 lb ball?

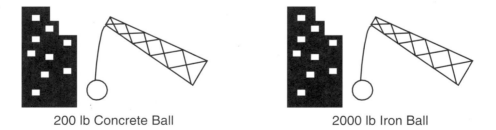

200 lb Concrete Ball   2000 lb Iron Ball

Answer: The 2000 lb wrecking ball will do more damage.

Fluid Power

Since liquids and gasses have similar characteristics they can be studied together as fluids.

DEFINITIONS:

Force (F) — a push or pull that has the ability to cause motion. Weight units are used with force values.

Pressure (P) — a force applied to an area. It is the concentration of force. Pressure is measured in weight per unit of area. N/m^2 (Newtons per meter squared or pascal Pa) and lb/in^2 (pounds per square inch or psi) are typical examples of pressure units.

Area (A) — the surface of an object. Squared length units are used for area measurements.

General Rule of Liquids

Liquid pressure is directly proportional to the depth of the liquid, where depth is the distance from the point of the bottom of the liquid to the surface of the liquid.

EXAMPLE 1: Where is the pressure the greatest?

a. X
b. Y
c. equal

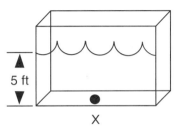 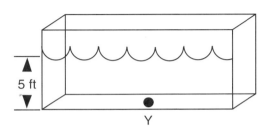

Answer: C — equal. Even though the right-hand tank is wider it does not affect the pressure at the bottom of the tank. Only vertical depth affects liquid pressure.

All fluids are compressible. If a force is applied to a fluid in a container the force is evenly distributed to all surfaces in contact with the fluid. A force applied to a specific area of surface is called pressure.

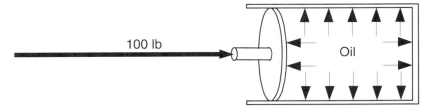

If the surface area of the piston in the above diagram is 1 in² then 100 lbs of force will be applied evenly to every square inch of surface in contact with the oil.

Fluid Pressure

$$P = \frac{F}{A}$$

Where: P = Pressure   F = Force   A = surface area

EXAMPLE 2: If the surface area of the piston is 10 in² what is the pressure inside the tank?

Given:

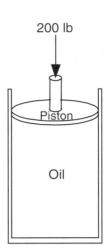

$\quad$ F = 200 lb
$\quad$ A = 10 in²
$\quad$ P = ?

Substitute and solve:

$\quad P = \dfrac{F}{A}$ $\qquad$ state the formula for pressure

$\quad P = \dfrac{200 \text{ lb}}{10 \text{ in}^2}$ $\qquad$ substitute given information and divide

$\quad P = 20 \text{ psi}$ $\qquad$ answer

This means that 20 pounds of force is applied to every square inch of surface area inside the tank.

EXAMPLE 3: If the surface area of piston 1 is 1 m² and the surface area of piston 2 is double the size of piston 1, how much force can be lifted with piston 2?

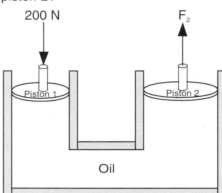

Given:

$\quad F_1 = 200 \text{ N}$
$\quad A_1 = 1 \text{ m}^2$
$\quad F_2 = ?$
$\quad A_2 = 2 \text{ m}^2$

Substitute and solve:

$\quad \dfrac{F_1}{A_1} = \dfrac{F_2}{A_2}$ $\qquad$ state the formula as a proportion

$\quad \dfrac{200 \text{ N}}{1 \text{ m}^2} = \dfrac{F_2}{2 \text{ m}^2}$ $\qquad$ substitute given information

$\quad F_2 = \dfrac{(200 \text{ N}) \, (2 \, \cancel{\text{m}^2})}{1 \, \cancel{\text{m}^2}}$ cross multiply then divide and cancel like units

$\quad F_2 = 400 \text{ N}$ $\qquad$ answer

EXAMPLE 4: Using the diagram in Example 2 if piston 1 is pushed down 2 cm, how far will piston 2 move up?

$\quad$ a. 2 cm
$\quad$ b. more than 2 cm
$\quad$ c. less than 2 cm

$\quad (F_E) \, (d_E) = (F_R) \, (d_R)$ $\qquad$ state the formula
$\quad (200 \text{ N}) \, (2 \text{ cm}) = (400 \text{ N}) \, (d_R)$ $\qquad$ substitute given information and solve
$\quad d_R = 1 \text{ cm}$ $\qquad$ answer

The correct answer is c. Using the law of simple machines; the ability to lift a load is doubled, however, the distance it is lifted is about ½ the distance piston 1 is moved.

Mechanical Physics

The Six Simple Machines

Machines help us do work. They move or change the direction of an object. People use machines in the office, kitchen, and garage, garden, trades work, school, leisure, hobbies, and so on. It would be impossible to include all types of machines in one book, much less one chapter, so to simplify things lets start with the 6 simple machines. All other machines, no matter how complex, are combinations of two or more of these 6 simple machines. Break down any complex machine into its individual components and you will find in its fundamental working parts two or more of these 6 simple machines. With a good understanding of the fundamental workings of the 6 simple machines you will have a better grasp of the more complex machines. The 6 Simple Machines are:

1. Lever
2. Inclined Plane
3. Wheel and axle
4. Screw
5. Pulley
6. Wedge

1. Lever

2. Inclined Plane

3. Wheel and Axle

4. Screw

5. Pulley

6. Wedge

Terms, Abbreviations, and Formulas

In every machine there are two forces at work, the Effort Force, and the Resistance Force.

1. The **Effort Force** is the amount of effort applied to the machine to make it work. In the example of a lever it is the amount of effort applied to lift the object. The Effort Force is measured in weight units of either pounds in the English system or Newtons for the metric weight system. The abbreviation for the Effort Force is F_E.

2. The **Resistance Force** is the combined weight of the object being moved by the machine. In the example of the lever it is the weight of the object being lifted. The Resistance Force is measured in weight units of either pounds or Newtons. The abbreviation for the Resistance Force is F_R.

$$\text{Effort Force} = F_E \qquad \text{Resistance Force} = F_R$$

In the diagram below, a 30 lb weight (Force of effort) is applied to one end of the teeter-totter to lift a weight (Force of Resistance) of 60 lbs on the resistance end of the teeter totter. The F_E is 30 lbs and the F_R is 60 lbs.

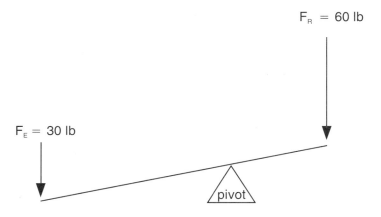

$F_R = 60$ lb

$F_E = 30$ lb

pivot

There are two distances to be considered in all machines, the Effort Distance, and the Resistance Distance.

1. The **Effort Distance** is the distance the effort force is moved in a machine. In the case of the lever the Effort Distance is measured from the fulcrum, or pivot, to the point where the EFFORT is applied. Effort distance is measured in length units such as feet, inches, centimeters, meters etc. The abbreviation for the Effort Distance is d_E.

2. The **Resistance Distance** is the distance the resistance force is moved. In the case of the lever it is the distance from the fulcrum, or pivot, to the point where the RESISTANCE is applied. Resistance Distance is measured in length units such as feet, inches, centimeters, meters, etc. The abbreviation for the Resistance Distance is d_R.

Effort Distance = d_E Resistance Distance = d_R

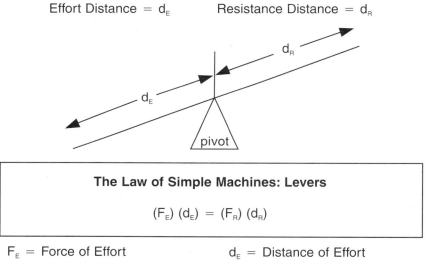

d_R

d_E

pivot

The Law of Simple Machines: Levers

$$(F_E)(d_E) = (F_R)(d_R)$$

Where:

F_E = Force of Effort	d_E = Distance of Effort
F_R = Force of Resistance	d_R = Distance of Resistance

Given any 3 of the variables and a basic knowledge of Algebra you should be able to solve for the missing variable.

EXAMPLE 1: A bar is used to raise a 700 lb tree and root ball. The fulcrum is placed 10 in. from the root ball. The worker pushes 70 in from the fulcrum. How much effort must the worker apply to raise the tree and root ball?

Given:

F_E = unknown
d_E = 70 in
F_R = 700 lb
d_R = 10 in

Substitute and solve:

$(F_E)(d_E) = (F_R)(d_R)$ state the law of simple machines

$(F_E)(70 \text{ in}) = (700 \text{ lb})(10 \text{ in})$ substitute given information

$(F_E)(70 \text{ in}) = 7000 \text{ lb in}$ multiply

$F_E = \dfrac{7000 \text{ lb } \cancel{in}}{70 \cancel{in}}$ divide and cross cancel like units

$F_E = 100 \text{ lb}$ answer

EXAMPLE 2: A wheelbarrow has a concrete statue placed .25 meters from the axle. The gardener lifts with 200 Newtons of force on the wheelbarrow handle that is 2 meters long from the axle to the point where the effort is applied. What is the maximum weight the gardener can lift?

Given:

$F_E = 200 \text{ N}$
$d_E = 2 \text{ m}$
$F_R = \text{unknown}$
$d_R = .25 \text{ m}$

Substitute and solve:

$(F_E)(d_E) = (F_R)(d_R)$ state the law of simple machines

$(200 \text{ N})(2 \text{ m}) = (F_R)(.25 \text{ m})$ substitute given information

$400 \text{ Nm} = (F_R)(.25 \text{ m})$ multiply

$\dfrac{400 \text{ N}\cancel{m}}{.25 \cancel{m}} = F_R$ divide and cross cancel like units

$F_R = 1600 \text{ N}$ answer

Machines are used to help us do work because they offer an advantage. This is called **Mechanical Advantage**. And, depending how the machine is used, the advantage gained comes in one of two types: one advantage is to make the job easier; the second advantage is to move an object over a greater distance. Here is an example of how the same type of machine can be used to obtain the two types of mechanical advantages:

Ease of Use: The wire cutter pictured below has a 4.5 in long handle (d_E) and a .75 in (d_R) cutting end which allows this machine to multiply the effort applied to the handle by about 6 times. So, for each pound of effort applied to the handle the cutting end applies 6 pounds of force. This is a good design for a tool used to cut dense objects such as wire.

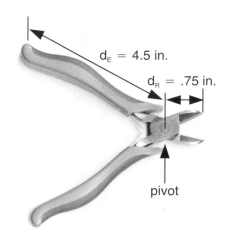

$d_E = 4.5$ in.

$d_R = .75$ in.

pivot

Move an Object over a Distance: The handle length on the scissors below is 4.25 in (d_E) and the cutting end is 4.3 in (d_R). So, for every pound of effort applied to the handle, the cutting end applies about .99 pounds of cutting force. The advantage to this machine is distance. The scissors provides a long cut with each squeeze of the handle. This is a good design for a tool used to cut thin materials such as paper or fabric.

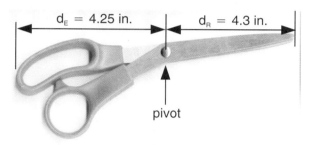

$d_E = 4.25$ in. $d_R = 4.3$ in.

pivot

The advantage gained from a machine is called the Mechanical Advantage. Mechanical Advantage is abbreviated MA. There are two formulas used to calculate Mechanical Advantage:

Mechanical Advantage Formulas: Levers

$$MA = \frac{F_R}{F_E} \qquad\qquad MA = \frac{d_E}{d_R}$$

Which mechanical advantage formula you use to solve a problem will depend upon the information given in the problem. If the problem includes numbers with either pounds or Newtons units, remember that these are weight units and Forces are measured in weight units, use the MA = FR ˜ FE formula. If the problem includes measurement units, remember that distances are measured in distance units so use the MA = dE ˜ dR formula.

• Mechanical Advantage has no unit. The units cancel.

• Mechanical Advantage can be written as a Ratio, a fraction, or a number.

EXAMPLE 3: A jack was used to lift a 2050 lb car. Only 25 lb of effort was needed on the jack handle to lift the car. What is the Mechanical Advantage of the jack?

Given:

$F_R = 2050$ lb
$F_E = 25$ lb
MA = unknown

Substitute and Solve

$$MA = \frac{F_R}{F_E}$$ state the appropriate Mechanical Advantage formula

$$MA = \frac{2050 \cancel{lb}}{25 \cancel{lb}}$$ substitute, cross cancel, and reduce the fraction

$$MA = 82 : 1 = {}^{82}\!/_1 = 82$$ answer

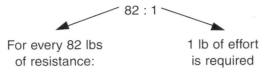

82 : 1

For every 82 lbs   1 lb of effort
of resistance: is required

EXAMPLE 4: How much effort must be applied to the jack in example 3 to lift an 1148 lb car?

Given:

$$F_R = 1148 \text{ lb}$$
$$MA = 82 : 1$$
$$F_E = \text{unknown}$$

Substitute and Solve

$$MA = \frac{F_R}{F_E}$$ state the appropriate Mechanical Advantage formula

$$82 = \frac{1148 \text{ lb}}{F_E}$$ substitute

$$F_E = \frac{1148 \text{ lb}}{82}$$ multiply both sides by F_E and divide each side by 82

$$F_E = 14 \text{ lb}$$ answer

Lever

There are many examples of levers. A lever is any device that has an arm that rotates or moves about a pivot point or fulcrum. Examples include all types of hand-held instruments such as, scissors, tin snips, wire cutter, bolt cutter, tree limb cutters, grass shears, pliers, pry bar, pop top, old fashioned can opener, teeter totter, hammer, claw end of a hammer, wheelbarrow, etc. Even though there are many examples of levers, all levers can be divided into 3 classes. Which class a lever belongs to depends upon the location of the pivot point in relation to the forces and distances.

General Rule of Levers

In any lever the Distance of Effort is ALWAYS measured from the point where the effort is applied to the center of the fulcrum or pivot. The Distance of Resistance is ALWAYS measured from the point where the resistance sits on the lever to the center of the fulcrum or pivot. These rules apply regardless of the class of lever used.

Use the following diagrams to help you determine the distance of effort and the distance of resistance in a lever.

First class lever:

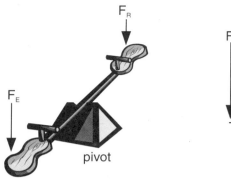
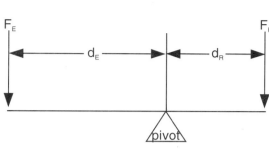

Second class lever:

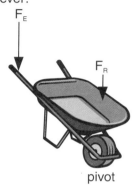
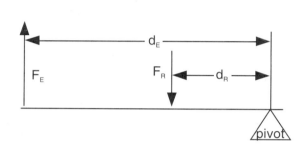

Third class lever:

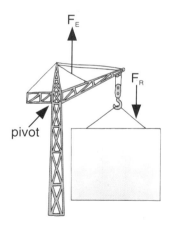
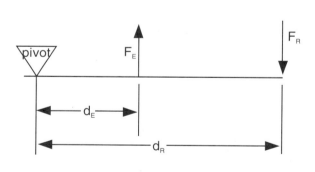

EXERCISE 1

Directions: On a separate sheet of paper, solve for the unknown in each of the following problems using the Law of Simple Machines or the Mechanical Advantage formulas. Place your answer in the space provided.

Answers

1. A pipe is used to pry an 1800 lb concrete block loose from a parking lot. If the effort is applied 108 in from the pivot and the block is 9 in from the pivot point, how much effort must be applied to the pipe?

1. _____

2. Find the mechanical advantage of the machine in problem 1.   2. _____

3. A certain wheelbarrow is 3.00 m long from the axle to the handle. If the
   wheelbarrow is used to move a 650.00 N load located 0.25 m from the
   axle, what force is needed to lift the load?   3. _____

4. What is the mechanical advantage of the wheelbarrow in problem 3?   4. _____

5. Which of the following teeter totters has a greater mechanical advantage? 5. _____
   a. A
   b. B
   c. equal

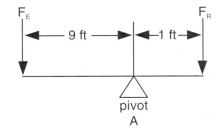
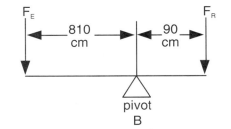

Inclined Plane

Inclined planes are used to raise objects that are too heavy to lift vertically. Examples include gangplanks, chutes, and ramps.

The Law of Simple Machines and the two Mechanical Advantage Formulas still apply.

┌───┐
| **The Law of Simple Machines: Inclined Plane** |
| |
| $(F_E)(d_E) = (F_R)(d_R)$ |
└───┘

Where F_E = Force of Effort d_E = length of the plane
               F_R = Force of Resistance d_R = height of the plane

┌───┐
| **Mechanical Advantage Formulas: Inclined Plane** |
| |
| $MA = \dfrac{F_R}{F_E}$ $MA = \dfrac{d_E}{d_R} = \dfrac{length}{height}$ |
└───┘

MA = Mechanical Advantage

Example 1: A 10 ft plank is used to help two movers push a 120 lb couch into the back of the moving van 4.5 ft above the ground. Ignoring friction, how much effort must each worker apply?

Given:

F_R = 120 lb
d_R = 4.5 ft
d_E = 10 ft
F_E = unknown

Moving

4.5 ft

10 ft

120 lb

Substitute and solve:

$(F_E)(d_E) = (F_R)(d_R)$ state the law of simple machines

$(F_E) (10 \text{ ft}) = (120 \text{ lb}) (4.5 \text{ ft})$ substitute given information

$(F_E) = \dfrac{(120 \text{ lb}) (4.5 \text{ ft})}{(10 \text{ ft})}$ divide both sides of equation by 10 lb
cancel out like units

$(F_E) = \dfrac{540 \text{ lb}}{(10)}$ multiply 120 × 4.5, then divide by 10

$F_E = 54 \text{ lb}$

Answer: Each worker must apply 27 lbs of effort (54 divided by 2)

EXERCISE 2

Directions: Apply the Law of Simple Machines or the Mechanical Advantage Formulas to solve the following problems. Solve on a separate sheet of paper and write your answers in the spaces provided.

Answers

1. A worker is using an 18.00 ft ramp to move a carton onto a platform 5.25 ft above the ground. What is the mechanical advantage of the machine?

1. _____

2. If the carton in problem 1 weighs 350.00 lb, how much effort must the worker apply?

2. _____

3. An inclined plank is 10 m long and is 2.5 m high. What is the mechanical advantage?

3. _____

4. If an effort force of 800 N is applied to an object being pushed up the plank in problem 3, what is the maximum possible weight of the object?

4. _____

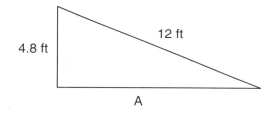

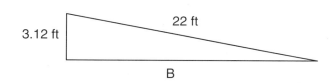

5. In the above diagrams which ramp can lift a heavier load?
   a. A
   b. B
   c. Equal

5. _____

Wheel and Axle

A Wheel and Axle consists of a wheel attached to an axle so that both turn together. Examples include bicycle sprocket, steering wheel, winch, doorknob, water faucet, screwdriver, etc. The wheel is the object to which the effort is applied and the axle is the object on which the resistance is applied. The law of Simple machines and the Mechanical Advantage Formulas still apply to the Wheel and Axle with a modification to the distance abbreviations. In place of the D_E and the D_R substitute r_w and r_a respectively

Law of Simple Machines: Wheel and Axle

$$(F_E)\,(r_w) = (F_R)\,(r_a)$$

Where:

F_E = Force of Effort
F_R = Force of Resistance

r_w = Radius of the Wheel
r_a = Radius of the Axle

Mechanical Advantage Formulas: Wheel and Axle

$$MA = \frac{F_R}{F_E} \qquad\qquad MA = \frac{r_w}{r_a}$$

MA = Mechanical Advantage

EXAMPLES:

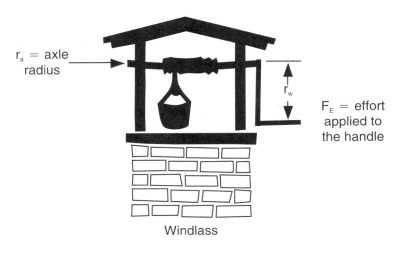

r_a = axle radius

r_w

F_E = effort applied to the handle

Windlass

Hand Drill

Sprocket

Spigot

EXERCISE 3

Directions: Apply the Law of Simple Machines or the Mechanical Advantage Formulas to solve for the unknown in the following problems:

PROBLEM #	MA	F_E	r_w	F_R	r_a
1	unknown	unknown	12"	60 lb	4"
2	3 : 1	unknown	9"	90 lb	3"
3	unknown	50 lb	unknown	125 lb	5"
4	4 : 1	20 N	2 m	unknown	unknown
5	unknown	8 N	unknown	48 N	0.6 m

6. Which windlass will require less effort?
   a. A
   b. B
   c. Equal

A

B

Screw

Think of a screw as an inclined plane wrapped around a cylinder. Examples include sheet metal screw, wood screw, and the jackscrew. The circumference of the handle where the effort force is applied is considered the Distance of Effort or the d_E. The circumference of a circle can be found by multiplying the radius times twice pi, so we will use $2 \pi r$ in place of d_E. The distance the screw advances with each revolution is called the **pitch**. The pitch of a screw is the distance between two successive threads. The pitch is the Distance of Resistance or the d_R.

Law of Simple Machines: Screw

$$(F_E)(2 \pi r) = (F_R)(pitch)$$

Where:
   F_E = Force of Effort $d_E = 2 \pi r$ = Circumference of the handle
   F_R = Force of Resistance d_R = pitch = Distance between two successive threads

---

Mechanical Advantage: Screw

$$MA = \frac{F_R}{F_E} \qquad\qquad MA = \frac{2 \pi r}{pitch}$$

MA = Mechanical Advantage

EXAMPLES:

Screw

Corkscrew

Scissor Jack

Directions: Use the Law of Simple Machines or the Mechanical Advantage Formulas as they apply to a screw to solve for the unknown in the following problems:

PROBLEM #	MA	F_E	$2 \pi r$	F_R	PITCH
1	unknown	unknown	15"	300 lb	.25"
2	unknown	5.00 N	5.50mm	20.00 N	unknown
3	unknown	20 lb	60"	unknown	5"
4	10:1	50 lb	20"	unknown	unknown

Pulley

A pulley is a wheel with a grooved rim, into which a rope is fitted, that turns on an axle and is supported in a frame. Pulleys can be used individually or in sets. It can be attached to a fixed object or it may be fastened to the resistance that is to be moved. If the pulley is attached to a fixed object, it is called a **fixed pulley**. If the pulley is fastened to the resistance, the pulley is called a **movable pulley**.

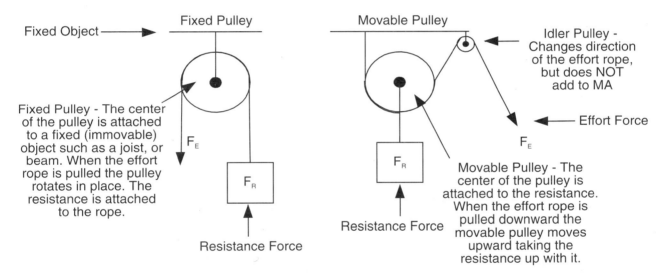

Example 1: How many fixed and movable pulleys are in the pulley system below?

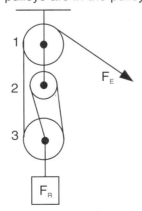

Answer: There are 2 fixed pulleys. The centers of pulleys 1 and 2 are attached to a fixed object. They do not move when force is applied to the effort rope. There is one movable pulley. The center of pulley 3 is attached to the resistance and will move upward when force is applied to the effort rope.

Example 2: How many fixed and movable pulleys are in the pulley system below?

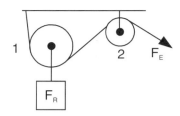

Answer: There are 0 fixed pulleys. Even though the center of pulley 2 is attached to a fixed object it is considered an idler pulley. The function of the idler pulley is to change the direction of the effort rope. In this case it is easier to pull the rope down rather than up. The idler pulley does not add any mechanical advantage to the system, whereas a true fixed pulley would add to the mechanical advantage. There is one movable pulley. The center of pulley 1 is attached to the resistance and will move upward when force is applied to the effort rope.

EXERCISE 5

Using the definitions for fixed and movable pulleys, count the number of fixed and/or movable pulleys in the following diagrams. Place your answers in the spaces provided.

1. # fixed = _____

   # movable = _____

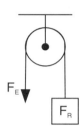

2. # fixed = _____

   # movable = _____

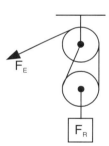

3. # fixed = _____

   # movable = _____

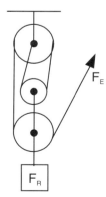

4. # fixed = _____

   # movable = _____

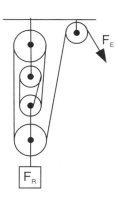

5. # fixed = _____

   # movable = _____

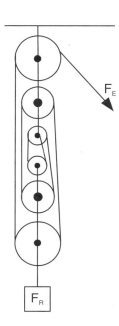

6. # fixed = _____

   # movable = _____

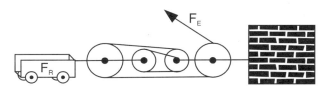

7. # fixed = _____

   # movable = _____

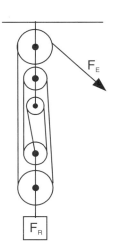

8. # fixed = _____

   # movable = _____

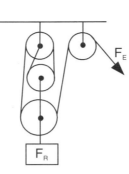

9. # fixed = _____

   # movable = _____

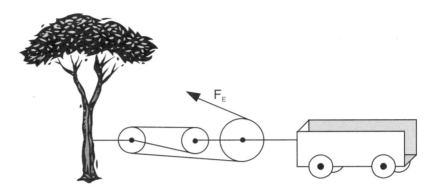

10. # fixed = _____

    # movable = _____

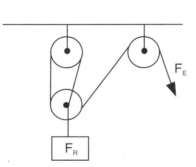

CALCULATIONS OF A PULLEY SYSTEM

The law of simple machines applies to pulleys in its basic format:

$$(F_E)(d_E) = (F_R)(d_R)$$

d_E = length of rope pulled out by the force of effort

d_R = height the load is lifted

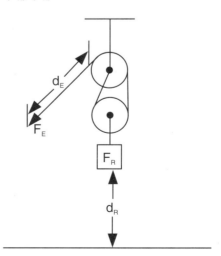

The mechanical advantage formulas also apply:

$$MA = \frac{F_R}{F_E} \qquad\qquad MA = \frac{d_E}{d_R}$$

However, when one continuous cable is used, as in a pulley system, mechanical advantage can be determined by counting the number of ropes directly supporting the load F_R.

Using # of Support Ropes to Determine MA of a Pulley System
MA of a pulley system = number of support ropes holding the resistance

Step 1: Draw a line crossing the ropes between the last fixed and the first movable pulley. The number of ropes the line crosses equals MA of the system.

Step 2: If the effort rope is pulled towards the fixed object it gets counted in the MA. If the effort rope is pulled away from the fixed object it does NOT add to the MA.

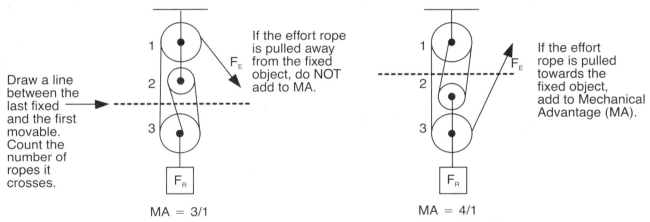

Draw a line between the last fixed and the first movable. Count the number of ropes it crosses.

If the effort rope is pulled away from the fixed object, do NOT add to MA.

MA = 3/1

If the effort rope is pulled towards the fixed object, add to Mechanical Advantage (MA).

MA = 4/1

EXERCISE 6

Calculate the mechanical advantage of the pulley systems drawn in Exercise 5.

1. MA = _____

2. MA = _____

3. MA = _____

4. MA = _____

5. MA = _____

6. MA = _____

7. MA = _____

8. MA = _____

9. MA = _____

10. MA = _____

EXERCISE 7

Answer the following using the pulley systems drawn in Exercise 5.

1. The pulley set drawn in problem 4 is used to lift a 500 N load. How much effort must be applied?

2. Compare the pulley set in problem 5 to the pulley set in problem 7. Which set requires less effort? Which set will lift the load higher?

Wedge

The friction generated between surfaces should be considered when a wedge is used to do work. For example an axe blade encounters friction when it is used to chop wood. Calculations must include the friction factor of the wedge and the material of which the load is made. Since different materials have different friction coefficients it is impractical at this stage to compute mechanical advantage and the law of simple machines for a wedge.

Gear Trains And Belt- Driven Pulleys

While neither are one of the six simple machines, gear trains and belt driven pulleys are included here because you are likely to encounter them on some mechanical comprehension tests.

When two gears mesh, they turn in opposite directions. If gear A turns clockwise, then gear B turns counterclockwise.

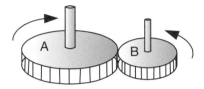

If a third gear is inserted between the two gears, then gear A and B turn in the same direction while gear X turns in the opposite direction. Gears A and B turn clockwise and gear X turns counterclockwise.

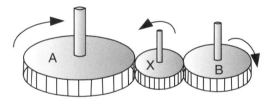

LAW TO DETERMINE GEAR ROTATION

Count the number of **SHAFTS**

If the number of shafts is **Even** then the first and last gears turn in **Opposite** directions
If the number of shafts is **Odd** then the first and last gears turn in the **Same** direction

---

EXAMPLE 1: If gear A turns counterclockwise, give the gear directions for:

Gear B = _____
Gear C = _____
Gear D = _____

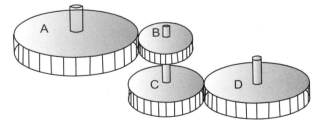

Answers:

      Gear B = clockwise (number of shafts from gear A to B is 2, which is even, so it turns in the opposite direction as gear A)

      Gear C = clockwise (it is physically fixed to the same shaft as B, so it must turn in the same direction as gear B)

      Gear D = counterclockwise (number of shafts from gear A to D is 3, which is odd, so it turns in the same direction as gear A)

Determine the gear directions for the following gear trains. You may use the abbreviations CW for Clockwise and CCW for Counterclockwise:

1. Gear A = Clockwise
   Gear B = _____
   Gear C = _____
   Gear D = _____

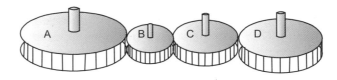

2. Gear A = clockwise
   Gear B = _____
   Gear C = _____
   Gear D = _____

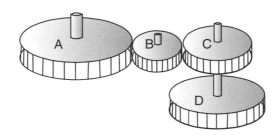

3. Gear A = Counterclockwise
   Gear B = _____
   Gear C = _____
   Gear D = _____
   Gear E = _____
   Gear F = _____

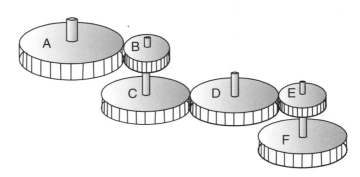

4. Gear X = Clockwise
   Gear A = _____
   Gear B = _____

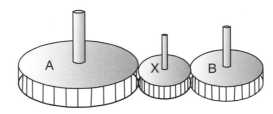

5. If gear A turns in the direction shown, gear C will turn in which direction X or Y? _____

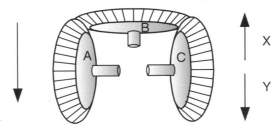

BELT-DRIVEN PULLEYS

LAW TO DETERMINE PULLEY ROTATION

Count the number of **TWISTS** in the belt

If the number of twists is **Even** then the pulleys turn in **Same** direction
If the number of twists is **Odd** then the pulleys turn in the **Opposite** direction

*Notice that this is the opposite of the gear rotation formula.

No twists in the belt, the pulleys turn in the same direction. No need to count open or non-twisted belts.

One twist, one is an odd number, the pulleys turn in opposite directions.

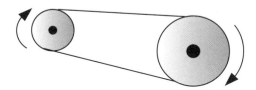
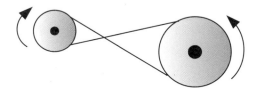

EXAMPLE 1:

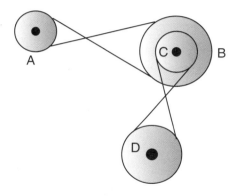

If A is turning clockwise, then:

B is turning counterclockwise
C is turning counterclockwise (fixed to B)
D is turning clockwise

EXERCISE 9

Determine the pulley direction:

1. If A is turning counterclockwise, in what direction is gear D turning?

    Gear D = _____

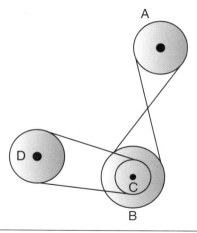

2. Find the direction of pulley D if pulley A is turning clockwise.

Gear D = _____

3. If pulley A is turning clockwise, find the direction of:

Pulley B = _____
Pulley C = _____
Pulley D = _____
Pulley E = _____
Pulley F = _____

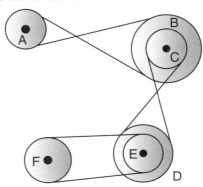

4. If pulley A is turning in the direction shown, which pulley(s) are turning in the same direction as pulley A?

_____

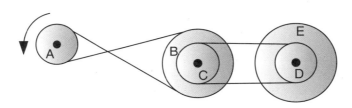

5. If pulley A is turning clockwise, name the pulley(s) that are turning counterclockwise. _____

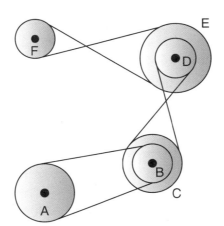

TIME: 10 minutes

Answer

1. Which direction will pulley X be going?
   a. Same as B
   b. Same as C
   c. Same as A
   d. Same as B and C

1. _____

2. Which pulley will turn fastest?
   a. Pulley A
   b. Pulley B
   c. Pulley C
   d. Pulley D

2. _____

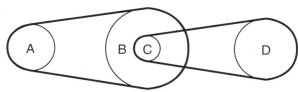

3. Which holds more?
   a. Container A
   b. Container B
   c. Equal

3. _____

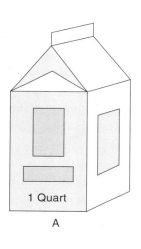

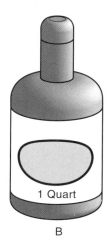

A

B

4. In which direction will boat M go if the two boats collide at point X?
   a. A
   b. B
   c. C
   d. D

4. _____

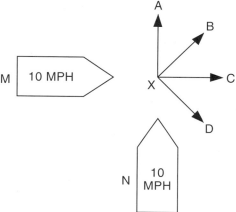

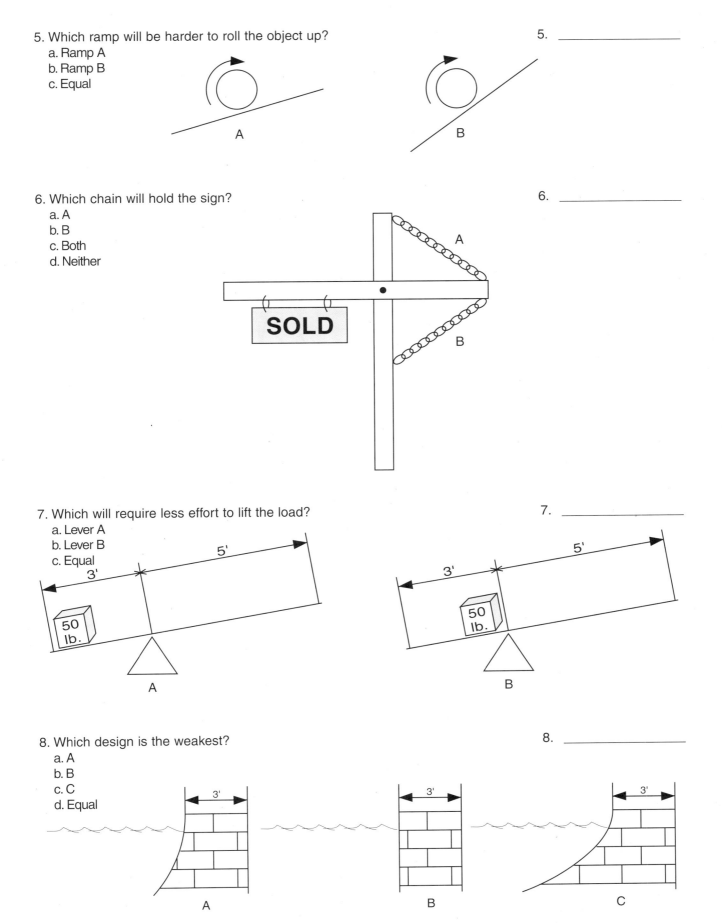

5. Which ramp will be harder to roll the object up?
   a. Ramp A
   b. Ramp B
   c. Equal

5. _____

6. Which chain will hold the sign?
   a. A
   b. B
   c. Both
   d. Neither

6. _____

SOLD

7. Which will require less effort to lift the load?
   a. Lever A
   b. Lever B
   c. Equal

7. _____

8. Which design is the weakest?
   a. A
   b. B
   c. C
   d. Equal

8. _____

9. Which gauge will read the highest pressure?
    a. A
    b. B
    c. C
    d. Equal

9. _____

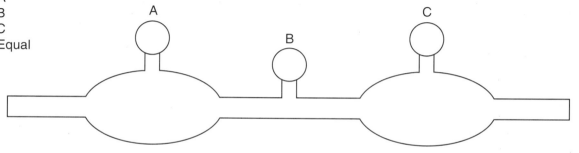

10. Which pulley system will lift the load easier?
    a. A
    b. B
    c. Equal

10. _____

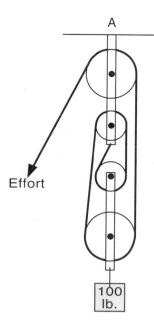

Effort

100 lb.

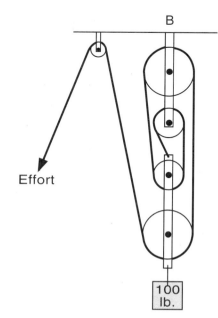

Effort

100 lb.

11. Which of the following shows the correct position once the object comes to rest?
    a. A
    b. B
    c. C
    d. All

11. _____

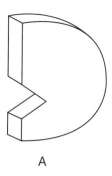

A

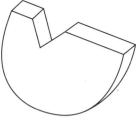

B

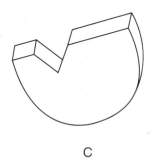

C

12. Which point on the record is moving fastest:
    a. A
    b. B
    c. C
    d. Equal

12. _____

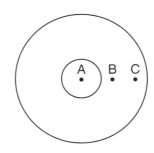

13. Which pulley system will lift the load the highest?
    a. A
    b. B
    c. Equal

13. _____

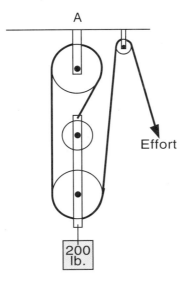

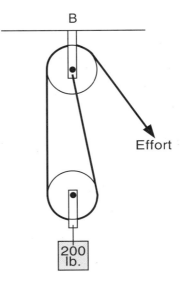

14. Which weighs more?
    a. A
    b. B
    c. Equal

14. _____

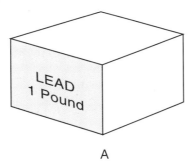

15. At which point will an object weigh more?
    a. A
    b. B
    c. Both A & B are equal

15. _____

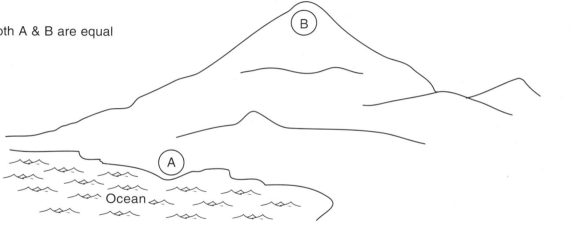

16. Which will roll the farthest?
    a. A
    b. B
    c. Equal

16. _____

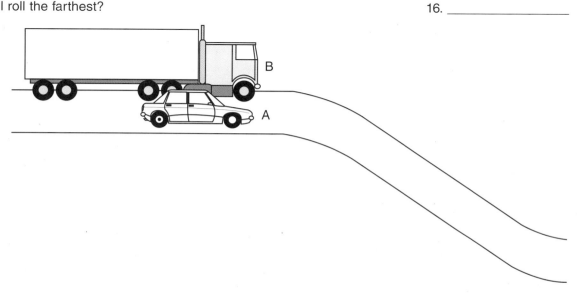

17. If the 3 men push equally on the ball, in which direction is it most likely to roll?
    a. A
    b. B
    c. C

17. _____

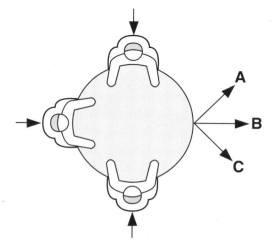

18. Which container will have the greatest pressure at the bottom of the container? 18. _____

a. A
b. B
c. C
d. Equal

A

B

C

19. If each hole is equally spaced, in which hole should the 8 pound weight be placed to balance the 6 pound weight? 19. _____

a. 1
b. 2
c. 3
d. 4

8 lb.

6 lb.

20. If the cars are identical, which jack will be harder to use? 20. _____

a. A
b. B
c. Equal

A

B

21. Which car is stopping abruptly from a forward motion? 21. _____

a. A
b. B
c. Neither

A

B

22. Which gear is rotating in the same direction as gear D?
    a. A
    b. B
    c. Neither

22. _____

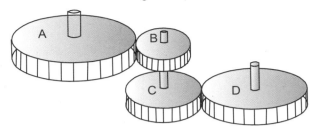

23. Which direction is the plane going to go?
    a. A
    b. B
    c. C

23. _____

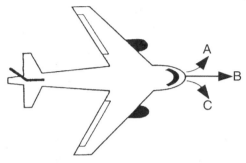

24. At which elevation will a cake baked from a cake mix require a higher oven temperature?
    a. A
    b. B
    c. C

24. _____

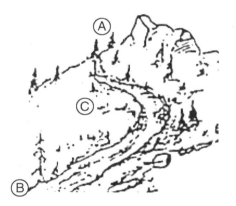

25. Which windlass will be able to lift a heavier load?
    a. A
    b. B
    c. equal

25. _____

A   B

CHAPTER 14

Technical Reading

It may surprise you to know that the skilled trades require reading skills beyond what you learned in school. Technical reading is more difficult than general reading because of the specialized vocabulary required to read diagrams, charts, blueprints, schematics, tables, and graphs. Consequently, many apprenticeship entry exams include the reading and analyzing of technical charts and graphs in order to solve problems.

Reading in the skilled trades is fundamental to being a successful tradesperson. It starts with reading a ruler (Chapter 4) and progresses to reading blueprints and being able to visualize objects in 3-dimensions (Chapter 10). Reading is required to understand job specifications in order to estimate and prepare job quotes. Purchase orders must be read before materials can be ordered and work can begin. Not all trades test for reading skills, but those that do require a demonstration of your ability to read technical material. The following is a description of two of the more commonly used charts and graphs and how to interpret the data that they provide.

Bar Graphs

Bar graphs are used to compare data. The vertical axis (Y-axis) measures the items being compared. The horizontal axis (X-axis) is for the units being measured. Examples include time, dates, etc. The Y-axis values increase at regular intervals, i.e.: 5, 10, 15, 20, etc. Bar graphs may be vertical or horizontal.

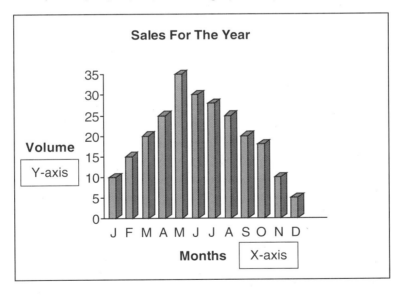

Based on the above bar graph you can begin to make several observations:

1. The graph measures sales volume over a one year period of time
2. Sales are best during the summer months.
3. Sales decline during the winter months.
4. The best month for sales is May.
5. The worst month for sales is December.

Line Graphs

Line graphs are used to show change or trends over time. The vertical (Y-axis) shows change that occurs and the horizontal (X-axis) measures time.

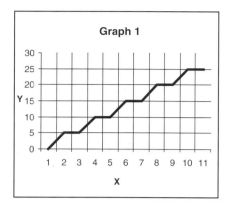

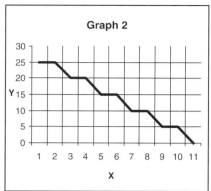

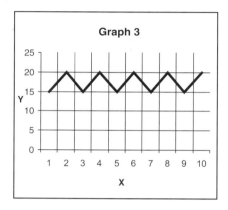

Based on the above line graphs you can make several obserations:

1. Graph #1 shows an increasing trend.
2. Graph #2 shows a decreasing trend.
3. Graph #3 shows variation but no change in the trend.

How To Read A Graph

A graph is information presented in picture form. It enables us to see information rather than having to read tables of data. The following steps will help you understand the information presented in a graph and will help you answer technical questions on the apprenticeship test:

1. First read the title of the graph.
2. Read to understand the scales along the graphís sides (X and Y axis).
3. Determine the units of measurement.
4. Examine the graph for patterns, differences, and trends.

TIME: 5 Minutes

Use the above graph to answer questions 1-5 below:

1. The information given in the chart can best be described as:
    a. Total number of people employed in manufacturing jobs in the U.S. for the years 2003 and 2004 month-by-month.
    b. New positions available in manufacturing jobs in the U.S. for the years 2003 and 2004 month-by-month.
    c. The gain or loss in the number of manufacturing jobs in the U.S. for the years 2003 and 2004 month-by-month.
    d. The loss of jobs due to overseas competition in manufacturing jobs in the U.S. for the years 2003 and 2004 month-by-month.
    e. None of these

2. Which month and year shows the greatest decline in manufacturing employment?
    a. 04/2003
    b. 04/2004
    c. 02/2003
    d. 02/2004
    e. None of these

3. Would you say that the increases in employment for the year 2004 make up for the losses sustained in 2003?
    a. YES
    b. NO

4. Approximately how many manufacturing jobs were gained or lost in August of 2004?
    a. 250,000 gained
    b. 25,000 lost
    c. 250 gained
    d. 2,500 lost
    e. None of these

5. Which of the following statements can be concluded from the graph?
    a. There was a gradual decrease in the number of people employed in manufacturing jobs for the year 2003.
    b. There were 60 fewer people employed in manufacturing jobs in May of 2003.
    c. The number of people employed in manufacturing jobs in June of 2003 was greater than the number of people employed in manufacturing jobs for the same month in 2004.
    d. Every month in the year 2003 shows a loss of employment in manufacturing jobs.
    e. None of these

EXERCISE 2

TIME: 6 Minutes

FREEZER PACK TEST

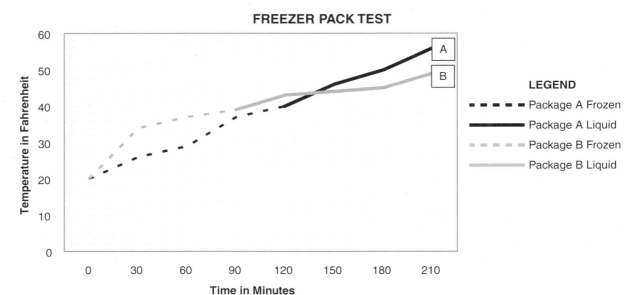

Use the above drawing to answer the following questions 1-5:

1. What was the temperature of package A at the start of the test?
    a. 0° F
    b. 10° F
    c. 15° F
    d. The same as Package B
    e. None of the above

2. At what time did Package B become liquid?
    a. 30 minutes after Package A liquefied
    b. 30 minutes before Package A liquefied
    c. At the same time Package A liquefied
    d. 2 hours after the start of the test
    e. None of the above

3. At what temperature does the Package A line cross over the Package B line?
    a. Between 40° F and 50° F
    b. Between 30° F and 40° F
    c. Between 120° F and 150° F
    d. 10° F below the freezing point of Package A
    e. None of the above

4. Package B shows the sharpest increase in temperature between what two time increments?
    a. 0 - 30 minutes
    b. 30 - 60 minutes
    c. 1 hour - 1 hour 30 minutes
    d. 1 hour 30 minutes - 2 hours
    e. None of the above

5. In general, which statement best applies to the test?
    a. Package A stays colder than Package B after 3 hours
    b. You can assume that the Freezer packs were set out at room temperature for the duration of the test
    c. Package A is the better Freezer Pack
    d. Package A and Package B do not contain the same concentration of coolant
    e. Not enough information is given to conclude which Freezer Pack is the best

Reading and Solving Story Problems

Technical reading problems on an apprenticeship test may be presented in several formats. You may be asked to interpret a graph as in exercise 1 and 2 or problems may be presented in a story or combination of story and graph format. Success on the apprentice test requires adapting a reading strategy tailored to solving the type of technical problem presented.

The following seven-step strategy will help you to organize your approach:

1. Identify what the problem is asking you to do by reading the questions first.
2. Scan the problem including any visuals before reading the content.
3. Read the story problems carefully and underline the key facts.
4. Answer any obvious questions first.
5. With multiple choice questions, narrow your choices by eliminating any obvious wrong answers.
7. Skip any uncertain or difficult problems and return to them if you have time.

EXERCISE 3

Time: 6 Minutes

COMMON NAILS

The success of most construction projects depends on using the right nails. Read the following paragraphs and study the chart before answering questions 1 through 6.

A common nail is used most often in wood construction when two pieces must be fastened together. The nail size and shape are important. The shaft of the common nail is thick, making it easy to drive without bending; the head is broad, preventing the nail from pulling through and groves on the shaft keep the nail from pulling loose.

When ordering common nails, you use the term penny for length. The symbol "d" stands for penny. A tradesperson ordering eight-penny nails will write "8d nails". Each penny designation refers to the length, shaft diameter, head size and weight. For example, an order for 10 pounds of 20d common nails will always mean 300 nails that are 4 inches long.

The chart below can be used to obtain length, estimate the number of nails per pound and determine the proper nail for the job. The length of the nail should be at least two times the thickness of the board being nailed. A board that is one inch thick requires a nail that is at least two inches long. For structural integrity and safety, it is important that the nail does not protrude through the pieces being fastened together. The chart below shows that anything less than a 6d nail would be too short to nail a one-inch thick board.

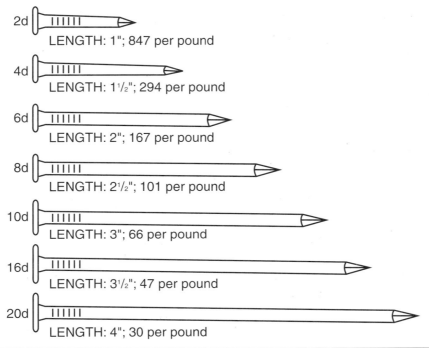

2d — LENGTH: 1"; 847 per pound

4d — LENGTH: 1½"; 294 per pound

6d — LENGTH: 2"; 167 per pound

8d — LENGTH: 2½"; 101 per pound

10d — LENGTH: 3"; 66 per pound

16d — LENGTH: 3½"; 47 per pound

20d — LENGTH: 4"; 30 per pound

Use the preceding paragraphs and chart to answer the following multiple choice questions:

1. How many nails would you get in two pounds of 8d common nails?
   a. 167 nails
   b. 202 nails
   c. 61 nails
   d. 1,010 nails

2. When ordering ten penny nails, you would write:
   a. 10 nails
   b. 10 pounds of nails
   c. 10 common nails
   d. 10d nails

3. You need to nail a board that is 1" thick. What size nails would be best to use?
   a. 2d
   b. 4d
   c. 6d
   d. None of the above

4. Which word best describes a common nail?
   a. Inexpensive
   b. Scarce
   c. Foreign
   d. None of the above

5. Grooves in a common nail are important because:
   a. They don't bend easily
   b. The head is broad
   c. They prevent the nail from pulling loose
   d. All of the above

6. A 10d nail should be used to fasten a _____" board
   a. 3"
   b. 4"
   c. 1½"
   d. 1"

EXERCISE 4

Time: 6 Minutes

WHERE DOES ELECTRICITY COME FROM?

Where does electricity come from? Some of you may smartly reply, "Electricity comes from the outlet in the wall". If only it was that simple! Let us dig deeper into the making of the electrical power that we take for granted. Electricity is a property of atoms, so to understand where electricity comes from; you will need a general knowledge of atoms.

Atoms are the building blocks of all matter. Everything from the book you are reading to the air you are breathing is made up of millions of tiny atoms. Atoms contain several types of electrically charged particles whose structure can be compared to a miniature solar system. An atom contains a large central core (like our sun) called the nucleus. Orbiting around the nucleus are tiny negatively ($-$) charged particles called electrons. There is a lot of empty space between the nucleus and the orbiting electrons. The nucleus contains two types of particles; neutrons which have no electrical charge (thus the name neutrons for neutral), and protons which have one unit of positive ($+$) charge each. The electrons orbiting the nucleus are much smaller in size than the neutrons and protons, but have equally as strong a negative electrical charge as the proton has in positive charge. When equal numbers of protons and electrons are found in an atom their charges cancel or balance each others effect to give the atom an overall zero charge. Atoms can be made to lose or gain electrons, which offsets the electrical balance of charges. Atoms with more electrons than protons are said to have a negative overall charge, and atoms with fewer electrons than protons are said to posses a positive charge. Materials made with these charged atoms have electrical potential, which means that they have the ability to produce electricity.

So how do you make atoms give up electrons? There are three ways to make an atom lose electron(s) and, thus, gain an overall electrical positive charge. The first method is friction; rub off the outer orbiting electron(s). The second method is chemical action. The third method involves the use of magnets and wire. These are the three methods used to generate electrical power.

The term static means stationary or non-moving, so, static electricity is non-moving electricity. Static electricity is produced by friction. As two materials rub together electrons are rubbed off from one substance and are picked up by the other substance. You have probably used this technique as a child to make a rubber balloon "stick" to a wall by rubbing it on your hair (your hair picked up a charge too). Sliding across leather car seats in a nylon suit, or walking across a wool rug also generates static electricity from friction. Walking across a wool rug generates friction between your shoes and the rug. Electrons are rubbed off the carpet, so the carpet takes on a positive charge. Your body picks up the electrons removed from the carpet, so your body gains a negative charge. Your body holds that charge (static) until it can be transferred by contact with another object. The sudden release of charge from your body is the static discharge or shock. Lightning is another form of static discharge when huge numbers of atoms become charged. Lightning is generated when rain clouds move rapidly through the atmosphere. The lightning bolt is the immense release of static charge.

Dry cells, lead storage batteries, and all sorts of chemical batteries use chemical action to produce large numbers of free electrons at the negative pole. When the negative pole of a battery is connected to the positive terminal via a conductor (wire), electrical current "flows" through the circuit due to the attraction of unlike charges and the imbalance of charges (electromotive force) of the poles from the chemical action. Batteries produce a current that flows in one direction. Electrical current that flows in one direction is known as direct current or DC.

Motors, meters, generators, transformers, and electromagnets all produce electricity from magnets and wires. As the magnetic fields of the magnet "cut" across a coil of wire the atoms in the wire become electrically charged and flow in the wire. In the devices mentioned one of two methods are applied; either a coil of wire rotates around a stationary magnet, or a magnet rotates inside a coil of wire. In either case the north pole of the magnet generates electrical current in one direction and the south pole causes the current to reverse and flow in the opposite direction. The direction of the flow of atoms in the conductor alternates as the north then the south magnetic fields cut the coil of wire. This is called alternating current. The electricity in your home is probably generated by the use of a magnetic core surrounded by a coil of wire.

1. What are the 3 types of particles found in atoms?
   a. Orbits, core, and charges
   b. Protons, nucleus, and electrons
   c. Matter, space, and nucleus
   d. Protons, neutrons, and electrons
   e. None of the above

2. A proton has a single unit of _____ charge and an electron has a single unit of _____ charge.
   a. Neutral, positive
   b. Negative, positive
   c. Positive, negative
   d. Negative, neutral
   e. None of the above

3. Lightning is a form of _____ electricity.
   a. Chemical
   b. Solar
   c. Alternating
   d. Magnetic
   e. None of the above

4. Batteries generate electricity from _____.
   a. Chemical action
   b. Friction
   c. Magnets and wires
   d. Transformers
   e. All of the above

5. The article mentioned which three methods commonly used to separate electrons from atoms to generate electrically charged particles?
   a. Chemical, nuclear, and atomic
   b. Solar, magnetic, and lightning
   c. Hydraulic, static, and nuclear
   d. Friction, chemical, and magnets and wires
   e. All of the above

15 Test-Taking Techniques

Preparation for the Test

Test-taking is a skill that can be learned. There is no magic in learning how to take tests - just hard work. If you have studied the material in this text, you are already ahead of the game. Your chances for success have been increased because you know what to expect.

A major reason for poor test performance is fear. To be afraid is natural when facing the unknown, but you know what to expect. You have studied the material, and you are adequately prepared. You are going to pass the examination because you have taken the time to study the kinds of things usually found on apprenticeship tests.

Preparation for a test begins with the development of a proper mental attitude. You must understand the purpose of the test and what it is trying to measure. Self-understanding will allow you to think positively about the test. Tests are not devices to trick you; they are trying to measure what you know. Approach the test positively. Rid yourself of any negative attitudes and you will surely do a better job.

TIP ONE

Think positively; get rid of any negative attitudes about tests. Approach the test with confidence and assurance because you are adequately prepared.

The proper frame of mind can do wonders, but not miracles. You must review and study in preparation for an exam. It is important that you not wait until the last minute to cram for the exam. Start your review about a week in advance and slowly build up steam. It is a good idea to study with a group. The group should be kept small, probably not more than four. Finally, a review of your notes on the day before the exam should conclude your study.

TIP TWO

Study and review, but don't cram for an exam.

Cramming in itself is isn't harmful; it's what it does to your mind and body that hurts your test performance. Imagine what staying up all night does to your mental and physical condition. Get sufficient rest, eat properly and plan exercise and recreation before a test. Keep your mind and body in top condition, and you won't have to worry about poor test performance because your "mind just didn't seem to work."

TIP THREE

Before a test get plenty of rest, eat properly, and keep you mind and body in top condition.

Now you are ready for the test. You have the proper mental attitude, your study is complete, and you are physically and mentally alert. Understanding the following rules will help your test performance.

TIP FOUR

Arrive early and get a good seat. Check the lighting and ventilation. Find a comfortable seat near the front so you can hear the directions.

TIP FIVE

Relax; try to eliminate any tenseness. Loosen your collar and clear your desk of anything that might distract you. Think positively about another time when you were very successful. If necessary, breathe deeply to get fresh oxygen to the brain.

TIP SIX

Listen carefully so that you understand the directions. If there is anything you don't understand, ask the person giving the test. Remember, once the test starts questions will not be allowed.

TIP SEVEN

Before you start, understand how the test is to be scored. Some test have a correction factor which penalizes for incorrect guessing. You should know if there is a correction factor, what it is, and if the odds favor an educated guess.

TIP EIGHT

Some tests are designed so that you are not expected to finish. Find out what the time limits are and pace yourself accordingly.

TIP NINE

Timed test require both accuracy and speed. One without the other will result in a poor score. Work as fast and as accurately as possible. don't get hung up on a difficult question; skip it, and if you have time, go back to it later.

TIP TEN

Find out if different parts of the test are weighted to give extra points. Some tests give more credit for the more difficult questions.

TIP ELEVEN

When the test starts, make sure that your answer sheet is arranged so that you don't have to make any unnecessary moves. Place your answer sheet as close to the test question as possible. This eliminates searching for a place to put your answer, and it saves time.

TIP TWELVE

Make sure you follow directions. If the test requires true and false questions to be answered with a "T" or "F", then don't take the time to spell them out. Some tests are also graded according to how you follow directions.

TIP THIRTEEN

Be careful not to make careless mistakes. If time allows, proofread for simple mistakes. If you're uncertain, don't change the answer - your first guess is probably correct.

TIP FOURTEEN

Don't become fatigued! Relax occasionally and release stress by taking your eyes off your paper.

TIP FIFTEEN

Ask the test administrator if they will let you know when the time is about to expire. This will give you time to guess at any unanswered questions.

TIP SIXTEEN

Don't guess haphazardly. Whenever possible, try to eliminate answers you're certain are wrong, then make an educated guess from the remaining answers.

Using a process of elimination, you can improve the odds.

TIP SEVENTEEN

Multiple choice tests usually instruct you to select the **best** answer. If all of the answers are incorrect, select the one that is closest to correct.

TIP EIGHTEEN

When guessing, consider all of the following:
1. Your first guess is usually correct.
2. Complex answers are usually wrong.
3. Make sure you pick a plural word if a question asks for a plural answer, or a singular word when a question asks for a singular response.
4. When a question uses limiting words like all, never, must, seldom, etc. The best answer is usually false.
5. When general terms like some, usually, could, might, etc. are used, the best guess is usually true.
6. Exaggerated answers are most likely false.

TIP NINETEEN

Answer as many questions as possible. Work as fast and as accurately as you can, and don't pay attention to what the other people are doing. If time permits reread the directions and double check your answers.

Test-taking is a skill that can be learned. It requires patience, persistence, and lots of practice. This text has been designed to give you the practice. If you have stayed with it to the bitter end, you have learned patience. Persistence means not giving up. If your first attempt at taking the apprenticeship test doesn't produce positive results, don't give up. Find out what your weakness is and seek to correct it. Separate classes in each of the areas covered in this text are available through most local adult education programs and community colleges. It may take longer, but the end result will be worth the effort.

16

The Apprenticeship Selection Interview

Not all apprenticeship applicants that complete an apprenticeship test receive an interview. Some companies only interview the top test scoring candidates. If you do well on the apprentice selection test, it is important that you carefully prepare for the interview. This chapter is designed to give you an idea of what to expect.

The apprenticeship interview is usually conducted by an employer or a joint apprenticeship committee. The committee represents both labor and management. They have responsibility to interview and select the most qualified applicants for the job without regard to their race, sex, religion, national origin, disability or sexual orientation. Usually, the interview is conducted by people with experience in the trade for which the interview is being conducted. Given the highly competitive nature of the apprenticeship selection process, it is to your advantage to prepare for the interview so that you present yourself in the best possible way.

Preparing For The Interview

The apprenticeship interview will usually include three broad areas. It is your responsibility to come to the interview prepared to discuss each of the following topics:

1. Previous education and training – be sure to bring all transcripts, diplomas, and certificates of completion from high school, college, military service or any other work-related training programs.

2. Prior related work experience– compile a list of your work experience that includes any full or part-time jobs and obtain letters from former or current employers that highlight the following information:

   • Job duties performed
   • List of tools and machinery used
   • Time on the job
   • Current and previous employer's name, address and phone number

   Be sure to include any experience with farm equipment, hobbies, community service, self-employment and volunteer work such as building homes for Habitat for Humanity.

3. Knowledge of the trade(s) - first, do some research. Learn as much as you can about the trade and the employer to whom you are applying:

   • Search the Internet by trade and potential employers
   • Learn the proper names for the tools and equipment
   • Learn about the job requirements and working conditions
   • Interview journeypersons to learn about the work content and safety requirements
   • Be prepared to answer specific questions about the trade and its requirements.

The Actual Interview

First impressions are important so it's necessary to be on time, dress appropriately for the situation and follow the interviewer's lead. A firm hand shake while looking directly at the interviewer starts the process. Always wait for the interviewer to offer their hand first, and wait to be offered a chair before you sit. If you are female, don't hesitate to offer your hand to a male interviewer. If you are seated before the interviewer enters the room, always rise and greet the interviewer with a smile.

The interview is intended to help evaluate your qualifications for the job. Consequently, it is important that you present yourself in a positive, organized manner, lead with a positive attitude and don't be afraid to sell yourself as a competent and qualified potential employee. Be open and honest in all of your answers, but be able to conclude any negative answers on a positive note. For example, if you don't have a high school diploma, say so, but be able to add, "However, I have since received my GED and I have successfully completed several adult education courses."

It is also important in the interview to listen carefully to the interviewer's questions. This is your chance to show that you are a good listener by responding directly to the questions asked. If you're unsure, it's alright to ask the interviewer to clarify or rephrase the question. This sometimes gives you time to organize your thoughts before responding.

During the interview be relaxed, but maintain good eye contact and sit up straight in your chair. Don't make the interviewer drag questions out of you. Respond with more than a Yes or No by adding details that fit the trade or the skills required by the job. For example: if asked "What was your favorite class in high school?" Explain what your favorite class was and how it helped prepare you for the skilled trades.

The primary purpose of the interview is to learn about your qualifications for a skilled trades apprenticeship. A secondary purpose is to provide you with information about the job for which you are applying. Consequently, most interviewers will allow time for your questions about the job or hiring process. You can demonstrate your organizational skills by having prepared a short list of questions that you would like to have answered. Don't, however, waste the interviewer's time with frivolous questions.

Anticipating Questions During The Interview

To help prepare for the interview, make a list of the kinds of questions that you would ask if you were going to hire a skilled trades apprentice. Begin by thinking about the qualifications and job responsibilities of the trade or trades for which you are applying and make a list of questions that you can practice answering. Your list should include some general questions such as the following:

- Why are you applying for a skilled trades apprenticeship?
- What are your qualifications for the trade or trades?
- Describe your ideal job. What parts of the job did you most enjoy?
- What courses have you had that helped to prepare you for the trades?
- What work experience have you had related to the trades?
- What type of tools, equipment or machinery have you had experience with?
- Do you prefer to work alone or with others?
- What are your major strengths and weaknesses?
- Why are you interested in working for this company and/or trade?
- Do you prefer to work indoors or outside?
- Are you able to move if the job requires it?
- Describe any hobbies you have that may be related to the skilled trades.
- Do you have any questions that you would like me/us to answer?

It is alright to be a little nervous when the interview starts. Most interviewers understand and usually will ask some icebreaker questions to calm you down. Remember that this is your chance to show your qualifications, preparedness and readiness for the job. The more prepared you are, the better you will do!

Following Directions

It is extremely important that you follow all directions exactly as they are given. Some employers will eliminate you from consideration if directions aren't carried out to the letter. Apprenticeships are highly sought after jobs with as many as twenty applicants for every opening. The competition is tough but the reward of a satisfying, good paying job is worth the effort.

Formulas

Perimeter of any polygon	$P = s_1 + s_2 + s_3 + ...$
Perimeter of an equilateral triangle	$P = 3s$
Perimeter of a rectangle	$P = 2w + 2L$
Perimater of a square	$P = 4s$
Area of a triangle	$A = \dfrac{bh}{2}$
Area of a rectangle	$A = bh$
Area of a square	$A = s^2$
Circular measure	$r = \dfrac{D}{2}$ or $2r = D$
Circumference of a circle	$C = \pi D$ or $C = 2\pi r$
Area of a circle	$A = \pi r^2$
Volume of a square	$v = s^3$
Volume of a rectangle	$v = lwh$
Pythagorean Theorem	$c^2 = a^2 + b^2$ (for right triangle only)
Gear and Belt driven pulley Proportion	$\dfrac{Speed_1}{Speed_2} = \dfrac{Size_2}{Size_1}$
Speed	$Speed = \dfrac{distance}{time}$
Total internal angles of any closed polygon	$(\text{\# sides} - 2)(180°)$
Mechanical Advantage	$MA = \dfrac{d_E}{d_R}$
Mechanical Advantage	$MA = \dfrac{F_R}{F_E}$
Simple Machines	$F_R \cdot d_R = F_E \cdot d_E$
Gear Direction	Count the number of Shafts # Shafts ODD = Same direction # Shafts EVEN = Opposite direction
Belt Driven Pulleys	Count the number of belt twists # twists ODD = Opposite direction # twists EVEN = Same direction

Pre-Apprentice Answer Key

CHAPER 2 - PAGE 5 EXERCISE 1

1. 12	4. 16	7. 13	10. 11
2. 11	5. 17	8. 16	
3. 11	6. 11	9. 12	

PAGE 6 EXERCISE 2

1. 19	4. 28	7. 36	10. 25
2. 24	5. 28	8. 37	11. 46
3. 17	6. 31	9. 25	12. 33

PAGE 7 EXERCISE 3

1. 43	7. 127	13. 63	19. 53	25. 232,976
2. 33	8. 131	14. 111	20. 131	26. 280,346
3. 39	9. 99	15. 105	21. 146	27. 289,263
4. 102	10. 101	16. 93	22. 2,168	28. 222,545
5. 103	11. 63	17. 289	23. 1,924	29. 118,078
6. 64	12. 167	18. 414	24. 11,025	30. 301,381

PAGE 8 EXERCISE 4

1. 7	8. 9	15. 3	22. 5	29. 4
2. 5	9. 4	16. 5	23. 9	30. 4
3. 9	10. 9	17. 8	24. 8	31. 9
4. 6	11. 5	18. 7	25. 8	32. 7
5. 6	12. 8	19. 3	26. 7	33. 8
6. 9	13. 2	20. 6	27. 9	34. 7
7. 6	14. 8	21. 7	28. 6	35. 11

PAGE 9 EXERCISE 5

1. 42	5. 4	9. 18	13. 367	17. 534
2. 58	6. 65	10. 79	14. 6,467	18. 470,507
3. 117	7. 49	11. 289	15. 456	19. 3,888
4. 46	8. 36	12. 138	16. 2,163	20. 3,368

PAGE 12 EXERCISE 6

1. 44	8. 420	15. 2,277	22. 4,606	29. 8,988,483,771
2. 819	9. 1,816	16. 3,588	23. 30,186	30. 98,700,857,528
3. 492	10. 39,438	17. 7,396	24. 219,868	31. 32,493,356
4. 160	11. 168,436	18. 1,278	25. 16,616,222	32. 42,450,048
5. 312	12. 7,200	19. 1,375	26. 81,282	
6. 584	13. 1,073	20. 79,200	27. 234,208	
7. 1,050	14. 364	21. 6,302	28. 30,958,006	

PAGE 14 EXERCISE 7

1. 13
2. 8 r $\frac{1}{2}$
3. 12 r $\frac{5}{6}$
4. 13 r $\frac{1}{3}$
5. 10 r $\frac{2}{7}$
6. 28
7. 52
8. 147 r $\frac{1}{5}$
9. 534
10. 82
11. 293 r $\frac{1}{9}$
12. 2,061 r $\frac{3}{4}$
13. 6,734 r $\frac{1}{2}$
14. 879
15. 125,469

PAGE 15 PRE-APPRENTICE TEST - WHOLE NUMBERS

1. 79
2. 87
3. 108
4. 1,221
5. 4,759
6. 41
7. 38
8. 389
9. 49
10. 4,999
11. 129
12. 2,688
13. 31,434
14. 117,840
15. 42,474,540
16. 309
17. 21 r6 or $\frac{3}{4}$
18. 18
19. 104 r 2 or 104 r $\frac{2}{37}$
20. 182 r40

CHAPTER 3 - PAGE 19 EXERCISE 1

1. $\frac{1}{2}$
2. $\frac{1}{4}$
3. L.T.
4. $\frac{7}{8}$
5. $\frac{7}{16}$
6. $\frac{3}{8}$
7. $\frac{7}{16}$
8. L.T.
9. $\frac{1}{2}$
10. $\frac{7}{12}$
11. $\frac{1}{8}$
12. $\frac{53}{128}$
13. L.T.
14. $\frac{5}{8}$
15. $\frac{15}{16}$
16. L.T.
17. $\frac{16}{31}$
18. L.T.
19. $\frac{41}{100}$
20. $\frac{4}{9}$
21. $\frac{13}{16}$
22. $\frac{1}{64}$
23. L.T.
24. L.T.
25. $\frac{3}{50}$
26. $\frac{5}{49}$
27. $\frac{711}{1408}$
28. $\frac{71}{685}$
29. $\frac{1}{20}$
30. $\frac{11}{16}$

PAGE 20 EXERCISE 2

1. $1\frac{1}{4}$
2. $1\frac{1}{2}$
3. $1\frac{2}{3}$
4. $1\frac{7}{8}$
5. $1\frac{3}{4}$
6. $1\frac{3}{5}$
7. $12\frac{1}{11}$
8. $2\frac{11}{16}$
9. $3\frac{1}{32}$
10. $1\frac{23}{64}$
11. $2\frac{1}{8}$
12. 1
13. $6\frac{31}{66}$
14. $6\frac{9}{13}$
15. $10\frac{4}{5}$
16. $4\frac{1}{7}$
17. $4\frac{11}{17}$
18. $21\frac{7}{13}$
19. $19\frac{1}{7}$
20. 6
21. 100
22. $5\frac{17}{143}$
23. $1\frac{5}{16}$
24. $5\frac{1}{6}$
25. 65

PAGE 20-21 EXERCISE 3

1. $\frac{4}{8}$
2. $\frac{4}{16}$
3. $\frac{8}{32}$
4. $\frac{18}{24}$
5. $\frac{27}{36}$
6. $\frac{24}{60}$
7. $\frac{26}{128}$
8. $\frac{91}{448}$
9. $\frac{90}{144}$
10. $\frac{39}{96}$
11. $\frac{88}{144}$
12. $\frac{125}{1000}$
13. $\frac{161}{175}$
14. $\frac{3125}{100,000}$
15. $\frac{434}{896}$
16. $\frac{5}{10}$
17. $\frac{50}{100}$
18. $\frac{500}{1000}$
19. $\frac{35}{42}$
20. $\frac{10}{64}$
21. $\frac{35}{160}$
22. $\frac{121}{352}$
23. $\frac{600}{1000}$
24. $\frac{84}{189}$
25. $\frac{625}{10,000}$
26. $\frac{80}{100}$
27. $\frac{8125}{10,000}$
28. $\frac{135}{144}$
29. $\frac{30}{90}$
30. $\frac{180}{320}$
31. $\frac{16}{32}$
32. $\frac{24}{96}$

PAGE 22 EXERCISE 4

1. $\frac{14}{16}$, $\frac{11}{16}$
2. $\frac{12}{16}$, $\frac{13}{16}$
3. $\frac{15}{32}$, $\frac{28}{32}$, $\frac{10}{32}$
4. $\frac{15}{30}$, $\frac{15}{30}$, $\frac{12}{30}$
5. $\frac{28}{35}$, $\frac{10}{35}$
6. $\frac{15}{48}$, $\frac{34}{48}$
7. $\frac{45}{144}$, $\frac{24}{144}$
8. $\frac{35}{70}$, $\frac{56}{70}$, $\frac{30}{70}$
9. $\frac{35}{70}$, $\frac{8}{70}$, $\frac{15}{70}$
10. $\frac{35}{140}$, $\frac{16}{140}$, $\frac{30}{140}$
11. $\frac{62}{64}$, $\frac{63}{64}$, $\frac{60}{64}$
12. $\frac{56}{84}$, $\frac{24}{84}$, $\frac{21}{84}$, $\frac{21}{84}$
13. $\frac{35}{60}$, $\frac{48}{60}$, $\frac{28}{60}$
14. $\frac{375}{4000}$, $\frac{672}{4000}$, $\frac{2800}{4000}$
15. $\frac{1250}{4000}$, $\frac{875}{4000}$, $\frac{680}{4000}$, $\frac{132}{4000}$
16. $\frac{125}{200}$, $\frac{46}{200}$, $\frac{60}{200}$
17. $\frac{35}{140}$, $\frac{84}{140}$, $\frac{120}{140}$
18. $\frac{40}{120}$, $\frac{30}{120}$, $\frac{15}{120}$, $\frac{48}{120}$
19. $\frac{104}{234}$, $\frac{90}{234}$, $\frac{135}{234}$, $\frac{78}{234}$
20. $\frac{6760}{9360}$, $\frac{585}{9360}$, $\frac{1404}{9360}$, $\frac{3600}{9360}$
21. $\frac{9}{57}$, $\frac{5}{57}$, $\frac{19}{57}$

PAGE 23 EXERCISE 5

1. 1
2. $1\frac{1}{8}$
3. $\frac{1}{8}$
4. $\frac{1}{4}$
5. $\frac{11}{21}$
6. $1\frac{9}{64}$
7. $\frac{53}{60}$
8. $1\frac{29}{140}$
9. $\frac{19}{48}$
10. $\frac{19}{48}$
11. $1\frac{31}{84}$
12. $\frac{11}{144}$
13. $\frac{5}{12}$
14. $\frac{7}{120}$
15. $\frac{46}{147}$
16. $\frac{5}{64}$
17. $\frac{11}{24}$
18. $1\frac{17}{225}$
19. $\frac{2}{45}$
20. $1\frac{29}{32}$
21. $\frac{11}{19}$

PAGE 24 EXERCISE 6

1. $6\frac{3}{8}$
2. $3\frac{3}{16}$
3. $5\frac{9}{20}$
4. $2\frac{19}{30}$
5. $11\frac{15}{16}$
6. $7\frac{1}{6}$
7. $6\frac{23}{70}$
8. $\frac{3}{4}$
9. $1\frac{43}{48}$
10. $\frac{121}{144}$
11. $1\frac{49}{64}$
12. $\frac{3}{4}$
13. $4\frac{19}{64}$
14. $18\frac{23}{60}$
15. $3\frac{57}{64}$
16. $6\frac{11}{16}$
17. $1\frac{21}{40}$
18. $2\frac{167}{576}$
19. $4\frac{3}{16}$
20. $8\frac{119}{120}$
21. $\frac{11}{26}$
22. $1\frac{239}{315}$
23. $1\frac{103}{108}$
24. $3\frac{57}{64}$

PAGE 25-26 EXERCISE 7

1. $2\frac{191}{240}$
2. $3\frac{23}{80}$
3. $\frac{41}{60}$
4. $9\frac{173}{192}$
5. $3\frac{3}{8}$
6. $8\frac{3}{16}$
7. $\frac{7}{30}$
8. $3\frac{39}{80}$
9. $\frac{19}{32}$
10. $5\frac{1}{120}$
11. $2\frac{13}{120}$
12. $1\frac{26}{45}$

PAGE 27 EXERCISE 8

1. $1\frac{1}{2}$
2. $\frac{1}{5}$
3. $\frac{1}{12}$
4. $\frac{1}{10}$
5. $\frac{2}{7}$
6. $2\frac{1}{12}$
7. $\frac{1}{8}$
8. $\frac{1}{6}$
9. $\frac{4}{9}$
10. 15
11. 69
12. $10\frac{15}{16}$
13. $126\frac{2}{3}$
14. $\frac{1}{16}$
15. $81\frac{1}{4}$
16. $\frac{11}{24}$
17. $\frac{45}{512}$
18. $1\frac{1}{20}$

PAGE 28-29 EXERCISE 9

1. $1\frac{1}{3}$
2. $6\frac{2}{5}$
3. $\frac{5}{32}$
4. $2\frac{1}{2}$
5. 9
6. $1\frac{13}{21}$
7. $\frac{3}{16}$
8. $\frac{1}{6}$
9. 21
10. $\frac{39}{64}$
11. $1\frac{19}{27}$
12. 2
13. 48
14. 28
15. $\frac{7}{120}$
16. 36
17. 1
18. 10
19. $1\frac{11}{20}$
20. 6
21. $\frac{16}{25}$
22. $7\frac{1}{9}$
23. $\frac{55}{896}$
24. $\frac{3}{224}$

PAGE 30 EXERCISE 10

1. $10\frac{2}{3}$
2. $1\frac{97}{176}$
3. $1\frac{11}{20}$
4. 24
5. $\frac{861}{1024}$
6. $1\frac{13}{17}$
7. $\frac{77}{152}$
8. $40\frac{5}{8}$
9. $\frac{9}{70}$
10. $2\frac{3}{5}$

PAGE 32 EXERCISE 11

1. Seven Tenths
2. Twenty two hundredths
3. Two Hundredths
4. Three thousands
5. Three tenths
6. One thousand three hundred seventy five ten-thousandths
7. Six and one hundred thirty four thousandths
8. Ninety nine hundredths
9. Eight hundred eighty eight thousandths
10. Five and six hundred seventy five thousandths
11. Eight tenths
12. Seven and eight tenths
13. Seven and twenty three ten-thousandths
14. Four tenths
15. Three and twelve thousandths
16. One hundred-thousandths
17. One hundred twenty five thousandths
18. Nine thousand three hundred seventy five ten-thousandths
19. Twenty eight thousand one hundred twenty five hundred-thousandths
20. Five hundred thousandths

PAGE 33 EXERCISE 12

1. .2
2. .007
3. .0136
4. .15
5. 5.047
6. 1000.001
7. 225.225
8. .2124
9. 7.6545
10. 47.125

PAGE 33 EXERCISE 13

1. .5
2. .7
3. .43
4. .06
5. .0005
6. .125
7. .4875
8. .0125
9. 25.0125
10. 1000.001
11. 2.006023
12. 1515.015
13. 5.000007
14. .406
15. .5260
16. .832

PAGE 34 EXERCISE 14

1. .1875
2. .703125
3. .75
4. .0625
5. .625
6. .328125
7. .6
8. .84375
9. .421875
10. .333

PAGE 34 EXERCISE 15

1. $\frac{1}{2}$
2. $\frac{6}{25}$
3. $\frac{12}{125}$
4. $\frac{1}{16}$
5. $\frac{5}{8}$
6. $3\frac{1}{20}$
7. $4\frac{15}{16}$
8. $\frac{11}{16}$
9. $\frac{1}{64}$
10. $3\frac{13}{160}$

PAGE 35 EXERCISE 16

1. .157
2. 2.1265
3. 3.5
4. .881
5. 4.7395
6. 2.975
7. .086
8. 10.36525
9. 3.060603
10. 5.460
11. 5.22835
12. .0225
13. 136.653
14. .4125
15. 5.269275
16. 167077.395423
17. 895.571
18. .86784205632
19. 1241.7375
20. 9.6356

PAGE 35-36 EXERCISE 17

1. 8.0634
2. 47.85
3. 8167.0875
4. .04
5. 5.9325
6. 986.44984
7. .196875
8. .2299375
9. 1.53125
10. 20.20914
11. 67.53
12. 675.3
13. 6753
14. 5.175
15. .015625
16. 27.2

PAGE 36 EXERCISE 18

1. 1.75
2. 1
3. .1
4. .1
5. 5
6. about 2.43
7. .01
8. 286.7
9. 28.67
10. 2.867
11. .2867
12. 1222.5
13. .001
14. .5
15. 1.6

PAGE 37 EXERCISE 19

1. 5/8
2. 6/8
3. 7/8
4. 3/4
5. 3/4
6. 1/2
7. .069, .635, .65, 6.1
8. .2485, .253, 2.249, 2.25
9. .51, .5126, .583, .6
10. .071, .076, .7, .76
11. .006, .1483, .503, 5.02
12. 2.04395
13. 4.5, 4.504
14. .0909, .091
15. .201, .21

PAGE 38 PRE-APPRENTICE TEST - FRACTIONS & DECIMALS

1. 19
2. 52
3. 40
4. 117
5. 9
6. 28
7. 1.733
8. 131
9. 72
10. 1.957
11. 3.528
12. 26
13. 4.5
14. 5/6
15. 187
16. 30
17. .521
18. .012
19. $\frac{1}{60}$
20. 1.296
21. $1\frac{11}{42}$
22. 1.2525 or $1\frac{101}{400}$
23. 90
24. 21
25. 1.4
26. $\frac{1}{3}$
27. 32
28. $\frac{19}{72}$
29. 204
30. 8.55
31. 16
32. .1 or $\frac{1}{10}$
33. 72
34. 3.75 or $3\frac{3}{4}$
35. 94
36. .003616
37. 7.283
38. .48 or $\frac{12}{25}$
39. 2
40. 24

CHAPTER 4 - PAGE 41 EXERCISE 1

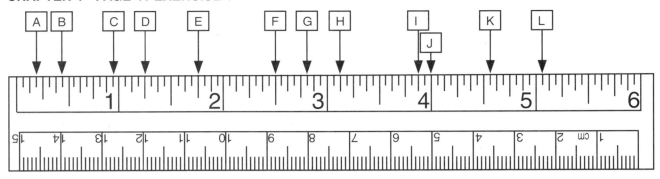

PAGE 42 EXERCISE 2

A. $\frac{3}{16}$ in
B. $\frac{9}{16}$ in
C. $\frac{15}{16}$ in

D. $1\frac{1}{4}$ in
E. $1\frac{5}{8}$ in
F. $2\frac{1}{8}$ in

G. $2\frac{7}{16}$ in
H. 3 in
I. $3\frac{3}{8}$ in

J. $3\frac{7}{8}$ in
K. $4\frac{5}{16}$ in
L. $4\frac{3}{4}$ in

PAGE 43 EXERCISE 3

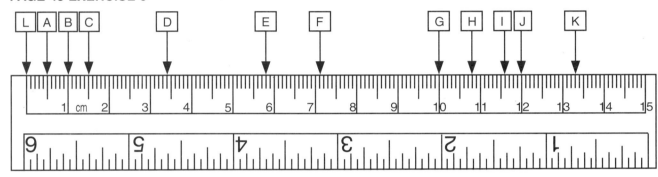

PAGE 44 EXERCISE 4

A. 1 mm
B. 7 mm
C. 20 mm

D. 33 mm
E. 42 mm
F. 53 mm

G. 65 mm
H. 77 mm
I. 96 mm

J. 112 mm
K. 124 mm
L. 140 mm

PAGE 44-45 EXERCISE 5

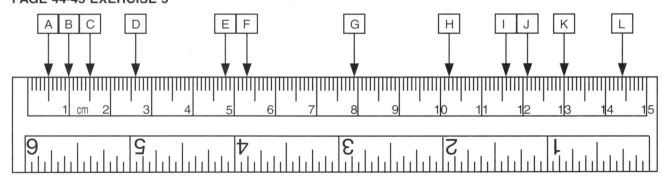

PAGE 45 EXERCISE 6

A. 1.3 cm = 13 mm
B. 2.1 cm = 21 mm
C. 3.4 cm = 34 mm

D. 4.4 cm = 44 mm
E. 5.5 cm = 55 mm
F. 6.9 cm = 69 mm

G. 8.2 cm = 82 mm
H. 10.3 cm = 103 mm
I. 11.0 cm = 110 mm

J. 11.7 cm = 117 mm
K. 12.7 cm = 127 mm
L. 14.7 cm = 147 mm

PAGE 46-47 EXERCISE 7

1. 16' 4"
2. 6' 2"

3. 13' 3"
4. Yes, he has 8' 6" total

5. A = 4' B = 12' 2"
6. 32' 4"

PAGE 47-48 EXERCISE 8

1. 1' 2"
2. 3' 7"
3. 4' 7"
4. 5' 7"
5. A = 2' 10" B = 2' 11"
6. 1"

PAGE 49 EXERCISE 9

1. 85 cubic inches
2. 42½ cubic inches
3. 161½ cubic feet
4. 403¾ cubic feet
5. 69³⁄₁₀ cubic feet
6. 64 days

PAGE 51 EXERCISE 10

1. 1³¹⁄₃₂ inches
2. 1⁵⁄₁₆ feet
3. 13⅓ cubic feet
4. 1⅛ feet
5. 14 feet
6. 3 whole stars

PAGE 55 EXERCISE 11

1. 1.89
2. 720
3. 59
4. 30,000
5. 17,300
6. 48
7. 1.19
8. 0.00006
9. 819
10. 7.642
11. 580
12. .00142
13. 46,000
14. 0.07
15. 27,100
16. 3050
17. 380,000
18. 0.003
19. 0.9
20. 19.37

PAGE 59 EXERCISE 12

1. 629.92
2. 31
3. 2.301
4. 15.748
5. 19.32
6. 45.72
7. 120.75
8. 48,300

PAGE 60-62 PRE-APPRENTICE TEST - MEASUREMENT AND METRIC CONVERSION

1.

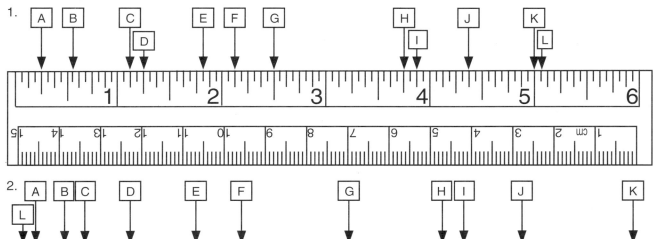

2.

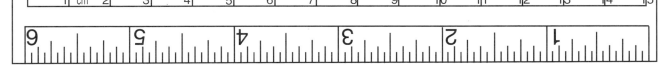

3. 5' 1⅜"
4. 4⅜"
5. 2' 11⅛"
6. 16' 5¼"
7. 4' 4⅞"
8. 1' 7"
9. 5' 6⅞"
10. 44.9
11. 54,000
12. 0.0075
13. 0.0163
14. 40
15. 9,790
16. 19.84
17. 7.02
18. 4.4196
19. 136.85
20. 196.85
21. 121.92

CHAPTER 5 - PAGE 64-65 EXERCISE 1

1. ⅔
2. ½
3. ⁵⁄₁
4. ¹⁴⁄₉
5. ¼
6. ⅔
7. ³⁄₁
8. ⁸⁴⁄₈₅
9a. ¼
9b. 2 lb.
9c. 8 lb
9d. ⅕

PAGE 66-67 EXERCISE 2

1. 14
2. 9
3. 3
4. 2.5
5. 24
6. 5.8
7. $9\frac{11}{19}$
8. 2
9. 5
10. 1725 rpm
11. 4480 screws
12. 4.07 ohms
13. base = 8
    leg = 12
14. $4\frac{2}{3}$ gallons

PAGE 67-68 EXERCISE 3

	percent	whole	part		percent	whole	part
1.	22	108	23.76	5.	3	136,000	4080
2.	44	96	42	6.	16.63	145 lb.	24 lb.
3.	$12\frac{1}{2}$	1500	187.5	7.	112	60	67.2
4.	33	$565.00	$186.45				

PAGE 69 EXERCISE 4

1. 2.08
2. .208
3. 12.25
4. .0208
5. $73\frac{1}{3}$%
6. 7.26
7. .12
8. 50%
9. 11.2 oz.
10. 3.125%
11. 33.3 lb.,
    .3 lb. carbon,
    .2 silicon,
    2.6 lb. chrome,
    .7 lb. nickel
12. 86.5%
13. 11
14. $13.25

PAGE 69 REVIEW EXERCISES - RATIO

1. $\frac{1}{2}$
2. $\frac{1}{3}$
3. $\frac{1}{9}$
4. $\frac{1}{2}$
5. $\frac{25}{34}$
6. $\frac{49}{10}$
7. $\frac{51}{31}$
8. $\frac{204}{65}$
9. L.T.
10. $\frac{840}{1}$

PAGE 70 REVIEW EXERCISES - PROPORTION

1. 15
2. 28
3. 10
4. 12
5. 36
6. 3
7. 2
8. 48
9. 20
10. .5

PAGE 70 REVIEW EXERCISES - PERCENT

1. 8
2. 121
3. 75
4. 380.9
5. 2
6. 30%
7. 12.25%
8. $6.16

PAGE 71 PRE-APPRENTICE TEST - RATIOS, PROPORTIONS AND PERCENTS

1. .88
2. $\frac{7}{3}$
3. 60¢
4. 5.25 yd
5. $20.92
6. .01
7. about 5
8. $\frac{48}{55}$
9. $11\frac{1}{9}$%
10. $\frac{1}{9}$
11. $3\frac{3}{4}$
12. 3 oz.

CHAPTER 6 - PAGE 75 EXERCISE 1

1. -7
2. 9
3. -10
4. -15
5. -14
6. 15
7. -4
8. 19
9. -14
10. 26
11. 15
12. -27
13. 11
14. 44
15. -35
16. -31
17. -18
18. -35
19. 29
20. -45
21. 37
22. 30.42
23. -7.125
24. -28.875
25. $5\frac{3}{8}$ or 5.375
26. 1.573
27. -6

PAGE 76 EXERCISE 2

1. 2
2. -4
3. -3
4. 2
5. 0
6. -1
7. -1
8. -7
9. 25
10. -18
11. -21
12. -2.25
13. -8
14. $5\frac{1}{5}$
15. -7.79
16. $-.025$
17. 122.489
18. -4.525 or $-4\frac{21}{40}$
19. -60.05
20. 563.11

PAGE 77 EXERCISE 3

1. -8
2. 11
3. -19
4. 12
5. -7
6. -11
7. 0
8. -19
9. 21
10. 28
11. -6
12. 15
13. 9
14. -47
15. -8
16. -6
17. 5.625
18. -6.875
19. 1.345
20. -18.23

PAGE 78-79 EXERCISE 4

1. 3	5. −112	9. −56	13. 21.70	17. 108
2. −35	6. 44	10. 42	14. −$\frac{3}{32}$	18. −27.3
3. −24	7. 108	11. 65	15. 48	19. .72
4. 40	8. −81	12. −4.2	16. −60	20. 120

PAGE 79 EXERCISE 5

1. 2	5. −7	9. −.3	13. −2	17. −0.25
2. 2	6. 5	10. 50	14. 1$\frac{1}{2}$	18. 0.6
3. −13	7. −48$\frac{1}{3}$	11. −.4	15. −$\frac{1}{4}$	
4. −6	8. 90	12. −1$\frac{1}{3}$	16. −$\frac{3}{5}$	

PAGE 80 PRE-APPRENTICE TEST - DIRECTED NUMBERS

1. −2	5. 73	9. −1070	13. −$\frac{3}{20}$	17. 1.7
2. 6	6. .9	10. 20	14. −15.9375	18. 2
3. −23	7. .7	11. −54	15. −8	19. −6
4. 8	8. 421	12. 528	16. −13	20. $\frac{2}{15}$

CHAPTER 7 - PAGE 83-84 EXERCISE 1

1. 26	7. 8	13. 18	19. 12	25. 22
2. 14	8. 26	14. −55	20. 30	26. 2 $\frac{1}{2}$
3. 20	9. 20	15. 20	21. 11	27. 26
4. 11	10. 24	16. 14	22. 2	28. 27
5. 16	11. −$\frac{1}{3}$	17. −48	23. 34	29. $\frac{5}{7}$
6. 25	12. 4	18. 38	24. 36	30. −6

PAGE 85 PRE-APPRENTICE TEST - ORDER OF OPERATIONS

1. 52	3. 13	5. 6	7. −56	9. −1
2. 72	4. 15	6. −9	8. 10	10. −6

CHAPTER 8 - PAGE 89 EXERCISE 1

1. x = 2	5. n = 5	9. x = 21	13. a = 26	17. x = 0
2. n = 7	6. n = 25	10. b = 19.2	14. c = 27	18. y = 58
3. a = 12	7. a = 13	11. y = 7	15. a = 13.265625	19. a = 71.6
4. y = 11	8. x = 10	12. h = 13.4	16. a = 128	20. x = 100

PAGE 90 EXERCISE 2

1. x = 3	6. y = 2	11. n = 11.6	16. k = 2.2	20. x = $\frac{5}{16}$
2. a = 4	7. b = 8	12. y = .02	17. y = 1.3125	
3. c = 4	8. x = 9	13. a = 3	18. x = −.025	
4. m = 1	9. c = 2	14. c = 5.625	or −1/40	
5. b = 0	10. n = 12	15. x = 7	19. m = .0625	

PAGE 91 EXERCISE 3

1. x = 2	5. c = 8$\frac{6}{7}$	9. y = 6	13. x = 2.7	17. b = 2$\frac{1}{5}$
2. a = 4$\frac{2}{5}$	6. k = 5	10. m = 13	14. m = 1.5	18. y = 7.5
3. b = 4	7. n = 12$\frac{1}{8}$	11. a = 90	15. c = .4	19. x = 110
4. m = 10$\frac{3}{4}$	8. x = 10$\frac{2}{7}$	12. b = 3	16. a = .1	20. c = 1

PAGE 92-93 EXERCISE 4

1. b = 8	5. n = 20	9. a = 8	13. b = 84	17. m = 1.5
2. x = 15	6. c = 36	10. d = 32	14. y = 6	18. c = 34
3. n = 30	7. x = 36	11. x = 90	15. a = 78	19. d = 13.4
4. a = 14	8. x = 16	12. y = 27	16. n = 3	20. b = 4

PAGE 94 EXERCISE 5

1. $y = 3$
2. $x = 2$
3. $c = 18$
4. $m = 1\frac{2}{3}$
5. $x = 2$

6. $x = 50$
7. $x = \frac{1}{2}$
8. $c = -3\frac{3}{5}$
9. $b = 66$
10. $n = 5$

11. $y = 3.5$
12. $x = 64$
13. $b = \frac{2}{13}$
14. $c = 2\frac{2}{3}$
15. $a = 21\frac{1}{3}$

16. $b = 15$
17. $y = -1\frac{7}{12}$
18. $d = -1.692$
19. $x = 10\frac{2}{7}$
20. $x = 2.033$

21. $z = .6$
22. $y = -.266$

PAGE 95 EXERCISE 6

1. $x = n - a$
2. $x = a/4$
3. $x = c + y$
4. $x = c + y$
5. $x = an$

6. $x = cy/a$
7. $x = b - 3a$
8. $x = 3b$
9. $x = \dfrac{7a - 7}{a}$
10. $x = a/b$

11. $x = 1$
12. $x = 2$
13. $x = -a + b + c + 2$
14. $x = c/2$
15. $x = -1/2b$

16. $x = c + cy$
17. $x = y$
18. $x = b/c$
19. $x = ac/b$
20. $x = dn/y$

PAGE 96 EXERCISE 7

1. $x = -1/2$
2. $x = -8$
3. $x = -1\frac{2}{19}$
4. $x = 4\frac{1}{2}$

5. $x = 1$
6. $y = -1\frac{13}{18}$ or -1.72
7. $y = -19$

8. $y = 12\frac{1}{2}$
9. $y = -4.75$
10. $a = -\frac{24}{25}$
11. $x = -8$

12. $y = -.8$
13. $x = \frac{11}{17}$ or $.647$
14. $x = 5\ b/a$
15. $x = 2\frac{3}{4}y$

PAGE 97 EXERCISE 8

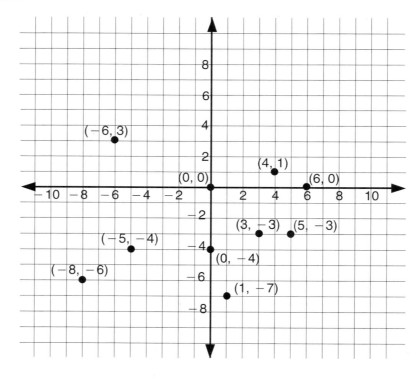

PAGE 100 EXERCISE 9

Answers are graphed using randomly chosen values for x or y including a positive value, a negative value, and zero. Your lines should still look the same ragardles of the values you choose.

1.

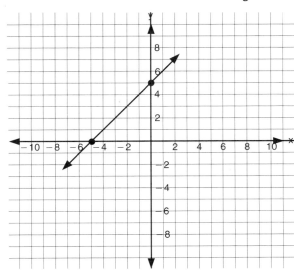

2.

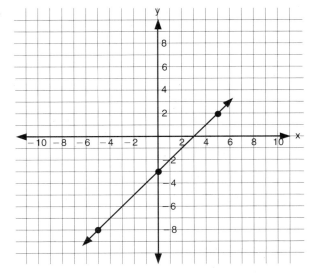

3.

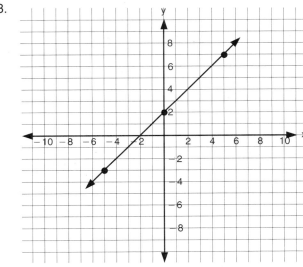

4.

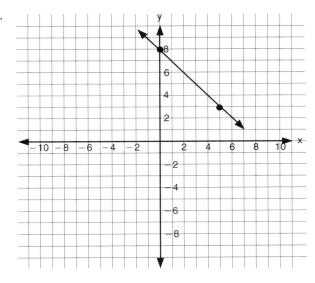

5.

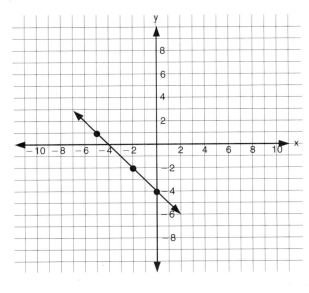

6.

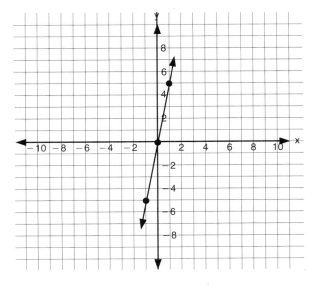

7.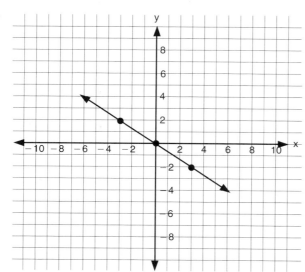

8.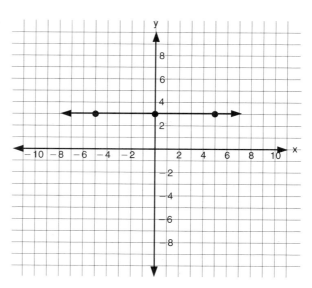

9.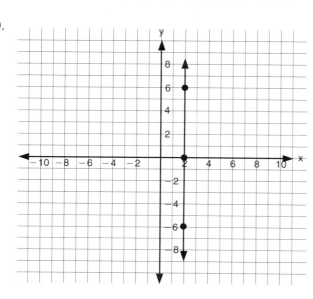

10.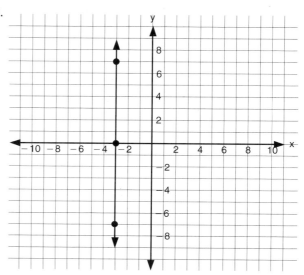

PAGE 101 EXERCISE 10

1. $x + 6$
2. $y - a$
3. $h + 5$
4. $9 - 4$
5. $17/c$
6. $\frac{4}{5}y$ or $\frac{4y}{5}$
7. $7 + z$
8. $\frac{1}{2}a$ or $\frac{a}{2}$
9. ty
10. $47y$

PAGE 101-102 EXERCISE 11

1. $13/y - 4$
2. $x + 4c$
3. $(y - 4)/a$
4. $xz/2$
5. $\frac{1}{2}cx$ or $\frac{xc}{2}$
6. $13 - x$
7. $x + 7$
8. $\frac{33}{y - 47}$
9. $3z + 2m$
10. $a + b - 5c$
11. $y/3 - 7$
12. $x/3 - 7$
13. $n/p - 7$
14. $\frac{2x - 5}{4}$

PAGE 102-103 EXERCISE 12

1. $x - 4 = 3, x = 7$
2. $y - 7 = 4, y = 11$
3. $x + y = 13, x = 13 - y$
4. $15 = 2x - 7, x = 11$
5. $16 - x = 7, x = 9$
6. $2(5)/x = 3, x = 3\frac{1}{3}$
7. $xy - a = z, x = \frac{z + a}{y}$
8. $(x + 3)/4 = 3, x = 9$
9. $y - x = z, x = y - z$
10. $2x/4 = 1, x = 2$
11. $1/2x/3 = 12, x = 72$
12. $3x/4 + 1/2 (y - z) = 30$, or $x = 40 - 2 (y - z)/3$
13. $1/2x/1/3 = 12, x = 8$
14. $x + 8/2 = 14, x = 20$

PAGE 104 EXERCISE 13

1. Bill = $34.28
   Jim = $17.14
   Sue = $68.56
2. 9 = Parts originally ordered
3. Corky = 36 lbs.
4. 6
5. $24
6. 11 red chairs
7. material cost = $175
8. 48
9. 25 girls
10. 33 lbs.
11. 9 hours
12. 12 and 16
13. 71, 120 &142
14. Father = 42 yrs., Son = 7 yrs.
15. 15 dimes, 11 nickels

PAGE 106 EXERCISE 14

1. x^6
2. a^9
3. c^6
4. 5^7
5. x^6y^{15}
6. x^4y^6
7. $a^4b^7c^{10}$
8. $-24x^2y$
9. $6a^2b^4c$
10. $18a^3b^2c^3$
11. $60axy^3z^3$
12. $-14abxy$
13. $72aby^3z^2$
14. $a^2bm^3n^5$
15. x^2y^2
16. $28mx^2y$
17. $126a^3x^4y^4$
18. $-48x^7y^{16}z^{15}$
19. $54a^8b^3c^2x^2$
20. $27a^6cwx^5yz$

PAGE 107 EXERCISE 15

1. $2a$
2. $2y$
3. $-2x^2z$
4. 3
5. $-3x^4y$
6. $-5y$
7. $-6\frac{1}{4}ab^2c^3n^{-1}$
8. $4m^3n$
9. $4a^{-1}b^{-1}c^6$
10. $8x^8y^{-1}z^{-1}$
11. $-3m^{-3}nx^2$
12. $4a^5y^3z^{-1}$
13. $-4a^3c^2d^{-2}$
14. $\frac{1}{3}xyz^7$
15. $5\frac{1}{3}a^{-2}m^2z^5$
16. $3bm^4z^6a^{-6}y^{-3}$
17. $-\frac{1}{4}a^7bm^9y^2z^5$
18. $1\frac{1}{2}x^6y^{-1}z^{-4}$

PAGE 108 EXERCISE 16

1. 2
2. xy^2
3. 5
4. $6ab^2$
5. $4x^2$
6. y^5
7. $\frac{8}{9}$
8. $2a\sqrt[5]{a^2}$
9. $2a\sqrt[5]{a}$
10. $\frac{3}{5}$
11. $4x^2\sqrt{2}$
12. $3a/4y$

PAGE 110 EXERCISE 17

1. $3(3m + 2)$
2. $4(3x + 1)$
3. $6(6y - 1)$
4. $8(3z - 1)$
5. $5p(4p + 3)$
6. $7r(r - 2)$
7. $13a(2a + 3)$
8. $17b(3b - 2)$
9. $e(13e + 1)$
10. $11p(4p^2 + 6p - 3)$

PAGE 112 EXERCISE 18

1. $12m^2 + 31m + 20$
2. $4x^2 + 26x - 14$
3. $12p^2 + 5p - 2$
4. $2d^2 + 4d - 6$
5. $12x^2 - 5x - 3$
6. $6t^2 - 19t + 15$
7. $3h^2 - 18h - 48$
8. $10w^2 - 29w + 10$
9. $3c^2 - 2c - 8$
10. $10b^2 + 9b + 2$
11. $x^2 + 2xy + y2$
12. $6m^2 + mh - 2h^2$
13. $3e^2 - ef - 2f^2$
14. $12c^2 - 11cd + 2d^2$
15. $4a^2 + 34am - 18m^2$
16. $3r^2 + 2rs - s^2$
17. $2x^2 - 5xy + 2y^2$
18. $r^2 - s^2$
19. $4j^2 + 13jk + 3k^2$
20. $y^2 - z^2$

PAGE 115 EXERCISE 19

1. $(x + 1)(x + 1)$
2. $(m + 2)(m + 3)$
3. $(p + 5)(p + 2)$
4. $(y + 2)(y - 1)$
5. $(a - 2)(a + 1)$
6. $(z - 3)(z - 1)$
7. $(2b + 3)(b + 1)$
8. $(3f + 1)(f + 3)$
9. $(2r - 1)(r + 1)$
10. $(5s + 3)(s - 2)$
11. $(3n - 1)(n - 1)$
12. $(5t + 3)(t - 5)$
13. $(2c - 3)(c - 1)$
14. $(g + 2)(g + 3)$
15. $(d + 1)(d - 4)$
16. $(2e + 3)(e - 2)$
17. $(5k - 2)(k + 1)$
18. $(7a - 2)(a - 3)$

1. d	6. c	11. d	16. e	21. a
2. a	7. b	12. b	17. b	22. d
3. b	8. b	13. d	18. c	23. b
4. b	9. c	14. c	19. e	24. d
5. d	10. a	15. a	20. b	25. a

PAGE 118-119 PRE-APPRENTICE TEST - ALGEBRA, FACTORING AND SEQUENCES

1. 100
2. .02
3. 90
4. 4
5. 1
6. 4
7. ½

8. yc/a
9. dn/y
10. 7
11. $3(3m + 1)$
12. $2a (3a - 1)$
13. $(2c + 3)(c - 2)$
14. $x^2 - y^2$

15. 33
16. $(2z + 3)(z - 1)$
17. $2m^2 - 3m - 2$
18. 80
19. $3m(m^2 + 3m - 6)$
20. $3b^2 - 8b + 4$
21. 23

22. $5k^2 - 14k - 3$
23. 15
24. 4
25. $(7t - 3)(t - 2)$

26.

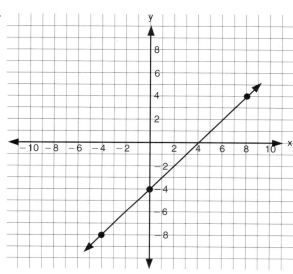

27.

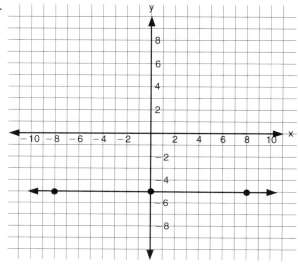

28.

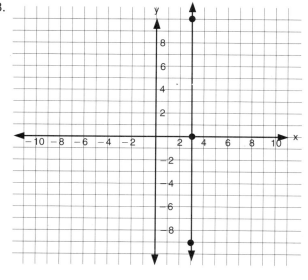

29.

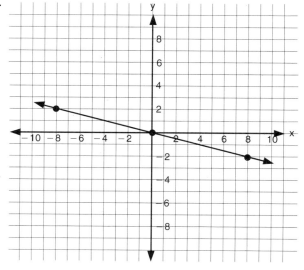

30.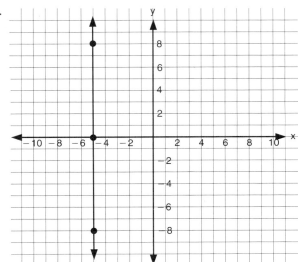

31.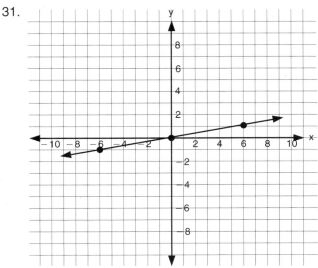

CHAPTER 9 - PAGE 127 EXERCISE 1

1. 69° 8' 44"
2. 91° 31' 30"
3. 20° 45' 19"
4. 59' 49"
5. 151° 6' 10"
6. 58' 59"
7. 54° 11' 35"
8. 1° 29' 41"
9. 65° 54' 57"
10. 8° 53' 34"

PAGE 127-130 EXERCISE 2

1. ∠C = 96° 43'
2. ∠C = 54° 31' 33"
3. ∠B = 45°
4. ∠A = 52° 3' 12"
5. ∠ABD = 79°
   ∠ADC = 105°
   ∠BAC = 68°
6. ∠C = 175°
7. ∠B = 26°
8. ∠A = 71°
9. ∠A = 54°
10. ∠CAD = 100°
    ∠ECB = 31°
    ∠ACB = 41°
11. ∠B = 105°
12. ∠ACF = 84°
13. ∠B = 7°
    ∠C = 19°
14. ∠X = 17°

PAGE 133 EXERCISE 3

1. ∠BDC = 52°
2. ∠BDE = 128°
3. ∠EDF = 52°
4. ∠DBG = 142°

PAGE 134 EXERCISE 4

1. ∠D = 50°
2. ∠A = 97°
3. ∠C = 83°
4. ∠B = 47°
5. Complement of ∠D = 40°
6. Supplement of ∠A = 83°
7. Complement of ∠C = 7°
8. Complement of ∠B = 43°

PAGE 135-136 PRE-APPRENTICE TEST - GEOMETRY

1. False
2. False
3. True
4. False
5. True
6. False
7. True
8. True
9. False
10. True
11. ∠ACD = 110°
    ∠DCE = 70°
    ∠ACD = 110°
12. ∠C = 50°
    ∠A = 97°
    ∠B = 47°
    ∠D = 36°
13. ∠B = 150°
    ∠C = 150°
    ∠D = 30°
    ∠E = 30°
    ∠F = 150°
    ∠G = 150°
    ∠H = 30°
14. ∠CAB = 45°
    ∠CA = 10"

CHAPTER 10 - PAGE 139-140 EXERCISE 1

1. 81 in²
2. 50.24 ft²
3. .785 in²
4. 24 yd²
5. 10.5 cm²
6. 12 mi²
7. 40 ft²
8. 324 ft²
9. 50 cars
10. 40 in²
11. 1.375 ft²
12. 4 rooms
13. 2880 tiles
14. 9 ft²
15. 1 ft²

PAGE 142-143 EXERCISE 2

1. a. 18 ft
   b. 72 cm
   c. 9.42 mm
   d. 43.96 in.

2. 5 cm
3. 50.24 ft
4. $416.00

5. 9, 18, 7
6. w = 9, l = 15
7. 21.25 ft

PAGE 144-145 EXERCISE 3

1. 512 in³
2. 30 ft³
3. 45 cm³
4. 266 ft³
5. 15 bags
6. 2310 in³
7. 12800 in³
8. 12 in.
9. yes
10. 128 in³
11. 8 blocks
12. 3240 in³

PAGE 146-147 PRE-APPRENTICE TEST - GRAPHIC MATH

1. c
2. a
3. a
4. b
5. d
6. b
7. b
8. d
9. e
10. b
11. c
12. e
13. a
14. b

CHAPTER 11 - PAGE 154-155 EXERCISE 1

1.
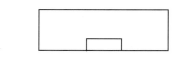

2.
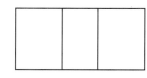

3.
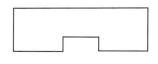
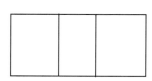

4.
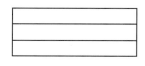
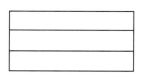

5.
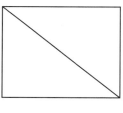

6.
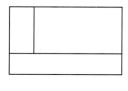

7.

8.

9.

10.

11.

12.

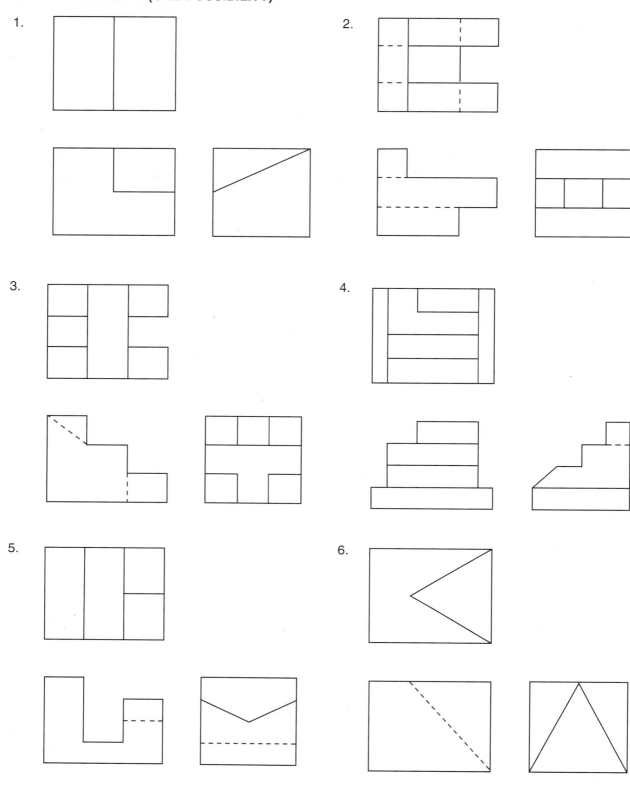

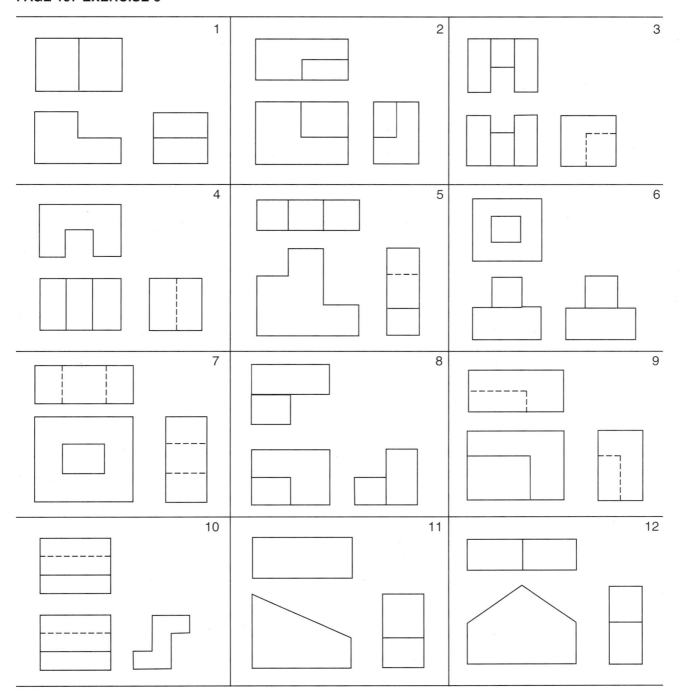

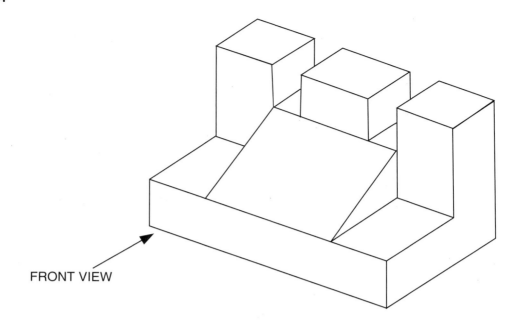

FRONT VIEW

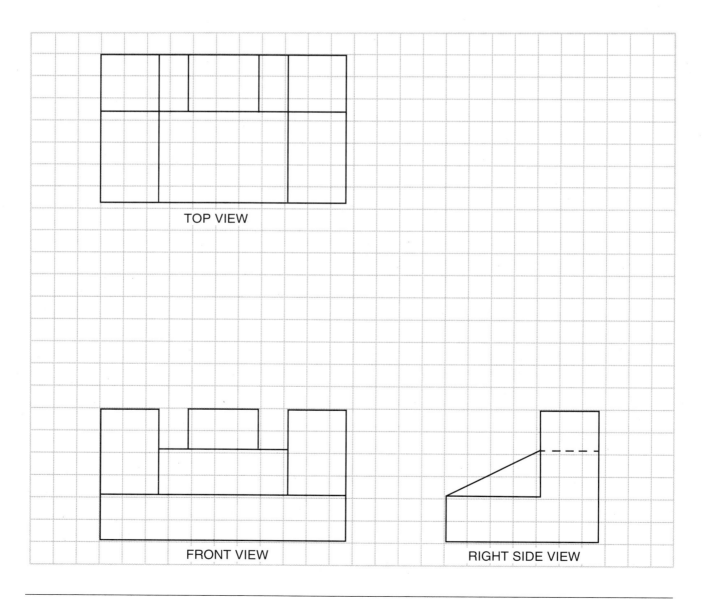

TOP VIEW

FRONT VIEW

RIGHT SIDE VIEW

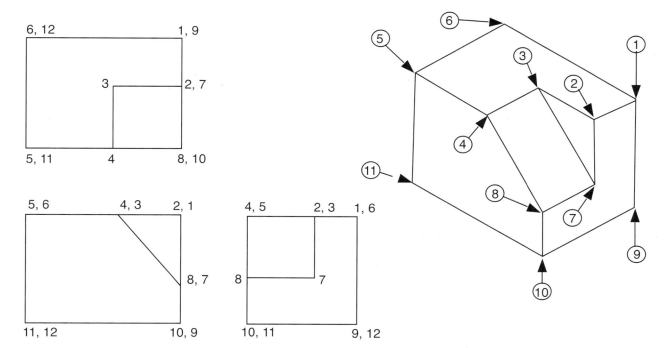

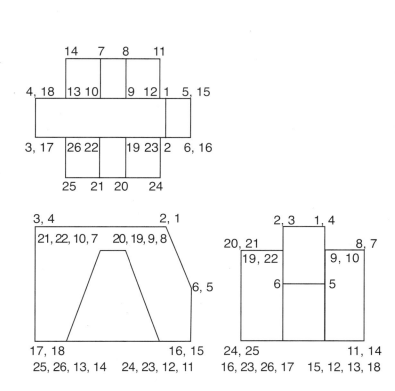

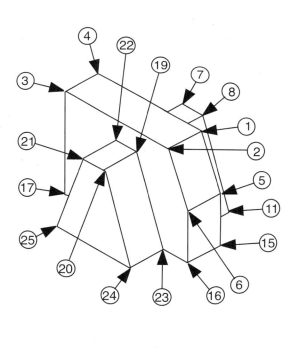

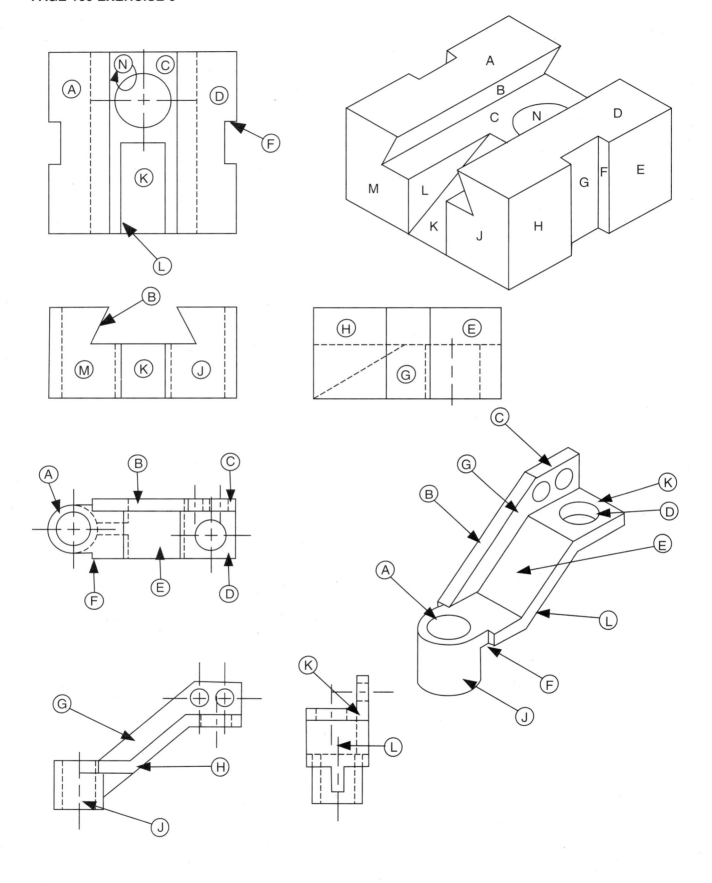

PAGE 161

1. c   2. a   3. b   4. d

PAGE 162

5. c   6. e   7. d   8. b

PAGE 163

9. e   10. d   11. d   12. c

PAGE 165-166 FORM Y PRE-APPRENTICE TEST - ROTATED/FLIPPED

1. a	10. a	19. b	28. b	37. a	46. b	55. b	64. b
2. a	11. b	20. b	29. a	38. a	47. b	56. b	65. a
3. b	12. a	21. b	30. b	39. a	48. b	57. a	66. a
4. b	13. b	22. b	31. b	40. b	49. b	58. a	67. b
5. a	14. a	23. a	32. a	41. a	50. b	59. b	68. b
6. b	15. b	24. a	33. a	42. b	51. b	60. b	69. b
7. a	16. a	25. b	34. b	43. b	52. b	61. b	70. b
8. a	17. b	26. b	35. b	44. a	53. b	62. b	
9. b	18. a	27. a	36. b	45. a	54. a	63. a	

PAGE 167-168 FORM Z PRE-APPRENTICE TEST - SAME OBJECT/DIFFERENT OBJECT

1. a	9. b	17. b	25. b	33. b	41. b	49. b	57. a
2. b	10. b	18. b	26. a	34. b	42. b	50. a	58. b
3. b	11. b	19. b	27. b	35. b	43. a	51. a	59. a
4. b	12. b	20. b	28. b	36. a	44. b	52. b	60. b
5. b	13. a	21. b	29. a	37. b	45. b	53. b	
6. a	14. a	22. b	30. a	38. b	46. b	54. b	
7. b	15. b	23. a	31. a	39. a	47. b	55. b	
8. b	16. b	24. b	32. b	40. a	48. a	56. b	

PAGES 170-171 CUBE FOLDING AND UNFOLDING PART A AND B

1. a   4. a   7. b   10. c
2. d   5. b   8. a   11. d
3. c   6. a   9. c

PAGES 172-173 CUBE FOLDING AND UNFOLDING PARTS C AND D

12. c   15. b   18. a   21. b
13. a   16. c   19. c   22. a
14. a   17. a   20. b

CHAPTER 12 - PAGE 181-182 PRE-APPRENTICE TEST - BASIC ELECTRICITY

1. b   3. c   5. a   7. a   9. b
2. a   4. c   6. d   8. d

CHAPTER 13 - PAGE 204-205 EXERCISE 1

1. 150 lb   2. 12/1   3. 54.17 N   4. 12/1   5. C equal

PAGE 206 EXERCISE 2

1. 3.43/1   2. 102.08 lb   3. 4/1   4. 3200 N   5. B

PAGE 207-208 EXERCISE 3

1. MA = 3/1, F_E = 20 lb
2. F_E = 30 lb
3. MA = 2.5/1, r_w = 12.5"
4. r_a = 0.5 m, F_R = 80 N
5. MA = 6/1, r_w = 3.6m
6. B

PAGE 209 EXERCISE 4

1. MA = 60/1, F_E = 5 lb
2. MA = 4/1, pitch = 1.38 mm
3. MA = 12/1, F_R = 240 lb
4. F_R = 500 lb, pitch = 2"

PAGE 210-212 EXERCISE 5

1. 1 Fixed, 0 Movable
2. 1 Fixed, 1 Movable
3. 1 Fixed, 2 Movable
4. 2 Fixed, 2 Movable
5. 3 Fixed, 3 Movable
6. 2 Fixed, 2 Movable
7. 3 Fixed, 2 Movable
8. 1 Fixed, 2 Movable
9. 1 Fixed, 2 Movable
10. 1 Fixed, 1 Movable

PAGE 213 EXERCISE 6

1. 1/1
2. 2/1
3. 4/1
4. 5/1
5. 6/1
6. 4/1
7. 5/1
8. 4/1
9. 4/1
10. 3/1

PAGE 213 EXERCISE 7

1. 100 N
2. # 5 less effort, # 7 higher

PAGE 215 EXERCISE 8

1. B = counterclockwise,
   C = clockwise,
   D = counterclockwise
2. B = counterclockwise,
   C = clockwise,
   D = clockwise
3. B = clockwise,
   C = clockwise,
   D = counterclockwise,
   E = clockwise,
   F = clockwise
4. A = counterclockwise,
   B = counterclockwise
5. X

PAGE 216-217 EXERCISE 9

1. clockwise
2. counterclockwise
3. B = counterclockwise,
   C = counterclockwise,
   D = clockwise,
   E = clockwise,
   F = clockwise
4. none
5. D and E

CHAPTER 13 - PAGE 218-224 - PRE-APPRENTICE TEST - MECHANICAL COMPREHENSION

1. c
2. a
3. c
4. b
5. b
6. b
7. b
8. b
9. d
10. b
11. b
12. c
13. b
14. c
15. a
16. b
17. b
18. d
19. d
20. a
21. b
22. a
23. a
24. a
25. b

CHAPTER 14 — PAGE 227 EXERCISE 1

1. c
2. a
3. NO
4. e
5. d

PAGE 228 EXERCISE 2

1. d
2. b
3. a
4. a
5. e

PAGE 229-230 EXERCISE 3

1. b
2. d
3. c
4. d
5. c
6. c

PAGE 230-231 EXERCISE 4

1. d
2. c
3. e
4. a
5. d